DATE DUE			

The Basic Business Library: Core Resources

The Basic Business Library: Core Resources

Edited by Bernard S. Schlessinger

 ORYX PRESS
1983

The rare Arabian Oryx is believed to have inspired the myth of the unicorn. This desert antelope became virtually extinct in the early 1960s. At that time several groups of international conservationists arranged to have 9 animals sent to the Phoenix Zoo to be the nucleus of a captive breeding herd. Today the Oryx population is over 400 and herds have been returned to reserves in Israel, Jordan, and Oman.

027.69
B29
142242
Sept. 1987

Library of Congress Cataloging in Publication Data

Main entry under title:

The Basic business library.

    Includes indexes.
    1. Business libraries.   2. Business—Bibliography.
I. Schlessinger, Bernard S., 1930–
Z675.B8B37   1983   027.6'9   82-14495
ISBN 0-89774-038-6

Contents

Preface

In the almost 20 years that the author has been involved with librarians of all types, one of the discussions in which he has most frequently participated has dealt with the need for lists of evaluated reference materials, rather than the usual lists of "all reference" materials that librarians are prone to produce. The author was familiar with the core lists of the medical field and was intrigued with the idea of applying the core list concept more broadly. The opportunity to develop a core list for business reference presented itself at a Business Reference Workshop in Albany in the summer of 1975, where a small group of practicing librarians agreed that such a list could be produced and, working with the author, produced it. That list eventually resulted in Part I of this book, the "Core List of Printed Business Reference Sources." Although the list has changed considerably from 1975 to the present, its twofold use remains the same:

1. As a checklist of essential business reference tools, which smaller libraries can use to test their business reference collections and to expand it if funds permit; and
2. For smaller libraries beginning a business reference collection, as a core list from which to choose in building the best collection possible within the limitations imposed by the available budget.

Part II, "The Literature of Business Reference and Business Libraries: 1976–1981," was added as a result of the many students, who, over the years, told the author that the exercise of finding appropriate literature for "show and tell" in the classroom, and the information derived from that literature, were most valuable in developing a familiarity with an unfamiliar field of librarianship. Since the book is aimed at practicing librarians and students, it seemed that a review of the literature should be included as a means for developing their familiarity with the business literature and business librarianship.

Finally, Part III, the series of state-of-the-art essays, was added so that the book could serve the student and the practicing librarian as a fuller introduction to the field. The commissioning of expert practicing librarians to write the essays was designed to present the most up-to-date and practical treatments for this purpose.

One of the author's great joys in his teaching, research, and writing has been involving himself with practitioners and students in joint efforts. This book gave ample opportunity for such interaction. In addition to the essayists, particular thanks are due to Virginia Vocelli, who organized the final work on the core list along with Katherine Roques; to Helen Jordan, who revised the original core list; to student assistants Kathleen Bessette, Margery Hudson, Emily Schuder, Margaret Thomas, and Jane Zande; and to the 1975 Business Reference Workshop attendees in Albany, all of whom provided valuable suggestions.

Whatever your use of this book, we hope that you will enjoy the fruits of our labor.

Part I
Core List of Printed Business Reference Sources

Introduction

by Bernard S. Schlessinger

The following core list of business reference sources was originally a selective list of sources for small and medium-sized libraries of which the total dollar value was below $5,000. It was developed by a small group of public and academic business librarians who attended the Business Reference Workshop at the State University of New York at Albany in the summer of 1975. After editing by the author, the original list was reviewed by all the attendees at the workshop and was distributed on demand for 3 years in mimeographed form. The response prompted the author to revise the original list in 1979 with the help of Helen Jordan, director of the Columbia College Library in Columbia, South Carolina. That revision, plus succeeding revisions and annotations, which involved Virginia Vocelli, director of the West Hartford Public Library in West Hartford, Connecticut, changed the list from one intended for smaller business libraries to a core list of business reference sources. The attendant increase in total price was unavoidable.

The total assignable cost of the 156 titles in the core list, based on November 1982 prices without discount, is now close to $11,000. This does not include titles such as the *Area Handbook Series* (in which prices of individual items vary in the series) or *Business Periodicals Index* (which is sold on a service basis).

There is some duplication of information within these various sources, but such titles have been included deliberately to allow for choice if desired. For example, although there is duplication of the publications of business services, it would be expected that the smaller library would buy selectively in accordance with its needs.

The list is arranged alphabetically by title, with letter-by-letter alphabetization. Data in citations, where applicable, include title, author or editor, edition, publisher and location, date of publication or beginning date, frequency of publication, and price.

To provide further access to the list, a subject index with broad classes has been included. Reference is to entry number. Also included is an Author/Editor/Publisher index.

As noted in the preface, this book is aimed at students and business reference practitioners. For the student, this core list will become meaningful only as the items are used. As with all reference tools, successful use transforms a lifeless title into an old friend. The student should use the list to become familiar with his/her basic helpers in the area of business reference. The business reference practitioner will recognize many of the titles, but should find the core list helpful in 2 other ways: (1) as a checklist for essential business reference tools, which may be used to test the completeness of the business reference collection and to expand it if funds permit, and (2) for smaller libraries beginning a business reference collection, as a core list from which to choose in building the best collection possible within the limitations imposed by the available budget. Although the readers will find that the majority of the tools included in the list are recommended for all (or almost all) librarians, it is unrealistic to assume that budget limitations will not be a factor in purchasing decisions. As a checklist and as a core list this volume should help in the efficient use of funds, but the individual librarian will know best what is affordable and what is only desirable.

In many of the annotations, the authors have indicated every-other-year purchase as a reasonable alternative to consider. We have also indicated, in some annotations, that the needs of the users would dictate the purchase decision. In addition, the reader should think carefully about other methods of resource sharing that are part of the prudent librarian's everyday operation. These might include:

1. Cooperating with a nearby library so that, by suitable alternate-year purchase by the 2 libraries, the latest edition of a tool would be available to the patrons of both.

2. Assigning subject area coverage to specific neighboring libraries so that the entire list could be accommodated by several libraries working together.

3. Arranging access to special corporate library collections.

4. Persuading businesses within the area to donate funds for purchase of specific items.

5. Suitable use of interlibrary loan or photocopying for items or parts of items that will not be heavily used.

The author recognizes that any such list begins to become out of date the day it is completed. Since there is every intention of updating the list, any recommendations from our readers for additions or deletions would be appreciated. At the same time, the reader may wish to comment on the annotation style. This type of structured annotation brief (STAB) has been experimented with by the author for 5 years in his classes with excellent results for beginners, especially in the shorter time required to produce satisfactory annotations.

Core List

1. Accountants' Index. American Institute of Certified Public Accountants. New York: American Institute Publishing, 1921–. Annual. $47.50.

Authority and scope: Published by the professional accounting association, the American Institute of Certified Public Accountants, this index covers books, pamphlets, government documents, and periodical articles dealing with all aspects of accounting published in English throughout the world. Authors, titles, and subjects are listed in a single alphabet, and entries are not annotated.

Evaluation: This is a convenient and comprehensive source for current literature in the field of accounting. Recommended especially for business and academic libraries.

2. Advertising Age. Chicago: Crain Communications, 1930–. Weekly. $30.00.

Authority and scope: A respected trade journal, this weekly paper covers the current scene of advertising and marketing and extends to television, broadcasting, and newspapers as well. Regular columns carry information on personnel shifts, account changes, ratings, and new products. Several times a year, special surveys, such as the top 100 national advertisers and top 100 leading media companies, are published.

Evaluation: Indexed in *Business Periodicals Index* (entry 20) and *Readers' Guide,* this is an excellent source for students and professionals following trends in the field or researching companies, and it is recommended for all libraries, except the smallest.

3. Advertising Cost Control Handbook. Ovid Riso. New York: Van Nostrand-Reinhold, 1973. $18.95.

Authority and scope: Ovid Riso, a corporate ad manager and former agency executive, has provided a fundamental text that covers advertising cost practices. Based on actual experiences of large and small companies, advertising agencies, and the media, the book is divided into 5 sections: management responsibilities, the creators and producers, the media, legal and international aspects, and evaluation and control.

Evaluation: Written primarily as a guide for the ad manager, this work can be helpful to anyone working in the field of sales promotion. A valuable addition to any public library.

4. Advertising Manager's Handbook. Richard H. Stansfield. Chicago: Dartnell, 1977. $52.50.

Authority and scope: Richard Stansfield, an authority in the field of advertising, presents a thorough treatment of modern advertising. All aspects of managing an advertising campaign are covered including agency selection, campaign planning, product identification, copy writing, headlines, media, research, surveys, and image building. An index is included.

Evaluation: This is a comprehensive treatise on the basic techniques utilized in a successful advertising campaign, and it can serve as the core source in this subject area for any reference collection.

5. Agent's and Buyer's Guide: The Markets Handbook. Cincinnati, OH: National Underwriter, 1947–. Annual. $11.50 paper.

Authority and scope: Compiled by the editors of the Fire, Casualty and Surety Bulletins and published by the National Underwriter Company, this is a guide to property and casualty insurance coverage. The largest section of the guide is the alphabetical listing of markets and the companies that handle this kind of insurance. The guide also includes an alphabetical listing by company with a complete address, territory and lines written; a directory of reinsurance companies; and other general information on life and health insurance and surplus line laws.

Evaluation: This useful directory could be purchased in alternate years by the smaller library but might find frequent use in a business library, warranting annual purchase.

6. Agricultural Statistics. U.S. Department of Agriculture. Washington, DC: Government Printing Office, 1936–. Annual. $9.50.

Authority and scope: Compiled and published by the U.S. Department of Agriculture, this is the authoritative source for statistics on all aspects of agricultural production and consumption. Included are statistics on costs and returns, farm resources, support programs, taxes, insurance, and credit. A historical series is included, generally limited to data for the last 10 years.

Evaluation: This report supplies an accurate summary of, and reference to, the current U.S. government agricultural information. It is necessary in any library interested in agricultural commodities, although purchase every other year would be adequate for libraries serving the nonspecialist.

7. Aljian's Purchasing Handbook. National Association of Purchasing Management. Paul V. Farrell, contributing ed. 4th ed. New York: McGraw-Hill, 1982. $46.50.

Authority and scope: In this handbook, formerly edited by George Aljian, retired purchasing executive Paul Farrell has brought together the contributions of 92 purchasing experts and has provided a comprehensive treatment of the policies, practices, and procedures used in purchasing and materials management. The information is presented in 32 sections and includes a glossary, bibliography and library suggestions, reference tables, and an index.

Evaluation: A good mixture of theoretical and practical information, this is the most comprehensive reference on this topic and belongs in all libraries.

8. American Bank Directory. Norcross, GA: McFadden Business Publications. 1836–. Semiannual. $60.00; $8.00 for single-state editions.

Authority and scope: Over 14,000 banks and holding companies in the United States are included in this directory. Information on bank name, address, Federal Reserve district, year established, transit number, officers and directors, and principal correspondents is given for each entry. The same type of information is provided in the single-state editions.

Evaluation: A useful alternative to more expensive banking directories, this reference is recommended to all libraries, especially those whose clientele would not have need for information on the foreign banking community.

9. American Statistics Index: A Comprehensive Guide and Index to the Statistical Publications of the U.S. Government. Washington, DC: Congressional Information Service, 1973–. Annual. $860.00.

Authority and scope: Published by a reputable firm specializing in providing access to government publications, the *ASI* provides access to federal statistics. The abstract volume, arranged by agency, is composed of entries that contain complete bibliographic citations and thorough descriptions of all tables and narratives contained in the government documents. The index volume is composed of 2 indexes: (1) subjects and names; and (2) categories: geographic breakdowns, economic breakdowns, and demographic breakdowns. Also included in the index volume are a title index, a guide to the Standard Industrial Classification code, the Standard Occupation Classification, and a list of Standard Metropolitan Statistical Areas (SMSAs). As a complement to *ASI*, CIS has produced since 1980 the *Statistical Reference Index; a Selective Guide to American Statistical Publications from Private Organizations and State Government Sources.*

Evaluation: Although comprehensive and thorough, price prohibits acquisition by many libraries. If, however, a library is centrally located, has heavy statistical demands, or is in an academic setting, this reference is essential.

10. Area Handbook Series. Washington, DC: U.S. Department of the Army. 1975–. Price varies.

Authority and scope: Published under the jurisdiction of the Department of the Army, this country study series is written by staff members of the Foreign Service Institute of American University. Still called the *Area Handbook Series,* each book covers the historical, political, economic, and military background of an individual country and includes a lengthy bibliography, a glossary, maps, and statistical information. New features include a 3- to 4-page profile at the beginning of the book and photographs. The studies are revised and updated on an irregular basis.

Evaluation: This is a basic, relatively inexpensive resource for information on various nations which will be of great use to the businessperson, student, and traveler. It is recommended that all libraries circulate these volumes rather than keep them on the reference shelf. The changes in design and added information make them much more appealing than the old series.

11. Area Wage Surveys. U.S. Bureau of Labor Statistics. Washington, DC: Government Printing Office, 1950–. Annual. Price varies.

Authority and scope: Since 1948, the U.S. Bureau of Labor Statistics has published surveys in which occupations common to a variety of manufacturing and other industries are studied on a community basis. The series has expanded through the years to include more occupations and more areas. Presently, approximately 71 smaller metropolitan areas and broad industry divisions (manufacturing, transportation, communication and other public utilities, wholesale trade, retail trade, finance, insurance and real estate, and services) are surveyed. Weekly and hourly earnings data are published annually, while a complete earnings and benefits survey is published every 3 years. A U.S. summary is published annually.

Evaluation: Libraries will be most interested if the metropolitan area in which they are located is included, and annual purchase of the report is recommended. Academic and larger business libraries will want the entire series.

12. ASPA Handbook of Personnel and Industrial Relations. Dale Yoder and Herbert J. Heneman, Jr. Washington, DC: U.S. Bureau of National Affairs, 1979. $45.00.

Authority and scope: Edited by 2 specialists in the area of personnel and management, this is the official handbook of the American Society for Personnel Administration. Seventy-two authors, all experts in the field, have contributed to 51 chapters divided into 8 sections: policy and program management, planning and auditing, administration and organization, staffing policies and strategies, training and development, motivation and commitment, employee and labor relations, and the professional in personnel and industrial relations (referred to as PAIR). Extensively footnoted, the handbook includes a literature survey, topical index, and name index.

Evaluation: Designed for the professional in personnel administration, this handbook belongs in all academic, business, and larger public libraries.

13. Ayer Directory of Publications. Philadelphia, PA: Ayer Press, 1869–. Annual. $79.00.

Authority and scope: Published by one of the oldest and most respected publishers in the U.S., this directory contains information about more than 21,000 newspapers, magazines, and trade publications in the U.S., Canada, the Bahamas, Bermuda, Panama, and the Philippines. Geographically arranged by state or province, and then by city, each entry contains cost, circulation, frequency, advertising rates, name of editor and/or publisher, and mailing address of each publication listed. A map for each state is included. An alphabetical index and several classified indexes are included: agricultural publications, magazines of general interest, college publications, trade and technical publications, and weekly, semi-weekly, and tri-weekly newspapers.

Evaluation: One of the best known and respected directories of its kind, this is recommended for all libraries as the authoritative source for data on commercially important publications.

14. Ayer Glossary of Advertising and Related Terms. Philadelphia, PA: Ayer Press, 1977. $11.95.

Authority and scope: Ayer Press has provided a lexicon for advertisers and anyone else interested in this field. A general listing in alphabetical order is followed by a relisting of terms under headings dealing with TV and radio, printing, photography and graphic arts, computer and data processing, research (advertising copy, media, marketing, etc.), and associations (unions and government bureaus, etc.).

Evaluation: This is a quick and easy-to-use reference source for the advertising and business library communities. The smaller library with a more general clientele may also find this relatively inexpensive item useful in its collection.

15. Best's Insurance Reports: Life-Health and Best's Insurance Reports: Property-Casualty. Morristown, NJ: Alfred M. Best, 1906–. Annual. $225.00 (Life); $375.00 (Property).

Authority and scope: Alfred Best & Co., a longtime publishing authority in the field of insurance, provides this reference source on the insurance companies in the U.S. and Canada. Information provided for each company includes history, management and operation, assets and liabilities, investment data, accident and health statistics, company growth, and Best's rating.

Evaluation: Together, these volumes form an extremely valuable source for information on the insurance industry, which is essential for any library where there is the demand for such information—be it from the businessperson or the consumer. Smaller libraries may economize by purchasing every other year.

16. Broadcasting Cable Yearbook. Washington, DC: Broadcasting Publications, 1935–. Annual. $60.00.

Authority and scope: Issued annually by Broadcasting Publications, this serves as a handbook and directory to the broadcasting industry in the U.S. and Canada. It is divided into several sections: broadcasting in general, television, radio, broadcast advertising, equipment and engineering, professional and trade and cable television. Included is such information as TV and radio call letters, principal FCC regulations, TV market maps, special programing, and audience statistics.

Evaluation: The combination and amount of information in this yearbook justify its place in all reference collections and merits annual purchase for larger libraries.

17. Business Books and Serials in Print. New York: Bowker, 1977. $37.50.

Authority and scope: One of the leading companies in library publishing has provided this listing from its extensive database. Over 37,500 titles from some 1,580 publishers are included in an attempt to provide author, title, and subject access to current business literature. According to the publisher, the full scope of economic literature is included: economic history, theory, and conditions; agriculture; industry finance; investment; insurance; and taxation. Economic indicators such as prices, employment, wages, production, income spending and forecasting, and all managerial functions are also covered. Emphasis is given to administrative and commercial titles, rather than those covering the industrial aspects of business operation. In the latest edition, over 6,000 serials are included for the first time.

Evaluation: Essential for business libraries, this is a reference tool recommended for all libraries desiring a strong business collection.

18. Business Information Sources. Lorna M. Daniells. Berkeley, CA: University of California Press, 1976. $18.50.

Authority and scope: Daniells, head reference librarian at Harvard University's Graduate School of Business and a noted authority and bibliographer in the business field, has compiled this basic guide to business sources and reference materials. The sources are arranged by subject area and then by type of material: handbook, periodical, etc. Brief but descriptive annotations are included for each entry. A ''basic bookshelf'' of recommended titles for company libraries comprises the final chapter. An index is provided.

Evaluation: An important contribution to the business bibliographic field, this is an essential purchase for all libraries.

19. Business Organizations and Agencies Directory. Anthony Kruzas and Robert C. Thomas, eds. Detroit, MI: Gale, 1980. $110.00.

Authority and scope: Noted business bibliographers Kruzas and Thomas have arranged this directory in 26 sections by type of organization, with each entry providing a complete address and description. Included are trade and business organizations, stock exchanges, Better Business Bureaus, Chambers of Commerce, diplomatic representations, trade and convention centers, educational institutions, data banks and computerized services, and franchise companies. There are separate indexes to some of the larger sections.

Evaluation: Although much of the information contained in this volume can be found in other publications, many of them Gale-produced, the combination of material included makes this a very useful source of business information for business libraries and larger public libraries.

20. Business Periodicals Index. New York: H. W. Wilson, 1958–. Monthly except July, with periodic cumulations. Sold on service basis.

Authority and scope: H. W. Wilson, a leading publishing house, provides this subject index to over 17 periodicals in the fields of accounting, advertising and public relations, automation, banking, communications, taxation, economics, marketing, finance and investments, labor, management, and specific businesses. Periodicals covered come from trade and professional associations and government agencies.

Evaluation: This is a valuable resource for businesspeople, students of business administration, or anyone interested in researching a particular area of business or economics. However, for institutions without a major interest in this area, the field is sufficiently covered by other more general indexes.

21. Business Serials of the U.S. Government. Richard King, ed. Chicago: American Library Association, 1978. $13.00 paper.

Authority and scope: Prepared by ALA's Business Reference Services Committee and Adult Service Division, this is an annotated checklist of 100 recommended business reference titles that are U.S. government serial publications. The entries are arranged by subject area, and each includes a descriptive paragraph and order information. A title index is included.

Evaluation: While not extensive, this is a handy reference tool for some very important sources of business information which would be useful in all libraries.

22. Business Services and Information: The Guide to the Federal Government. Philadelphia, PA: Management Information Exchange, 1978. $41.50.

Authority and scope: This guide to business information available from federal agencies is arranged by business subject area. When appropriate, the publications listed include price and GPO stock number. Thorough descriptions of available services, such as computer tapes or consultants (with direct dial telephone number given), are also presented.

Evaluation: Particularly useful for the businessperson or researcher, this guide is recommended for medium-sized and larger libraries. It is comprehensive in its attempt to provide access to the vast array of information and services offered by the federal government.

23. Business Statistics. U.S. Department of Commerce. Washington, DC: Government Printing Office, 1932–. Biennial. $9.50.

Authority and scope: Published by the Bureau of Economic Analysis of the Department of Commerce, this volume is a biennial supplement to the periodical *Survey of Current Business* (entry 135) and presents historical data for approximately 2,500 series that appear in the S-pages of that periodical. Data are shown on an annual basis for early years, quarterly for the last decade, and monthly for the most recent 5 years. Also included are sources and explanatory notes to tables.

Evaluation: This is a basic statistical report useful for any library, whether or not the *Survey of Current Business* is received. It is an economical purchase for the smaller library with business statistical needs going beyond the *Statistical Abstract of the United States* (entry 132).

24. Canadian Trade Index. Toronto, ON: Canadian Manufacturers' Association, 1968–. Annual. $82.50.

Authority and scope: Published by the Canadian Manufacturers Association, the representative organization of Canadian manufacturers, this index provides basic information for approximately 13,000 Canadian manufacturers, including addresses, branches, export representatives, trademarks, and brands. It also includes a classified list of products, a classified and geographical list of manufacturers, an alphabetical list of agricultural producers, French translations of product headings, and an alphabetical list of trademarks, trade names, and brands.

Evaluation: An international directory of basic information on manufacturers, this is a good reference source for any library, though alternate years of purchase would suffice for the smaller library.

25. Commodity Prices: A Source Book and Index. Paul Wasserman and Diane Kemmerling, comps. Detroit, MI: Gale, 1974. $30.00.

Authority and scope: Noted editors in the business field Paul Wasserman and Diane Kemmerling have compiled current commodity prices for more than 5,000 consumer, commercial, agricultural, and industrial products in the U.S. and Canadian markets. The arrangement is alphabetical by commodity, and entries include the following information: source (title of periodical where price is found), frequency of price listings, and pertinent market.

Evaluation: A valuable source for anyone interested in the analysis of commodity market. Alternate years of purchase would suffice for the smaller library.

26. Commodity Yearbook. New York: Commodity Research Bureau, 1939–. Annual. $30.95.

Authority and scope: Published since 1939, this source presents pertinent data about more than 100 raw commodities (aluminum, apples, cattle, etc.) and manufactured products and resources (burlap, currencies, electric power, etc.). Data included are prices, production, shipment, etc.—in most cases for better than a 10-year period. Also included are general articles on topics such as commodity price trends and futures markets.

Evaluation: As a reliable, inexpensive source of data on commodities, this reference belongs in all but the smallest public libraries.

27. Computer Dictionary and Handbook. Charles J. Sippl and Roger J. Sippl. 3rd ed. New York: Howard Sams & Co., 1980. $29.95.

Authority and scope: The authors—professors, consultants, and business writers—have compiled a dictionary that is updated to reflect the changes in this area. Half of the book is composed of definitions of terms and concepts important to understanding a complex field. The definitions range in length from one sentence to 7 or 8. The second part is a handbook consisting of several appendixes, ranging from an introduction to computer principles and procedures to sections on computer languages, flow charting, and acronyms used in the field.

Evaluation: Comprehensive and up to date, this reference is recommended for all libraries. Because of the nature, amount, and combination of material, it would be wise to purchase a copy for circulation as well.

28. Consultants and Consulting Organizations Directory: A Reference Guide to Concerns and Individuals Engaged in Consulting for Business and Industry. Paul Wasserman and Janice McLean, eds. 5th ed. Detroit, MI: Gale, 1982. $190.00.

Authority and scope: Compiled by noted business bibliographers, this directory contains information on more than 7,000 firms, individuals, and organizations active in over 130 fields. The first part contains the main listing for each organization: complete name, address, telephone number, principal officers and management, and a description of specialties and activities. The information is arranged geographically for the U.S. (by state and city), Canada, Australia, the United Kingdom, and other foreign countries. The second part is a subject index of firms arranged by geographical location; the third part is composed of 2 indexes: listing of individuals and a listing of firm names.

Evaluation: The most extensive of its kind, this directory is recommended for all but the smallest public libraries.

29. County and City Data Book. U.S. Bureau of the Census. Washington, DC: Government Printing Office, 1949–. Irregular. $21.00.

Authority and scope: Published as a supplement to the *Statistical Abstract of the United States* (entry 132), this volume presents a large and varied selection of items taken from the major decennial and quinquennial censuses and other statistical series. Subjects included are agriculture, vital statistics, business, city finances, education, housing, climate, health, manufacturing, population characteristics, retail and wholesale trade, and services. Geographical areas covered are cities, congressional districts, divisions, states, SMSAs, and smaller urban areas. Also includes a special appendix on congressional districts.

Evaluation: A valuable reference source for any library, this book provides general and in-depth overviews of communities and their vital statistics.

30. County Business Patterns. U.S. Bureau of the Census. Washington, DC: Government Printing Office, 1943–. Annual. $6.00.

Authority and scope: Issued by the U.S. Bureau of the Census, this report series contains employment and payroll statistics by county and by industry, classified by 2-, 3-, and 4-digit Standard Industrial Classifications. A separate report is issued for each state, Puerto Rico and outlying areas, the District of Columbia, the U.S., and Standard Metropolitan Statistical Areas.

Evaluation: This is a handy reference tool for any library interested in annual employment and payroll statistics. Small libraries might consider limiting purchase to their own states, surrounding states, and the U.S. Although the reports are issued annually, the statistics lag by approximately 2 years.

31. Demographic Yearbook. New York: United Nations. Department of Economic Affairs, 1949–. Annual. Price varies.

Authority and scope: Published by the United Nations and internationally recognized as authoritative on population statistics, this compilation presents detailed information on selected subjects: natality, mortality, population distribution, trends and censuses, marriage and divorce, ethnic and economic characteristics, etc., for approximately 250 geographical entities.

Evaluation: This source provides a quick reference to international population statistics. Smaller libraries may economize by buying every 2 or 3 years.

32. A Dictionary for Accountants. Eric L. Kohler. 5th ed. Englewood Cliffs, NJ: Prentice-Hall, 1975. $26.00.

Authority and scope: Kohler, a respected accountant, has provided the standard dictionary in the field. Over 3,000 terms and concepts in accounting and related areas are included, with many definitions running to several pages in length. Graphics are used effectively.

Evaluation: Authoritative and readable, this reference will be useful in all libraries.

33. Dictionary of Business and Management. Jerry M. Rosenberg. New York: Wiley-Interscience, 1978. $29.95.

Authority and scope: Rosenberg, a professor and consultant in the field of management, has compiled a reference source for terms currently used in business and management. More than 8,000 entries are included in alphabetical order, with an average entry length of 2 or 3 sentences. Terms, acronyms, and some slang are included. The appendix includes Celsius and Fahrenheit tables, a metric conversion table, a compound interest table, a list of programs of graduate study in business and management, and relevant business quotations.

Evaluation: Useful for general access to business terms, this dictionary is readable, easy to use, and recommended for all libraries.

34. Dictionary of Insurance. Lewis E. Davids. 5th ed. Totowa, NJ: Littlefield, Adams & Co., 1977. $4.95 paper.

Authority and scope: Lewis Davids, a university professor and business author, has compiled a practical guide defining terms used in the insurance business. The definitions are brief and often limited to one sentence. Abbreviations used in insurance are defined as well. Titles and locations of many of the nonbook sources of information on insurance are also included.

Evaluation: This dictionary provides quick access to the terms most often used in insurance and can be recommended as a convenient and relatively inexpensive purchase for all libraries.

35. Direct Mail and Mail Order Handbook. Richard S. Hodgson. 3rd ed. New York: Dartnell, 1980. $52.50.

Authority and scope: Richard Hodgson, a well-known person in the field of direct mail marketing strategies, has compiled this handbook covering all aspects of direct mail promotion. Discussed in chapter format are basic elements and applications, a direct mail campaign, the influence of technology, and public reaction to this segment of business. Includes an index.

Evaluation: Comprehensive and expensive, this is considered the "Bible" of direct mail business and is recommended for all libraries where there is interest in this field.

36. Directory of American Savings and Loan Associations. Baltimore, MD: T.K. Sanderson Organization, 1955–. Annual. $50.00.

Authority and scope: This comprehensive listing of all active savings and loan associations and cooperative banks in the U.S. is arranged alphabetically by state and city. Each entry includes street address, mailing address, branches, telephone number, key personnel, and assets.

Evaluation: This directory provides easy access for those interested in savings and loans associations. Business libraries with a banking clientele would find it most useful.

37. Directory of Corporate Affiliations. Skokie, IL: National Register Publishing. Annual. $197.00.

Authority and scope: One of the many directories published by the National Register Publishing Co., this directory is a "who owns whom" listing of about 3,000 American parent companies. In Section 1, the parent companies are listed alphabetically, followed by a list of divisions, subsidiaries, and affiliates. A brief listing of executive officers, products, and total sales is included for each company. Section 2 is a complete index to all listed entries in the directory by state and city.

Evaluation: A valuable source of information for those interested in the corporate structure of the U.S. business community, it is one of the few published sources in which to identify a smaller company. Necessary for all but the smallest reference collections.

38. Directory of Directories: An Annotated Guide to Business and Industrial Directories, Professional and Scientific Rosters and Other Lists and Guides of All Kinds. James M. Ethridge, ed. Detroit, MI: Gale, 1980. Supplement. $65.00.

Authority and scope: Noted business bibliographer James M. Ethridge has compiled a reference source to over 5,000 directories of all types. Arranged in 15 major subject classifications, each entry includes title, publisher name and address, description, frequency, and price. There is a title index and a detailed subject index with many cross-references. Periodic supplements keep the subscriber up to date on new editions of established directories, as well as brand-new directories.

Evaluation: Useful in all libraries but the smallest, this directory is strong in business and technical areas as well as current "social" topics.

39. Directory of Obsolete Securities. New York: Financial Information, 1927–. Annual. $100.00.

Authority and scope: Compiled from the publishing company's Financial Daily Card Service and Financial Stock Guide Service, this is a list of companies whose identities have been lost as a result of name changes, mergers, acquisitions, dissolutions, liquidations, organizations, bankruptcies, charter cancellations, and related changes. Each listing indicates the manner in which the company's identity has been changed, the name of the new company (if any), and the year in which the action took place. It is cumulative since 1927.

Evaluation: Recommended for all libraries except the smallest public libraries; economy may be sought by alternating years of purchase.

40. Directory of Shopping Centers in the United States. 22nd ed. Chicago: National Research Bureau, 1981. $168.00.

Authority and scope: This directory is published in 4 regional books, plus an index, and it is compiled from information from questionnaires sent to the management of shopping centers. The information in each regional volume is presented in 4 sections with access provided by state, city, metro areas, and name of shopping center. From this directory, one can learn name, location, owner/developer, leasing agent, shopping center management, architect/engineer, tenants, and miscellaneous statistical data.

Evaluation: Larger business-oriented libraries should hold this valuable directory but may economize by buying in alternate years. Smaller public libraries may want to lease if use warrants, and otherwise should simply be aware of its availability in the area.

41. Directory of Trust Institutions. New York: Fiduciary Publishers, 1959–. Annual. $10.00.

Authority and scope: Issued by the publishers of *Trusts and Estates,* this directory is a geographical listing of active trust institutions in the U.S. and

Canada. Each entry provides names, addresses, trust assets, and key personnel.

Evaluation: This is an inexpensive practical guide which provides quick reference to over 3,800 trust institutions in the Northern Hemisphere, and is recommended for all libraries.

42. Dow Jones Investor's Handbook. Maurice Farrell, ed. Princeton, NJ: Dow Jones Books, 1966–. Annual. $12.95; $5.95 paper.

Authority and scope: Data on the well-known Dow Jones averages for the most recent year are compiled in this handbook. Industrials, transportation, and public utility stocks are covered, with data including monthly closing averages, quarterly earnings, dividends, yields, and price-earning ratios for over 10 years. The activities of the New York Stock Exchange, American Stock Exchange, and Barrons Group stock are reviewed, with the year's high and low prices, net change, volume, dividends, and most active stock identified.

Evaluation: Convenient and easy to use, this is recommended for all business and medium-sized to large public libraries.

43. The Dow Jones-Irwin Business Almanac. Summer N. Levine, ed. Princeton, NJ: Dow Jones Books, 1977–. Annual. $16.95.

Authority and scope: Summer Levine, finance professor and business author, has compiled a handy source of information on business, economics, and investments. Essays, charts, graphs, chronologies, and statistical tables cover such topics as regulatory agencies, finance, largest corporations, stock market, employment wages and productivity, advertising and international business, and financial comparisons. Includes an index.

Evaluation: Recommended for all libraries, this volume is a handy ready-reference tool with an extremely useful and up-to-date combination of information.

44. Dun and Bradstreet's Principal International Businesses. New York: Dun and Bradstreet, 1974–. Annual. $395.00.

Authority and scope: Over 50,000 leading enterprises in over 130 countries are listed in this directory published by one of the most respected publishers in the business world. Arranged in 3 sections (geographical, by Standard Industrial Classification [SIC] number, and alphabetical, by company name), the most complete entry is provided in the first section and includes company name, address, product, number of employees, sales, executive officers, and SIC number. The other sections give name and location only.

Evaluation: As one of the most complete listings of international businesses, this directory certainly belongs in business and academic libraries. The price would probably prohibit small libraries from considering it.

45. Economic Census. U.S. Bureau of the Census. Washington, DC: Government Printing Office, 1929–. Quinquennial. Price and number of volumes vary.

Authority and scope: Published by the U.S. Bureau of the Census, the *Economic Census* includes individually published censuses of retail trade, wholesale trade, service industries, construction industries, manufacturers, mineral industries, and transportation, as well as the censuses of outlying areas (Puerto Rico, the Virgin Islands, and Guam), the Enterprise Statistics Program, the Survey of Minority-Owned Business Enterprises, and the Survey of Women-Owned Businesses. Published at 5-year intervals (covering the years ending in ''2'' and ''7''), the economic censuses constitute the most comprehensive and periodic canvass of the nation's industrial and business activities. The data for the economic censuses are tabulated on the basis of the Standard Industrial Classification system. Geographic coverage varies, with the most detailed data published at the national level and fewer statistics appearing for states and smaller areas in order to avoid disclosure of individual firms.

Evaluation: Recommended for all business and academic libraries, selection of the individual reports would depend on projected interest. Smaller, more general libraries should consider obtaining reports for their own states for each census and perhaps the U.S. summary volume.

46. Economic Indicators. U.S. Council of Economic Advisers. Washington, DC: Government Printing Office, 1948–. Monthly. $15.00.

Authority and scope: Prepared with an emphasis on concise presentation of factual data in tabular and chart form. Data, covering latest months, quarters, and in some cases as long a period as 10 years, are compiled from statistics collected by various government agencies on total output, income, and spending; employment, unemployment, and wages; production and business activity; prices; and currency, credit, security markets, and federal finance.

Evaluation: Of value to statisticians and economics and business analysts for up-to-date information on economic conditions, *Economic Indicators* is easy to read, and the table and chart format can be a useful combination. Data are available in other sources, however, and purchase is necessary only if format and combination of data are found valuable by patrons.

47. Economic Report of the President. Transmitted to the Congress, February (each year); Together with the Annual Report of the Council of Economic Advisors. U.S. Council of Economic Advisors. Washington, DC: Government Printing Office, 1947–. Annual. $5.50.

Authority and scope: This annual review of the nation's economic conditions reports projections of the current economic policy, a review of the existing economic conditions, and prospective changes in economic policies.

Evaluation: This prospectus will be of interest to students of political science, to economists, and to historians. Particular data or data combinations may be useful to the nonspecialist.

48. Editor and Publisher Market Guide. New York: Editor and Publisher, 1924–. Annual. $40.00.

Authority and scope: Published since 1924, this book surveys over 1,500 daily and weekly newspaper markets in the U.S. and Canada, as well as selected foreign markets. Arranged by state and city, the information includes population, location, trade areas, principal industries, retail businesses, colleges and universities, climate, and newspapers. Includes a map for each state and rankings by Standard Metropolitan Statistical Area.

Evaluation: This is a good reference source for people interested in the factors that make up a potential market or a place to live. It is easy to use, up to date, and warrants annual purchase by all but the smallest libraries, considering the general interest nature of the material.

49. Employment and Earnings. U.S. Bureau of Labor Statistics. Washington, DC: Government Printing Office, 1909–. Annual. $31.00.

Authority and scope: Published by the Bureau of Labor Statistics, this compilation presents detailed statistics on the work force in the U.S. Included are data on both employed and unemployed persons, embracing characteristics such as age, sex, race, occupation, and industry attachment. Also covered is information on nonagricultural wages and salaries, including average weekly hours, average hourly earnings, and average weekly earnings for the nation, states, and metropolitan areas. Data from 1909 to 1978, structured on the 1972 Standard Industrial Classification System, may be found in the historical databook *Employment and Earnings, United States 1909–1978,* also published by the bureau.

Evaluation: This is recommended for all business and academic libraries. Smaller public libraries should consider alternate year purchase, or at least be aware of the amount of useful data in this reference tool.

50. Encyclopedia of Advertising. Irvin Graham. 2nd ed. New York: Fairchild Publications, 1969. $20.00.

Authority and scope: Graham, advertising manager and professor for over 30 years, has compiled an encyclopedia of over 1,100 entries grouped according to subject and covering all major aspects of advertising, marketing, public relations, and media. The length of entries ranges from one or 2 sentences to 3 pages.

Evaluation: While dated in some respects, this is a basic reference source in its field and is recommended for all libraries.

51. Encyclopedia of Associations. Denise Akey, ed. 17th ed. Detroit, MI: Gale, 1981. (3 vols.) vol. 1, $140.00; vol. 2, $125.00; vol. 3, $140.00.

Authority and scope: Editorial consultant Denise Akey has prepared a classified directory of over 16,000 organized groups of people who have voluntarily associated themselves for stated purposes. Details for each group include name, address, acronyms, chief officer, membership, purpose and activities, staff size, special committees, and meetings and publications. Entries in Volume 1 are arranged by category, and there is a key word index. Volume 2 is a geographic-executive index, and subscribers can also receive Volume 3, a quarterly updating service.

Evaluation: This is an indispensable reference tool for all libraries. Annual purchase for Volume 1 is recommended, while less frequent purchase of Volumes 2 and 3 would be possible.

52. Encyclopedia of Banking and Finance. Glenn G. Munn and Ferdinand L. Garcia. 7th rev. ed. Boston: Bankers Publishing, 1973. $49.75.

Authority and scope: First edited by Glenn G. Munn, and followed by equally recognized authorities, the latest being F. L. Garcia, this comprehensive work contains brief definitions of terms such as cheque, money order, etc.—and a number of encyclopedia articles on money, credit, banking practices, pertinent business laws and federal regulations, investment, insurance, brokerage, and other topics that require in-depth coverage.

Evaluation: The encyclopedia has no competitor. It furnishes authoritative and readable information on the whole spectrum of banking and related subjects and is an indispensable reference work for all libraries.

53. Encyclopedia of Business Information Sources. Paul Wasserman, ed. 4th rev. ed. Detroit, MI: Gale, 1980. $98.00.

Authority and scope: Paul Wasserman, a leading editor in the business field, has compiled this comprehensive guide to sources of information on over 1,300 specific topics to meet the research needs of executives and researchers. Categories are in alphabetical order and range from abbreviations and abrasives to zoning and zoological gardens. Complete citations are provided for each source. Arrangement is by type of source such as handbooks and manuals, directories, price sources, and trade associations. A geographical listing, included in previous editions as Volume 2, is not present in this edition.

Evaluation: Excellent as a place to start when researching unfamiliar topics, this is an essential purchase for all reference collections. The specificity of subjects, as well as the different types of sources covered, is particularly useful.

54. Encyclopedia of Economics. Douglas Greenwald, ed. New York: McGraw-Hill, 1982. $49.95.

Authority and scope: Greenwald, a well-known consulting economist and author, together with 178 experts in this area has compiled this comprehensive reference source covering the entire field of economics. The length of entries range from one page to several, and each includes definition, explanation, relationship to other concepts, and charts and graphs where appropriate. There are references at the end of most entries, and the work is liberally cross-referenced and indexed.

Evaluation: Because of its timeliness and comprehensiveness, this reference is recommended for most libraries. Though expensive for a one-volume book, it is readable, easy to use, and thorough.

55. Encyclopedia of Information Systems and Services. Anthony T. Kruzas and J. Schmittroth. Detroit, MI: Gale, 1980. $190.00.

Authority and scope: Compiled by business bibliographers Kruzas and Schmittroth, this is an international guide to over 2,000 organizations that produce, process, store, and use bibliographic and nonbibliographic information. It covers computer-readable databases, database producers, online vendors and time-sharing companies, consultants, networks, government agencies, libraries, etc. The main body of the encyclopedia is arranged in alphabetical order by parent organization. Each entry contains complete address, name of director, description of system or service, scope, input sources, holdings, storage media, publications, computer-based products, clientele, and contact. Twenty-two indexes provide access to this information.

Evaluation: Although expensive, this is a basic resource providing access to a fast-growing field and is essential for any library serving a substantial number of patrons with an interest in this field.

56. Encyclopedia of Long Term Financing and Capital Management. John F. Childs. Englewood Cliffs, NJ: Prentice-Hall, 1976. $34.95.

Authority and scope: Childs, noted adviser, lecturer, and writer in the field of finance, is the author of this reference tool on financing and capital investment in the corporate world. Encyclopedic in length and coverage, it is more like a textbook in arrangement and approach. Part 1 outlines financing or raising of capital, and Part 2 covers putting the capital to work, monitoring the results, and setting standards for performance. At the beginning of each chapter, the contents are outlined. Examples are used heavily, along with tables and graphs when appropriate. An index is also included.

Evaluation: Readable and direct, this is an excellent resource, usable either as an educational text or for review. It is recommended for all business libraries and medium-sized public libraries.

57. Encyclopedia of Professional Management. Lester R. Bittel. New York: McGraw-Hill, 1979. $29.50.

Authority and scope: Bittel, business author, consultant, and professor, has edited the contributions of 232 experts in the field to provide a thorough treatment of management techniques, terms, practices, and philosophy. Each entry, under 2 pages in length, supplies a definition of underlying principles, a description of concrete applications and procedures, and evaluations of the usefulness of the concept. Illustrations are included when applicable, and most entries are accompanied by a list of references. It is generously cross-referenced and indexed.

Evaluation: This up-to-date and comprehensive treatment of management concepts useful to managers and students should be included in all library collections.

58. Europa Year Book: A World Survey. Detroit, MI: Gale, 1926–. Annual. 2 vols. $110.00.

Authority and scope: Published for over 50 years, this has become a standard source for information on the countries of the world. Volume 1 covers European countries and international organizations, and Volume 2 covers all other countries. Information provided includes essential data, statistical tables, descriptions of political and judicial systems, media, trade and industry, tourism, and population.

Evaluation: This is a truly authoritative handbook known for its up-to-date, accurate, and comprehensive coverage of the political, economic, and commercial institutions of the world. It is recommended for all but the smallest libraries. Smaller libraries may wish to note its accessibility elsewhere in the immediate area.

59. Everybody's Business: An Almanac; The Irreverent Guide to Corporate America. Milton Moskowitz, Michael Katz, and Robert Levering, eds. New York: Harper, 1980. $24.95.

Authority and scope: The authors, all business writers and journalists, have compiled this compendium of facts, figures, and anecdotes about 317 of the nation's largest corporations. Each profile includes concise summaries of the company's history, products, successes and failures, a comparison with related markets, and a discussion of the future of the company. Includes a consumer brand name index and a general index.

Evaluation: Informative as well as entertaining, libraries should consider buying a reference and a circulating copy of this "resourceful resource."

60. Fairchild's Financial Manual of Retail Stores. New York: Fairchild Publications, 1980. Annual. $50.00 paper.

Authority and scope: Statistical information on retail stores in the U.S. is provided, including sales, net income, assets, and stocks. Listed for each unit are officers, directors, business activities, subsidiaries, branches (if existent), and transfer agents.

Evaluation: Recommended for all libraries, this provides easy access to this segment of business for all business professionals, students, and job hunters. Smaller libraries could economize by purchasing in alternate years.

61. Federal Reserve Bulletin. U.S. Board of Governors of the Federal Reserve System. Washington, DC: Government Printing Office, 1915–. Monthly. $20.00.

Authority and scope: Published by the U.S. Board of Governors of the Federal Reserve System, this monthly periodical presents current articles on economics, money and banking, policy, and other official statements issued by the board. The "Financial and Business Statistics" section is the second half of each issue and is composed of current U.S. banking and monetary statistics. The statistics are presented monthly or quarterly for the current year and annually for the previous 3 years.

Evaluation: An excellent source for a survey of U.S. banking and monetary statistics, this periodical would be particularly useful for academic and special libraries.

62. Financial Studies of the Small Business. 3rd ed. Washington, DC: Financial Research Associates, 1976. $31.00.

Authority and scope: Published in loose-leaf format, this resource provides financial data (such as sales volume, operating ratios, income statements, liabilities, and trends) on various types of small business. Data included cover the year of publication.

Evaluation: The emphasis on factual data will aid the businessperson, student, or researcher in analyzing smaller businesses. It is recommended for academic and larger public libraries.

63. Forbes, Annual Directory Issue. New York: Forbes, 1917–. Annual. $3.00.

Authority and scope: Forbes, a leading publisher in the field of business, provides a listing of the 500 largest companies in the U.S. Published in May each year, the issue ranks the companies separately by sales, profits, assets, and market values and then lists them in alphabetical order. Each entry in the latter summarizes all rankings and financial data for that company.

Evaluation: This is a quick, convenient source for any library and comes as part of the subscription to the magazine. The list might not be as well known as the *Fortune Magazine's* 500 (entry 65), but the companies listed are usually the same on both lists, or nearly so, and the information provided in the *Forbes* list is more varied. Subscribers to the magazine should also benefit from other studies published on a regular basis, such as the mutual fund survey.

64. Foreign Economic Trends and Their Implications for the United States. U.S. Bureau of International Commerce. Washington, DC: Government Printing Office, 1968–. Irregular. $55.00/yr.

Authority and scope: Published by the Bureau of International Commerce, Department of Commerce, as compiled by the various U.S. embassies abroad, this series of over 100 brief country-by-country reports surveys current economic situations and trends and short-term prospects. Data provided are gross national product, foreign trade, wage and price indexes, unemployment rates, and construction.

Evaluation: This is a basic series useful for a concise overview of overseas economic conditions and their implications for the U.S. economy. It is recommended for all business libraries that can afford it, especially those with clientele involved in overseas business.

65. Fortune Directory of the 500 Largest U.S. Industrial Corporations. Chicago: Fortune Magazine, 1967–. (Published first in 3 issues each year and then issued as a separate pamphlet.) $3.75.

Authority and scope: Published by one of the most well-known and prestigious business magazines, the "Fortune 500" lists the largest U.S. industrial corporations. Appearing in May each year, the rankings include sales, assets, net income, stockholder's equity, employees, net income as percent of stockholder's equity, earnings per share, and total return to investors. The magazine also publishes 2 other similar lists: in June, the second 500 and in July, the largest commercial banking, life insurance, diversified financial, retailing, transportation, and utility companies.

Evaluation: As a special feature of one of the best-known business magazines, this source is a handy and reliable ranking of America's largest corporations and should be in all libraries. (See also entry 63, *Forbes, Annual Directory Issue.*)

66. Franchise Opportunities Handbook. U.S. Bureau of Domestic Commerce. Washington, DC: Government Printing Office, 1967–. Annual. $10.00.

Authority and scope: The U.S. Bureau of Domestic Commerce has provided a handbook of equal opportunity franchisors with the following information: descriptive information, number of existing franchises, training provided, requirements, and a brief history. There is useful information on selecting and evaluating a franchise, a list of government assistance programs, and a bibliography. The franchises are listed by category, but there is an alphabetical index and an index by category.

Evaluation: This is a relatively inexpensive and up-to-date reference source for a growing field of business; recommended for all libraries because of its general-interest value.

67. Guide to American Directories: A Guide to the Major Business Directories of the United States. Bernard Klein, ed. Coral Springs, FL: B. Klein Publications, 1956–. Irregular. $45.00.

Authority and scope: Bernard Klein, a well-known editorial consultant, has compiled an extensive listing of over 6,000 directories arranged in several hundred categories. A descriptive annotation is provided, with publication data for each title.

Evaluation: Heavy in business listings, this is a useful guide to reference books of value to all types of libraries, with the exception of the smallest public libraries.

68. Guide to Special Issues and Indexes of Periodicals. 2nd ed. New York: Special Libraries Association, 1976. $14.50.

Authority and scope: Compiled by members of the Special Libraries Association and published by the same organization, this reference tool provides details on over 1,200 periodicals that publish special features or indexes on a regular basis. The periodicals are listed in alphabetical order, and each entry, in addition to providing complete subscription information, includes the following information: title of the special issue or index, description, release date, and price. Added features include a classified list of periodicals and a subject index to the special issues. Work on a third edition is underway.

Evaluation: A valuable tool for identifying regularly appearing issues and indexes that attempt to gather together statistical or other types of useful data on an area, this is recommended for all libraries.

69. Handbook of Accounting and Auditing. John C. Burton, Russell E. Palmer, and Robert S. Kay. Boston: Warren, Gorham, and Lamont, 1981. (Annual supplements planned.) $57.50.

Authority and scope: The authors have compiled this handbook with the help of over 50 contributors, all accounting professors or accountant professionals. It is composed of 49 chapters in 7 parts: general issues of accounting measurement and disclosure, overview of accounting concepts and procedures, specific areas of current financial accounting reporting and auditing, accounting for specialized industries, major accounting institutions, legal aspects of accounting and auditing, and an overview of research in both fields. Each chapter includes suggested readings, and these lists are combined into a bibliography at the end. It is indexed.

Evaluation: A basic resource in an important field, the approach, content and comprehensiveness of this handbook recommend it as an essential purchase for all libraries.

70. Handbook of Advertising Management. Roger Barton. New York: McGraw-Hill, 1970. $39.50.

Authority and scope: Roger Barton and nearly 40 other contributors, all experts in the field of advertising, examine in detail all aspects of advertising management. The book's sections, each containing from 2 to 6 articles, cover the role of advertising in our society, organization of the department, advertising role in marketing, planning and budgeting, copy, media planning, research, special kinds of advertising, and advertising terms. There is a glossary of advertising terms and an index.

Evaluation: This thorough and informative book is particularly useful in its examination of each topic from one or more viewpoints, with case studies or examples illustrating each point or concept. Though somewhat dated, it is still the basic resource in its field and is recommended for all business libraries and medium-sized public libraries.

71. Handbook of Basic Economic Statistics. Washington, DC: Bureau of Economic Statistics. Monthly; annual cumulation. $120.00.

Authority and scope: The Bureau of Economic Statistics, a private research organization, publishes this basic sourcebook for current statistical information on the national economic situation, including comparable data back to 1913, if available. Data on labor, prices, production, general business indicators, social security, and national product and income are included.

Evaluation: Comprehensive, reliable, and approachable, this handbook is useful when statistics are needed but the patron is unsure of availability and format wanted. Expensive, though plain in appearance, this is a basic reference tool for business, academic, and larger public libraries.

72. Handbook of Construction Management and Organization. Joseph P. Frein, ed. 2nd ed. New York: Van Nostrand-Reinhold, 1980. $44.50.

Authority and scope: Frein, along with other experts in their fields, has compiled a comprehensive handbook on every phase of organizing and operating a construction business. The information is divided into 32 chapters, beginning with the basics of contracting and following through to contract completion and settlement. There is also coverage on financing, equipment maintenance and repair, basic management techniques, bid strategy, taxes, and estimating. An index is included.

Evaluation: This is an invaluable reference work directed to the general contractor, specialty contractor, and subcontractor, as well as to the student and professor. It is recommended to the business and medium-sized public library as a basic resource in this area.

73. Handbook of Labor Statistics. U.S. Bureau of Labor Statistics. Washington, DC: Government Printing Office, 1924/26–. Annual. $9.50.

Authority and scope: Issued by the U.S. Bureau of Labor Statistics, this handbook presents in one volume all major statistical series produced by the bureau and related series from other government agencies. Contents consist of statistical tables relating to employment, unemployment, productivity, compensation, prices, unions, industrial injuries, and foreign labor. In most of the tables, data for the last 2 years are given by month and by year prior to that.

Evaluation: This indispensable publication of current U.S. labor statistics is useful for any library.

74. Handbook of Marketing Research. Robert Ferber. New York: McGraw-Hill, 1974. $52.95.

Authority and scope: With the help of over 80 subject specialists, Robert Ferber, the first editor of the *Journal of Marketing Research* and active in the field of marketing research for over 30 years, has compiled a comprehensive reference on marketing research methods and applications. It is divided into 4 major sections: introduction, techniques, behavioral science techniques, and major areas of application. There is an index, and most chapters are accompanied by a bibliography. Some of the bibliographies are extensive.

Evaluation: This is an excellent one-volume reference source on this subject and is recommended for all libraries.

75. Handbook of Modern Accounting. Sidney Davidson and Roman Weill. 2nd ed. New York: McGraw-Hill, 1977. $39.50.

Authority and scope: Sidney Davidson, professor of accounting, provides an encyclopedic treatment of the subject with a series of articles written by 49 specialists. Topics range from basic concepts of accounting to the more specialized areas of cost analysis and dividends. The information is contained in 44 chapters, most with bibliographies, and the volume is indexed. ·

Evaluation: This is one of the most useful professional handbooks in the field of accounting and provides a solid core of information for any library.

76. Handbook of Modern Marketing. Victor P. Buell, ed. New York: McGraw-Hill, 1970. $59.95.

Authority and scope: Victor Buell, an associate professor of marketing and an active member of professional marketing associations, has edited this comprehensive reference work in the field of marketing. Each of the 120 chapters is written by a different authority and covers aspects such as modern marketing concepts, classification of markets, planning the product line, distribution, pricing, marketing research, planning the marketing program, selling and sales management, communications, customer services, and international marketing. There is an index, and most chapters are accompanied by a bibliography.

Evaluation: Although particularly applicable to a business library, this handbook can be recommended for general library collections as well.

77. Handbook of Modern Office Management and Administrative Services. Carl Heyel, ed. New York: Krieger, 1980. reprint of 1972 ed. $59.00.

Authority and scope: Carl Heyel, with the help of 80 contributors, provides a basic reference handbook for efficient office organization and operation. The information is divided into 10 sections: modern office operations, office environment, staffing and office pay, central support services, managing and improving office operations, training, personnel relations, achieving supervisory effectiveness, data processing, and new challenges and opportunities. An index is included.

Evaluation: Though dated in light of recent developments in word processing in office management, this handbook is the basic source in its field for any library reference collection.

78. Historical Statistics of the United States, Colonial Times to 1970. U.S. Bureau of the Census. Bicentennial Edition. Washington, DC: Government Printing Office, 1976. 2 vols. $34.00.

Authority and scope: Prepared by the Bureau of the Census with the cooperation of the Social Science Research Council, this 2-volume set serves as a historical supplement to the annual *Statistical Abstract of the United States* (entry 132). Like the *Abstract,* it serves as a prime source for U.S. social, economic, political, and industrial statistics, with linkages made between data in the 2 reference sets. One major difference is that statistics here are presented on a national basis only, with no breakdowns by region, state, or local area.

Evaluation: This is essential for every reference collection. Issued just twice since the first edition in 1945, it remains an affordable and easy-to-use statistical source for any library.

79. Illustrated Encyclopedic Dictionary of Real Estate Terms. Jerome S. Gross. 2nd ed. Englewood Cliffs, NJ: Prentice-Hall, 1978. $19.95.

Authority and scope: Jerome Gross, real estate broker for over 25 years and author of 2 other books on real estate, has compiled this dictionary of over 2,500 terms in the real estate field. Technical terms, colloquial words and phrases, laws, and policies are included. Most of the entries are less than 5 sentences in length, are liberally cross-referenced, and are illustrated when appropriate. The book also contains sample forms in their entirety, tables of amortization, a list of national organizations active in this field, and the code of ethics and standards of practice of the National Association of Realtors.

Evaluation: Easy to use and understand, this book is recommended as a basic source for all libraries. Public libraries should find the sample forms particularly useful.

80. Industrial Real Estate Managers Directory. Woburn, MA: Capitol Advertising Agency, 1967–. Annual. 1982–83, $42.00.

Authority and scope: Compiled by questionnaire and solicitations, this directory provides access to the industrial/commercial side of real estate. It is composed of 7 sections: (1) an alphabetical listing of the largest real estate management companies in the United States, along with names of managers and addresses; (2) an alphabetical listing of companies involved in the business; (3) a property digest (a geographical listing of new development and surplus properties available); (4) a classified listing of industrial development organizations that specialize in everything from a aerial photography and air parks to government agencies, industrial parks and warehouses—the names of the companies, addresses, and telephone numbers are provided; (5 and 6) alphabetical listings of Canadian firms in real estate and industrial development; and (7) a limited listing of foreign firms and organizations in industrial commercial real estate.

Evaluation: Larger public and business-oriented libraries should hold this directory. Smaller public libraries will want to assess its potential use by their business communities before deciding whether to purchase.

81. Insurance Almanac: Who, What, When and Where in Insurance; An Annual of Insurance Facts. New York: Underwriter Printing and Publishing, 1912–. Annual. $40.00.

Authority and scope: Published by the Underwriter Printing and Publishing Company, a leading publisher of insurance publications, this directory provides names of officers, type of insurance written, and for a few larger companies, the corporate history and company statistics, all separated into the 6 major lines of insurance. It also lists names of agents and brokers, adjusters, organizations, state officials, and management and insurance groups.

Evaluation: This is a basic insurance directory, useful as a quick reference source for any library. Smaller libraries may economize by purchasing in alternate years.

82. Insurance Facts. New York: Insurance Information Institute, 1961–. Annual. Single copies free.

Authority and scope: Published by one of the leading professional insurance associations in the country, this booklet provides basic data relating to the property and liability insurance business. The "facts" are separated into 2 sections: (1) insurance statistics, i.e., number of premiums written by type of insurance, and (2) losses, i.e., numbers of boating accidents, losses suffered as a result of tornadoes, etc.

Evaluation: A brief, convenient source for quick and selective reference questions, this booklet would be useful in any library.

83. Insurance Literature. INA Corp. Insurance and Employees Benefits Div. Philadelphia, PA: Special Libraries Association, 1940–. 10 issues a year. $10.00.

Authority and scope: The contributors to this annotated list of books and government documents are librarians for insurance and accounting firms. All fields of insurance are covered. Complete citations and order information are included with one or 2 brief sentences describing the publication. Articles on insurance which appear in the nontrade press are also included.

Evaluation: This source provides a good review of literature in the field and is essential for insurance libraries and any academic library serving students of insurance.

84. International Dictionary of Management. Hano Johannsen and G. Terry Page, eds. New York: Nichols Publications, 1977. $11.50 paper.

Authority and scope: Hano Johannsen and Terry Page, both noted business researchers and authors in Great Britain, have compiled a dictionary of over 5,000 entries covering the language of management in international usage. Definitions are thorough, ranging in length from one sentence to several paragraphs. When necessary, examples, addresses, italicized cross-references, and colloquialisms are included.

Evaluation: This comprehensive, practical, and easy-to-use reference tool is recommended for all libraries.

85. International Yearbook and Statesmen's Who's Who. London: Kelly's Directories, 1953–. Annual. $140.00.

Authority and scope: First published by the esteemed Burke's Peerage and most recently by Kelly's Directories, Ltd., the first section generally covers, for each country listed, information on area and commerce, constitution and government, and communications. The second part gives biographical sketches of world leaders in government, religion, commerce, industry, and education. Also included is information on international organizations such as the United Nations and the Organization of American States.

Evaluation: This is recommended as an additional source for information on nations when other reference tools have been purchased and/or consulted. The information is valuable and reliable, but the unevenness of the data included detracts from its usefulness. Most useful is the biographical section on world leaders, which provides often hard-to-find information.

86. Kelly's Manufacturers and Merchants Directory. London: Kelly's Directories, 1880–. Annual. $90.00.

Authority and scope: With a long publishing history behind it, this directory contains an alphabetical and classified listing of the names, addresses, products, and services of over 90,000 British companies. Companies in the London postal area are first listed alphabetically, with a classified listing following. The next section lists companies in England (excluding the London postal area), Scotland, Wales, and Northern Ireland, with the classified trade listing following. The final section is a listing of United Kingdom exporters and overseas companies in a classified products section that is subdivided by countries within continents.

Evaluation: An old favorite for access to British companies, this directory is recommended for business libraries and public libraries whose clientele have an interest in foreign enterprise.

87. The Language of Real Estate. John W. Reilly. New York: Real Estate Education, 1977. $35.95; $19.95 paper.

Authority and scope: John Reilly, an instructor in real estate law and practice, has compiled this handy reference of current terminology in real estate. Presented in dictionary format, the entries range in length from one paragraph to one page. Examples are given when useful. It is liberally cross-referenced and includes an appendix of abbreviations, sample forms, and a glossary of building terms.

Evaluation: Comprehensive, readable, and affordable, this handbook is recommended for all libraries.

88. Lesly's Public Relations Handbook. Philip Lesly. 2nd ed. Englewood Cliffs, NJ: Prentice-Hall, 1978. $29.95.

Authority and scope: With the contributions of over 40 experts, Lesly, a noted consultant and author in the field of public relations, has produced this extensive introduction to public relations. Fifty-three chapters are subdivided into 7 sections: what public relations is, what it includes, how an organization utilizes public relations, the techniques of communication, the practice of public relations, emerging principles, and trends. A bibliography, a glossary, codes of practice, and an index are provided.

Evaluation: Long considered the most comprehensive resource in its field, this reference is recommended for all libraries.

89. Life and Health Insurance Handbook. Davis W. Gregg and Vane B. Lucas, eds. 3rd ed. Homewood, IL: Dow Jones-Irwin, 1973. $17.50.

Authority and scope: Davis Gregg and Vane Lucas, both of the American College of Life Underwriters, with the help of 123 insurance authorities, have compiled this handbook on all major phases of life and health insurance, including the fields of pension, profit sharing, and estate planning. It is composed of 10 sections and divided into 72 chapters, all of which are followed by selected references. The appendixes contain a variety of contracts, riders, forms, tables, and other materials, and the volume is indexed.

Evaluation: Although written for the practitioner, businesspersons, researchers, and students dealing with insurance problems will find this handbook useful. It is recommended for all libraries as a basic reference source in this field.

90. Life Insurance Fact Book. Washington, DC: American Council of Life Insurance, 1946–. Annual. Single copies free.

Authority and scope: First published in 1946, this booklet summarizes—with texts, tables, and charts—the year's developments in the life insurance business in the United States. The data are taken from annual statements provided by life insurance companies and include statistics in summary form on annuities, payments, pensions and retirement programs, assets.

causes of death, and mortality. In most cases, the statistics are presented for the present year, as well as for the previous 20–30 years.

Evaluation: Most useful as a single source of information about the life insurance business; no library would go wrong in obtaining a copy of this handy factbook every year.

91. Life Rates and Data. Cincinnati, OH: National Underwriter, 1971–. Annual. $13.50.

Authority and scope: More than 300 insurers have contributed information for this compilation of premium rates, cash values, dividends, costs, and policy conditions for the life plans of the insurers listed. It is a companion volume to *Life Reports: Financial and Operating Results of Life Insurers* (entry 92).

Evaluation: Recommended as an inexpensive source for financial data on life insurers, this publication is extremely useful for both the professional and the layperson and should be in all libraries.

92. Life Reports: Financial and Operating Results of Life Insurers. Cincinnati, OH: National Underwriter, 1971–. Annual. $29.00.

Authority and scope: This companion volume to *Life Rates and Data* (entry 91) presents basic financial information on over 1,000 life insurers, plus detailed corporate operating statistics on more than half of those companies.

Evaluation: Both the professional and the layperson will be interested in this reference tool which is recommended for all libraries.

93. MacRae's State Industrial Directories. New York: Sales Management, 1959–. Annual. Price varies from $15.00 to $148.50.

Authority and scope: Recently acquired by MacRae's, a reputable publisher of business directories, this series includes individual directories for all states and lists manufacturers and processors alphabetically, geographically, and by Standard Industrial Classification (SIC) number. The geographical listing includes the most complete information for each company: names and corporate affiliations, street and mailing addresses, telephone numbers, names and titles of key personnel, products manufactured, year of establishment, square footage of plant, SIC codes, number of employees, locations of branch plants and research facilities, and export-import status.

Evaluation: These directories are easy to use and up to date. All libraries should hold the directory for their own state and perhaps those for surrounding states.

94. Mail Order Business Directory: A Complete Guide to the Mail Order Market. 13th ed. Coral Springs, FL: B. Klein Publications, 1980. $55.00.

Authority and scope: Klein Publications has prepared this directory of over 6,500 of the most active mail order and catalog houses. Listed geographically, state by state, each company is described (address, specialty, etc.), with a list of buyers included.

Evaluation: While somewhat limited in scope, this directory is recommended for medium-sized libraries as a basic, relatively inexpensive resource in this popular field.

95. Marconi's International Register. New York: Telegraphic Cable & Radio Registrations, 1898–. Annual. $65.00.

Authority and scope: This is an international cable address directory with a long history of publication. The company name section includes name, address, nature of business, telex numbers, and cable address. Another section presents trade headings, arranged in alphabetical order with a list of companies dealing in that trade. Also provided are a product heading index and sections for trade names, brands and trademarks, law specialties and names of attorneys by country, and cable addresses (with references to the complete address in the front of the directory).

Evaluation: This is useful as a directory for international companies; the access to foreign trade names could be helpful to special and larger public libraries. The register attempts to be comprehensive but is not, and smaller libraries could forego purchase.

96. Marketing Manager's Handbook. Stewart Henderson Britt, ed. Chicago: Dartnell, 1973, $52.50.

Authority and scope: Stewart Britt, well-known author and lecturer and president of his own marketing research firm, is editor of this comprehensive handbook. Over 150 marketing experts have contributed to the 73 chapters, which cover such topics as marketing research, developing the marketing plan, putting it into action, promotion, and international marketing. There are suggestions for further reading at the end of most chapters, and the volume is indexed.

Evaluation: One of the most comprehensive handbooks in the field, this is recommended for all libraries as a basic resource.

97. Million Dollar Directory. New York: Dun and Bradstreet, 1964–. Annual. 3 vols. vol. 1, $245.00; vol. 2, $215.00; vol. 3, $215.00.

Authority and scope: Published by a leading provider of business information, this well-known directory is now available in 3 volumes. Volume 1 covers companies with a net worth of $1.2 million plus; Volume 2 covers companies with a net worth of from $900,000 to $1.2 million; and Volume 3 covers companies with a net worth of from $500,000 to $900,000. Industrial firms are listed as well as utilities, banks and trust companies, transportation companies, mutual and stock insurance companies, wholesalers and retailers, and domestic subsidiaries of foreign corporations. In each volume, the businesses are listed alphabetically with the following information: address; headquarters; annual sales and number of employees, when available; stock exchange number; company ticker symbol; Standard Industrial Classification (SIC) number; names, titles, and functions of officers, directors, and other principals; and principal product. Each volume has a master index to all 3 volumes and geographical and SIC number listings to all companies.

Evaluation: Although expensive, these directories are essential for all business libraries and academic libraries, and for the public library with a large business clientele.

98. Minerals Yearbook. U.S. Bureau of Mines. Washington, DC: Government Printing Office, 1932–. Annual. 3 vols. vol. 1, $17.00; vol. 2, $14.00; vol. 3, $20.00.

Authority and scope: Since 1932, the Bureau of Mines, which is under the Department of the Interior, has annually reported mineral industry activities in the United States and foreign countries. Presently, the series is issued in 3 volumes. Volume 1 reports on all metals and minerals individually and reviews mining and metallurgical technology, employment, and injuries. Annual statistics on domestic production, consumption and uses, prices, foreign trade, and reserves are included. Volume 2 contains chapters on the mineral industry of each of the 50 states, the outlying areas, and the Commonwealth of Puerto Rico. Volume 3 reports the latest available material on the mineral industry of more than 130 foreign countries and discusses the importance of minerals to the economics of these nations. Information contained in these volumes is about 3 years behind publication date.

Evaluation: Recommended for all libraries, this series contains the most comprehensive data on the mineral industries of the United States and foreign countries. Depending on use, however, libraries could economize by buying volumes individually.

99. Modern Accountants Handbook. James Don Edwards and Homer A. Black, eds. Homewood, IL: Dow-Jones Irwin, 1976. $37.50.

Authority and scope: James Edwards and Homer Black, both professors of accounting, have compiled the contributions of 65 experts in the field and produced this handbook dealing with all phases of accounting and reporting problems. Presented in 8 parts and subdivided into 47 chapters, the information includes objectives of corporate accounting, realization and measurement of earnings, special problems, publication of financial information, policy, standards, and planning. It is indexed.

Evaluation: This basic text is recommended for all libraries as a useful resource in this field.

100. Monthly Bulletin of Statistics. New York: United Nations, 1947–. Monthly. $105.00.

Authority and scope: Published by the Department of International Economic and Social Affairs of the United Nations, this comprehensive bulletin provides statistical data for the nations of the world in such areas as industrial production, trade, transportation, national accounts, wage and price indexes, population, manpower, forestry, mining, manufacturing, construction, electricity and gas, and finance. Where possible, figures are given for 5 years and for the most recent 18 months. This bulletin is the monthly update to the annual *Statistical Yearbook* of the United Nations (entry 133).

Evaluation: Comprehensive and relatively up to date, this reference is recommended for business and academic libraries with appreciable interest in materials about foreign countries.

101. Monthly Labor Review. U.S. Bureau of Labor Statistics. Washington, DC: Government Printing Office, 1915–. Monthly. $23.00.

Authority and scope: In its seventh decade as the official journal of the Bureau of Labor Statistics, *Monthly Labor Review* continues to provide authoritative coverage of employment, prices, wages, productivity, job safety, and economic growth. Data are also presented on developments in industrial relations, labor case law, and foreign labor developments. Book reviews and explanatory notes on the data also appear.

Evaluation: The authoritative nature and extent of statistical treatment make this a must for all libraries.

102. Moody's Investors Service: Moody's Manuals: New York: Moody's Investors Service, 1955–. Annual, with semiweekly supplements. $525.00.

Authority and scope: Issued by one of the best-known financial publishing companies, *Moody's Investors Service* provides information on every U.S., Canadian, and foreign company listed on U.S. exchanges. The information is presented in 6 separate manuals: *Bank and Finance, Industrial, International, OTL Industrial, Public Utility,* and *Transportation.* Included are company history, subsidiaries, properties, management individuals, income statement, balance sheet, financial ratios, and outstanding securities. Also available, and of interest to investors, is the *Municipal and Government Manual,* covering over 15,000 municipalities.

Evaluation: One of the most comprehensive sources for information of this kind, this service is recommended for all business, academic, and medium-sized public libraries. The price is restrictive, unfortunately, and smaller libraries will want to pursue sharing this resource with other libraries before making a final decision on purchase, or simply indicating to users its availability elsewhere if the price proves prohibitive.

103. National Roster of Realtors Directory. Cedar Rapids, IA: Stamats Publishing, 1919–. Annual. $45.00.

Authority and scope: In its 60th edition, this directory provides a listing by state of all realtors (members of the National Association of Realtors), and within states, by boards, in the United States and Canada. The listing includes names and addresses. Also provided is information on the institutes, councils, and societies of the National Association of Realtors, including officers, directors, and executive staffs.

Evaluation: While most of this information can be obtained from the yellow pages of the telephone book, this directory is a convenient resource for this information. Libraries may consider purchasing in alternate years or obtaining an earlier edition from a local realtor.

104. National Trade and Professional Associations of the United States and Canada and Labor Unions. Washington, DC: Columbia Books, 1966–. Annual. $35.00.

Authority and scope: This is a directory listing more than 6,000 trade and professional associations and labor unions with national memberships.

Excluded are fraternal, sporting, patriotic, hobby, and political organizations. The organizations are first listed alphabetically, including name, chief executive officer, size of staff, membership, year founded, annual budget, meetings, and publications. Four indexes provide access to the associations listed: key word, geographic, budget (8 categories—from under $10,000 to over $1,000,000), and executive.

Evaluation: Overshadowed by the *Encyclopedia of Associations* (entry 51), this directory nevertheless is useful and has been known to list organizations not included by other publications. It is recommended for purchase by business and larger public libraries.

105. The 1981 Franchise Annual Handbook and Directory. Lewiston, NY: Info Press, 1981. $14.95.

Authority and scope: A directory of over 1,300 listings for American, Canadian, and overseas franchises, this volume also includes consultants, distributors, and licensors. Arranged by categories, most entries include name, address, and telephone number of contact person, nature of franchise, number of units authorized, date of establishment, and investment cost. There are also 6 chapters that explore and explain the intricacies of the franchise industry.

Evaluation: The general interest potential and reasonable price would make this a recommended item for all public and business-oriented libraries.

106. Overseas Business Reports. U.S. Bureau of International Commerce. Washington, DC: Government Printing Office, 1962–. Irregular. $44.00 per year.

Authority and scope: Prepared by the U.S. Department of Commerce, working with material provided by U.S. Foreign Service Officers, each report covers detailed information on trade and investment conditions, and on marketing opportunities in the country reviewed. Areas included are trade patterns, industry trends, distribution channels, natural resources, population, transportation, trade regulations, market prospects, and finance and economy.

Evaluation: These readable analyses are recommended for any business library with patrons interested in overseas markets. They can also serve smaller libraries as sources of information about foreign countries.

107. Personnel Administration Handbook. Wilbert Scheer. 2nd ed. Chicago: Dartnell, 1980. $48.50.

Authority and scope: Wilbert Scheer, consultant, author, and speaker, has provided a handbook covering all aspects of personnel administration: personnel management, recruitment, employment, indoctrination, orientation, training and development, health and safety, employee services, wage and salary administration, benefits, labor relations, administration, policy, and statesmanship. It is indexed.

Evaluation: This handbook is recommended for all libraries as a basic resource in this field, although smaller public libraries may want to identify a patron interest, considering the price and the possibility of limited and special interest.

108. Polk's World Bank Directory. Nashville, TN: Polk and Co., 1895–. Issued twice per year at $67.50 per issue, with supplements.

Authority and scope: This geographic listing of world banks gives names of officers and directors, correspondents, assets, and liabilities. A map accompanies each state and country section. The U.S. volume is issued semiannually with supplements, with an international section issued annually at mid-year. Additional information supplied includes state banking officials, holidays, an explanation of the Federal Reserve System, transit numbers, and holding companies. The world volume includes a list of U.S. banks offering international banking services.

Evaluation: A basic banking directory is necessary for all libraries, and this is recommended as one of the best available. The ability to purchase this directory as opposed to leasing it may be a factor for some libraries.

109. Production Handbook. Gordon B. Carson, et al., eds. 3rd ed. New York: Wiley-Interscience, 1972. $49.95.

Authority and scope: Gordon Carson and his coeditors are professors and consultants in industrial engineering and finance and, with 40 contributing experts, have compiled this comprehensive text on every state of planning, operation, and control in modern industrial management. Its 22 sections cover all phases of production, and a helpful outline is provided at the beginning of each section. Diagrams, charts, and formulas are included where appropriate, and there is a list of references at the end, as well as an index.

Evaluation: Though somewhat dated, this is still recommended as the basic resource in its field, particularly for business libraries and medium-sized public libraries.

110. Public Affairs Information Service. Bulletin. New York: Public Affairs Information Service, 1915–. Issued twice a month with 3 cumulatives and an annual bound volume. $200.00.

Authority and scope: The Public Affairs Information Services (PAIS), a nonprofit association of libraries, provides this subject index to periodicals, pamphlets, government documents, society publications, mimeographed materials, and some yearbooks. PAIS attempts to identify public affairs information relating to economic and social conditions, public administrations, and international affairs. Complete bibliographic information is included for each citation. Annual cumulations include an author index with enough information to identify the source.

Evaluation: This is highly recommended for the use of library patrons interested in public affairs. The subjects and types of material covered make it particularly useful. However, the smaller library with a general clientele may want to forego purchase.

111. Pugh's Dictionary of Acronyms and Abbreviations. Eric Pugh, ed. Phoenix, AZ: Oryx Press, 1982. $85.00.

Authority and scope: Previously published in 3 separate noncumulating volumes, this reference is a combination of all editions and contains over 30,000 entries in management, technology, and information science. Arranged alphabetically by acronym, the full name associated with each acronym and abbreviation is given, plus the name of originating country and/or the organization that developed the acronym.

Evaluation: Comprehensive and covering useful areas, this reference is recommended for all business and academic libraries.

112. Quality Control Handbook. J.M. Juran, ed. 3rd ed. New York: McGraw-Hill, 1974. $42.50.

Authority and scope: Working with the contributions of over 40 experts, Juran—a consultant, professor, and manager—has compiled this handbook covering all aspects of quality control in industry. Designed as a reference source for the manager, supervisor, and engineer, the volume presents its information in 52 sections and 1,800 pages. General principles and concepts as well as standards and guidelines for specific industries are covered. Examples and illustrations are used throughout, and each section is followed by a bibliography. There are also extensive statistical tables, charts, and an index.

Evaluation: Comprehensive in scope, this handbook is recommended as a basic resource in this field and belongs in all but the smallest libraries.

113. Questions and Answers on Real Estate. Robert W. Semenow. 9th ed. Englewood Cliffs, NJ: Prentice-Hall, 1979. $14.95.

Authority and scope: Considered the foremost real estate license law expert in the United States, Robert Semenow has authored a text that has become the chief resource for individuals taking the real estate license examination. It covers the major aspects of real estate, such as agreements, financing, deeds, landlord-tenants relationships, valuation, condominiums, syndicates, and appraisal, and it includes a question-and-answer section.

Evaluation: Because of its importance to the real estate community, this is an essential purchase for every library. It is recommended that 2 copies be purchased: a reference copy and a circulation copy.

114. Rand McNally Commercial Atlas and Marketing Guide. New York: Rand McNally, 1876–. Annual. $135.00.

Authority and scope: Published by a company known by the general populace for its maps, the *Commercial Atlas* contains a map for each state, but it is especially valuable for its excellent statistical and demographic data. It provides statistical indicators of market potential for U.S. cities, counties, and regions. In addition it includes a list of colleges, a list of the largest corporations in America, postal information, and railroad and air distances. The place name index provides for each entry, population, elevation, zip code, post office (if different), and symbols to indicate commercial activity (e.g., banking town, principal business center, railroad). The *Road Atlas* appears as a supplement to the *Commercial Atlas* and is received with it.

Evaluation: This is a standard reference that belongs in all libraries.

115. Real Estate Desk Book. Institute of Business Planning. 6th ed. Englewood Cliffs, NJ: Prentice-Hall, 1979. $29.95.

Authority and scope: Researched and edited by the staff of the Institute of Business Planning, this handbook comprehensively covers all aspects of real estate. Intended for the investor, salesperson, and home buyer, it includes information on tax benefits, syndication, leasing, casualty losses, zoning laws, financing, and how to figure tax on a sale. Also included are a glossary, comparative depreciation tables, interest amortization tables, and an index.

Evaluation: Frequently revised, this is a useful reference, and it is recommended as a basic resource on real estate for all libraries.

116. Real Estate Handbook. Maury Seldin, ed. Homewood, IL: Dow Jones-Irwin, 1980. $37.50.

Authority and scope: Maury Seldin, a professor and consultant of finance and real estate, along with 78 authorities in the field, has compiled this handbook dealing with all phases of the real estate industry. It is divided into 5 sections: transactions, analyses, marketing, financing, and investments. Some chapters include a selected list of references. A lengthy appendix lists the requirements and certifications of professional designations in the field. An index is included.

Evaluation: Thorough and up to date, this reference tool is recommended to all libraries as an authoritative resource in this area.

117. Real Estate Law. Robert Kratovil. 7th ed. Englewood Cliffs, NJ: Prentice-Hall, 1979. $24.95.

Authority and scope: Written by a member of the Chicago Bar, this reference covers the basic principles of real estate law and includes such topics as sources of real estate law, aspects of land, titles, deeds, acknowledgements, contracts, sales, escrows, mortgages, and insurance. The coverage is thorough and follows an easy-to-use numbered paragraph format.

Evaluation: Recommended for all libraries, this will be useful to the general public, students, and professionals interested in real estate transactions.

118. Real Estate Today. Chicago: National Association of Realtors, 1968–. Bimonthly. $11.00, library rate.

Authority and scope: Published by the National Association of Realtors for the real estate professional, this periodical includes topical articles on real estate management and trends. Regular features are legal briefs, news developments, ''Washington Focus,'' sales ideas, and book reviews. Indexed in *Business Periodicals Index* (entry 20).

Evaluation: Readable and timely, this periodical should be included in any library collection.

119. Sales and Marketing Management. New York: Sales Management, 1918–. Biweekly. $24.50.

Authority and scope: Published for many years as *Sales Management*, this periodical offers information on all phases of the marketing process. In short- to medium-sized articles, it covers strategies, tactics, research and evaluation, and success stories. Of particular note are the 4 annual statistical issues, the most well-known being *Survey of Buying Power,* Parts 1 and 2. Part 1 reports statistical data on buying power; population; households; and income and retail sales for cities, counties, and metropolitan areas. Part 2 reports metropolitan market projections and growth rates for population, income, and retail sales; annual surveys of television, newspaper, and radio markets; and Canadian metropolitan market projections. Also published annually are: *Survey of Selling Costs,* a statistical report on a broad range of selling expenses, and *Survey of Industrial Purchasing Power,* which provides industrial data for approximately 2,800 countries with manufacturing activity.

Evaluation: Presenting information on all phases of the marketing process, this periodical is unsurpassed in its field and belongs in all but the smallest public libraries because of its general interest to the business community.

120. Sales Promotion Handbook. Ovid Riso. 7th ed. Chicago: Dartnell, 1979. $48.50.

Authority and scope: Ovid Riso, an active and leading authority in the field, has compiled this 44-chapter handbook covering all aspects of sales promotion. The book is divided into 4 parts: responsibilities of sales promotion, techniques and tools, channels of distribution, and special supplements to sales promotion. This volume makes extensive use of examples, charts, and actual cases. It is indexed.

Evaluation: Recommended as a basic resource in its field, this handbook is especially recommended for business libraries and medium-sized public libraries.

121. Savings and Loan Sourcebook. Chicago: U.S. Savings and Loan League, 1954–. Irregular. $2.50.

Authority and scope: Published by a major trade association in the United States, this booklet is a consolidation of factual information on savings, mortgage lending, housing, the savings and loans business, and related federal government agencies. Data are given for the latest year and, in some cases, for 10 to 20 years. A short text explains the basics of the savings and loans business, and a table of major federal laws affecting the business, a glossary of terms, and an index are provided.

Evaluation: This is a handy, useful booklet, whose easy availability makes it a recommended item for all libraries.

122. Security Dealers of North America. New York: Standard and Poor's, 1982. $212.00 set.

Authority and scope: A noted publishing company in the field of business, Standard and Poor's provides this listing of brokers/dealers and investment banking firms in the United States and Canada. Completely revised twice a year, it is a geographical listing of security administrators and active security dealters, with a separate listing of discontinued security dealers. Listings include names of partners, officers, branch managers, and department heads. In addition, complete address and telephone number for each office, exchange memberships, specialization, clearing facilities, and wire services are listed.

Evaluation: This is a necessary, although expensive, reference source for all business libraries and large public library systems. A current subscription is necessary and probably places the source out of the reach of smaller libraries.

123. Small Business Index. Wayne D. Kryszak. Metuchen, NJ: Scarecrow, 1978. $12.00.

Authority and scope: Wayne Kryszak, a business librarian in a public library, has compiled a listing of books, pamphlets, periodical articles, and government documents which contain information on starting a small business. Over 500 types of small businesses are covered in citations that include material varying in length from a page or 2 to complete books. Arrangement is alphabetical by type of business with one to a dozen or so listings for each. Also included are a list of publishers and a bibliography with complete bibliographic information.

Evaluation: Recommended for any library with clientele interested in small business, this volume is a handy, time-saving reference tool.

124. Standard and Poor's Register of Corporations, Directors, and Executives, United States and Canada. New York: Standard and Poor's, 1928–. Annual. $130.00.

Authority and scope: Standard and Poor's, a leading publisher in the field of business publications, has compiled this comprehensive directory to over 37,000 U.S. corporations. Volume 1 is an alphabetical listing of the companies; each entry includes addresses, names of officials, products, company accounting firm, primary bank and law firm, and number of employees, as well as total sales figures when available. Volume 2 is a straight alphabetical listing of over 72,000 individuals serving as chief officials or board members. Each entry includes name of company with which individual is affiliated, business and residence addresses, and when possible, date of birth, education received, and club memberships. Volume 3 is divided into 6 color-coded sections: Standard Industrial Classification (SIC) numbers and explanations, a list of companies by 4-digit SIC number, geographical index, obituary section, new individual listings, and new company additions.

Evaluation: One of the best-known of all directories, this is recommended for all libraries. If the library is limited to only one business directory, this should be it.

125. Standard Directory of Advertisers (Classified and Geographical Editions). Skokie, IL: National Register Publishing, 1980. $109.00 each.

Authority and scope: This directory lists over 17,000 companies allocating annual appropriations for national or regional advertising campaigns. The companies are listed in 50 product classifications, and each entry includes name, address, telephone number, type of business, key management executives, advertising agency, account executive, time and amount of appropriations, and advertising media. Also included are an alphabetical index, a trade name index, and a list of Standard Industrial Classification group numbers and their relation to the product classification used in the directory.

Evaluation: Recommended for all but the smallest libraries, this is a handy source of basic information on nationally known companies. While the same information can be found elsewhere, the arrangement of the information and the trade name expand the usefulness of this directory.

126. Standard Directory of Advertising Agencies. Skokie, IL: National Register Publishing, 1981. 3 vols. $52.00 each; $127.00 set.

Authority and scope: Over 4,500 companies are listed in this directory of advertising agencies in the United States and overseas. To keep up to date in a rapidly changing business, it is published 3 times a year and supplemented by a news sheet issued 9 times a year. Agencies are arranged alphabetically, and each entry contains the following information: address and phone number, chief officers, specialization, annual billing, number of employees, and names of clients. At the front of the directory are a geographical index of domestic agencies and an index of foreign advertising agencies, including U.S. companies with foreign branches.

Evaluation: An essential resource for researchers and individuals in the advertising business and related fields, this directory is recommended to libraries serving those patrons. Other libraries may elect to purchase only one volume per year or the entire set in alternate years.

127. Standard Handbook for Secretaries. Lois Hutchinson. 8th ed. New York: McGraw-Hill, 1969. $9.95.

Authority and scope: Hutchinson, a long-recognized authority in her field, has compiled this standard desk reference for secretaries, which covers a wide variety of topics, including reports, minutes of meetings, letter writing, filing, grammar, legal papers, patents, copyrights, trademarks, and weights and measures.

Evaluation: This is recommended as an essential handbook for all libraries. The combination of information and ease of use makes it a helpful reference.

128. Standard Industrial Classification Manual. U.S. Bureau of the Budget. Washington, DC: Government Printing Office, 1972. $15.00. 1977 supplement, $2.00.

Authority and scope: Issued by the Office of Management and Budget, the SIC manual is a guide to one of the most extensive classification systems in use in the United States. It divides U.S. industries by type of activity and assigns an industry code number that is determined by the product or service rendered. The entire field of economic activity (agriculture, forestry, construction, manufacturing, wholesale and retail trade, finance, real estate, etc.) is covered.

Evaluation: Because of the extensive use of this classification system in government and private industry, this is an essential purchase for all but the smallest libraries, especially considering its reasonable price.

129. Standard Periodical Directory. Patricia Hagood, ed. 7th ed. New York: Oxbridge Communications, 1981–82. Biennial. $120.00.

Authority and scope: Irregularly published at first, but now biennial, this directory contains information on over 65,000 periodicals published in the United States and Canada. It is arranged by subject, and each entry includes title, publishing company, address, telephone, key staff names, description of contents, book review acceptance, year established, frequency and circulation, advertising and subscription rates, printing method, size, and color if used. There is also an index by title.

Evaluation: Recommended for all libraries, this directory lists more periodicals than *Ulrich*'s (entry 140) and is easier to use. Since it does not contain foreign titles, libraries may want to purchase both on an alternate year basis.

130. Standard Rate and Data Service. Chicago: Standard Rate and Data Service, 1919–. Frequency and price vary with issue.

Authority and scope: This comprehensive source of information about media provides advertising rates and data information for newspapers, business publications, consumer magazines, farm publications, print media, community periodicals, co-op news types, co-op source directories, Canadian and international advertising media, spot television and radio, small markets, and networks. Information such as demographic characteristics, metro area rankings, spendable income, retail sales, and media market maps (when appropriate) is also useful.

Evaluation: Useful to larger libraries (which may also be better able to afford it), this is recommended to any library whose patrons are buyers of advertising time and space. Libraries may wish to subscribe selectively.

131. Statesman's Year-book. John Paxton, ed. New York: St. Martin's Press, 1864–. Annual. $30.00.

Authority and scope: With a long history of reliable publication, this manual provides a wide variety of information about the United Nations, other international organizations, and the nations of the world, in addition to statistical tables on some commodities. For each country, information includes history, area and population, constitution and government, defense, international relations, economy, energy and natural resources, industry and trade, communications, justice, religion, education and welfare, and diplomatic representatives.

Evaluation: Reliable and relatively inexpensive, this is recommended for all libraries.

132. Statistical Abstract of the United States. U.S. Bureau of the Census. Washington, DC: Government Printing Office, 1879–. $12.00.

Authority and scope: Published regularly by the U.S. Bureau of the Census since 1879, this is the "standard summary of statistics on the social, political, and economic organization of the United States." National data are featured, although data for regions, states, metropolitan areas, and cities, are sometimes provided as well. Included are tables of statistics for population, vital statistics, and statistics for immigration and naturalization, health and nutrition, education, law enforcement, geography and environment, public parks, federal and state and local government finances and employment, social insurance, national defense, labor, income, prices, elections, banking and finance, communications, energy, science, transportation, agriculture, forests, fisheries, mining, construction, manufactures, domestic trade, and foreign commerce. Most tables cover several years; some go back to the 1800s.

Evaluation: An indispensable and inexpensive source, this is a must for all libraries.

133. Statistical Yearbook. United Nations. Statistical Office. New York: International Publications Service, 1948–. Annual. $60.00.

Authority and scope: Published by the Statistical Office of the United Nations, this reference tool is a digest of statistics for over 200 countries. Arranged by broad subject areas and then presented by individual countries, the statistical tables include data on manufacturing, energy resources, agricultural production, finance, etc. In most cases, the data cover the last 10 years.

Evaluation: This is a valuable reference source for larger libraries; smaller libraries may rely on more general titles or may elect to purchase in alternate years.

134. Statistics Sources: A Subject Guide to Data on Industrial, Business, Social, Educational, Financial, and Other Topics for the United States and Internationally. Paul Wasserman and Jacquelyn O'Brien, eds. 7th ed. Detroit, MI: Gale, 1982. $130.00.

Authority and scope: Paul Wasserman and Jacquelyn O'Brien, noted business bibliographers, are editors of this guide to over 28,000 statistical sources issued by both the private sector and the government. Arranged in very detailed subject categories, some 12,000, each entry includes title, name of publisher, and address (where obtainable). While emphasis is on data in published form, sources of current information on fast-changing fields are also identified. Previous editions have concentrated on U.S. statistics, but the most recent edition includes expanded coverage on foreign nations and products.

Evaluation: Recommended for all libraries as a basic resource on which to base referrals, this is the purchase to be made if only one such reference tool can be afforded.

135. Survey of Current Business. U.S. Department of Commerce. Washington, DC: Government Printing Office, 1921–. Monthly. $22.00.

Authority and scope: Published by the Bureau of Economic Analysis of the Department of Commerce, this periodical presents significant economic indicators for business use. Each issue contains an analysis of the current business situation, and, as the other regular feature, current business statistics for the latest month, quarter, or year. In the latter section, categories are as follows: general business indicators (personal income, business sales, manufacturers' inventories, etc.), commodity prices, domestic trade, labor force, employment and earnings, finance, and production and export statistics for major industry categories. The rest of each issue is composed of articles on various aspects of the nation's economy, trends, and outlook. It is indexed in *Business Periodicals Index* (entry 20), and the current business statistics are cumulated in the biennial publications *Business Statistics* (entry 23).

Evaluation: Considered by many to be the most important single source for current business statistics, this is recommended for all libraries.

136. Television Factbook. Washington, DC: Television Digest, 1982–. Annual. 2 vols. $159.50.

Authority and scope: Published by a specialist in the industry, the *Factbook* provides access to all aspects of the business of television. The "Station" volume contains operating information for U.S. and Canadian television stations, and to a lesser degree, those in foreign countries. Arranged geographically, the information includes: personnel, ownership and history of station, technical facilities, a map indicating the market, and advertising rates. There is also a directory of public educational TV stations. The "Services" volume includes information on television stations (call letters, etc.), cable TV, networks, and related industries: production firms, advertising agencies, and equipment manufacturers.

Evaluation: This directory is the most comprehensive guide to the television industry and is recommended for all libraries. It could be purchased in alternative years by smaller libraries in order to economize or availability could be noted in other libraries in the area.

137. Thomas' Register of American Manufacturers. New York: Thomas Publishing, 1905–. Annual. 16 vols. $95.00.

Authority and scope: This comprehensive directory to American manufacturing firms is offered in 3 parts. Part 1 lists products and services in detailed subject categories with helpful cross-references. All known manufacturers or sources are listed alphabetically by state and by city within a state, with addresses and telephone numbers included. Part 2 lists, in alphabetical order, all companies included in the *Register* with complete addresses and phone numbers, asset ratings, subsidiaries, and affiliates. There is also a brand name listing with owner company's name and address. Part 3 is composed of reprints of company catalogs.

Evaluation: Somewhat like a "yellow pages," this is recommended for all libraries as a very comprehensive access to American manufacturing. Smaller libraries may alternate years of purchase or obtain the "next to the latest" set from a larger library or friendly local business.

138. Thorndike Encyclopedia of Banking and Financial Tables. Boston: Warren, Gorham, and Lamont, 1980–. Annual. $60.00.

Authority and scope: Published by a respected publishing firm, this yearbook is a comprehensive collection of tables of banking, investment, mortgage, and financial computations compiled by David Thorndike, Wall Street consultant. There are tables for interest rates or yields on mortgage and real estate, simple and compound interest on savings and bonds, and rates on various types of loans. The yearbook contains more tables, updated to reflect the changing monetary scene, and a revised section on state usury and bad-check laws, foreign exchange rates, and a glossary of terms.

Evaluation: Comprehensive and up to date, this reference is recommended for all libraries except the smallest public libraries (where similar information on a narrower scale, published in pamphlet form and usually available locally, might be all that is needed).

139. Trade Names Dictionary. Ellen T. Crowley, ed. 2nd ed. Detroit, MI: Gale, 1979. $145.00.

Authority and scope: With emphasis on consumer-oriented products, this dictionary contains over 130,000 entries for products, manufacturers, and distributors. Arranged in alphabetical order, each trade name appears in bold face and is followed by a brief description, the manufacturer's name, and a symbol indicating the source of information. The names of manufacturers are listed in regular type with brief addresses. The list of information sources includes complete name, publisher's address, and current price. It has been issued every 3 years, and supplements are published annually. Also available is a company index that lists all companies in the basic dictionary and the products they manufacture.

Evaluation: Recommended for all libraries, this easy-to-use reference is the most comprehensive such list in a single source.

140. Ulrich's International Periodicals Directory. New York: Bowker, 1932–. Annual. $78.00.

Authority and scope: Bowker, one of the largest and most respected companies in publishing, is responsible for this classified listing of over 63,000 periodicals published throughout the world. Arranged in 385 subject areas, each entry provides title, frequency, publisher name and address, cost, and indexing or abstracting information. Also included are a list of publications that have ceased publishing, an index to publications of international organizations, and a title index.

Evaluation: This comprehensive and up-to-date resource is considered a basic part of every reference collection. Its classified arrangement provides easy access to a large amount of information.

141. U.S. Government Manual. U.S. General Services Administration. Office of the Federal Register. Washington, DC: Government Printing Office, 1935–. Annual. $11.00.

Authority and scope: Published by the General Services Administration, this manual provides comprehensive information on the agencies of the federal government, as well as on the quasi-official agencies, commissions, committees, boards, and international organizations in which the United States participates. Each entry includes a list of principal officials, organization chart, agency purpose, history, legislative and executive authority, address, description of program and activities, and "sources of information." The appendixes offer additional, useful information: abolished or transferred agencies, commonly used abbreviations and acronyms, the text of several information acts, names of regional councils and boards, and a list of Code of Federal Regulation titles. Indexed by name, subject, and agency.

Evaluation: Recommended for all libraries, this handbook provides indispensable access to the agencies of the federal government.

142. U.S. Government Purchasing and Sales Directory. Washington, DC: Government Printing Office, 1977. $6.50.

Authority and scope: Compiled by the Small Business Administration (SBA), this is an alphabetical listing of the products and services bought by military departments and civilian agencies. Divided into 2 sections, military and civilian, the directory provides a list of products keyed to a separate listing of agencies with addresses. The directory also includes ways in which the SBA can help a business get government contracts and data on surplus property.

Evaluation: Informative and comprehensive, this relatively inexpensive directory is recommended for all libraries, particularly small and medium-sized public libraries serving the small business owner or entrepreneur.

143. [Year] U.S. Industrial Outlook for 200 Industries with Projections for [year]. U.S. Department of Commerce, Trade and Industry. Washington, DC: Government Printing Office, 1960–. Annual. $10.00.

Authority and scope: Published by the Department of Commerce, this report presents statistics and 5-year projections for 200 major U.S. industries, grouped by the Standard Industrial Classification system. Along with the statistics are included short descriptions and discussions of trends, international trade, research and development, and outlook. A list of additional references is included at the end of most chapters.

Evaluation: Recommended for all libraries, this is a reliable resource for information on recent trends and outlook for industries.

144. Value Line Investment Survey. New York: Arnold Bernhard, 1937–. Weekly. $330.00.

Authority and scope: This weekly review and analysis of over 1,630 stocks in 75 industries includes, for each stock, a stock chart, tabular statistics and opinions on longer-term quality, performance and income, and yield expectations. The statistics and charts are reviewed on a rotating basis, industry by industry, so that the information on every company is revised quarterly. A weekly ''Selection and Opinion'' newsletter includes an analysis of the stock market, prospects for business, and recommendations for investment strategy.

Evaluation: Considered to be one of the most popular and respected investment surveys, this reference tool is recommended for all libraries.

145. Vital Statistics of the United States. U.S. Department of Health and Human Services. Public Health Service. National Center for Health Statistics. Washington, DC: Government Printing Office, 1937–. Annual. vol. 1: Natality, $13.00; vol. 2: Mortality, part 1, $22.00, part 2, $22.00; vol. 3: Marriage & Divorce, $11.00.

Authority and scope: The U.S. government publishes this extensive report presenting tabulations of data on natality, marriage, divorce, and mortality. The statistics are tabulated in detailed demographic and geographic breakdowns (state, county, Standard Metropolitan Statistical Areas, and in some cases, towns of 10,000 or more) and extensive cross-tabulations. A monthly report is published to make up for the considerable time lag in the annual volumes.

Evaluation: Considered the authoritative source in this area, this reference is recommended for business libraries (particularly those specializing in insurance), academic libraries, and larger public libraries.

146. The Wall Street Journal. New York: Dow Jones, 1889–. Daily except Saturday and Sunday. $77.00/year.

Authority and scope: Generally recognized as the basic newspaper for the businessperson, the *Wall Street Journal* is also a useful source of information for the general reader. A summary of general news accompanies detailed factual reports on companies, industries, and business personalities. The latest stock market statistical information is included, as is a classified section that lists positions available.

Evaluation: Because of its coverage of all news important to business, this basic reference tool should be held by all libraries.

147. The Wall Street Journal Index. Princeton, NJ: Dow Jones Books, 1958–. Monthly with annual cumulations. $365.00.

Authority and scope: This index is compiled from the final eastern edition of *The Wall Street Journal* (entry 146) and is arranged in 2 parts: "Corporate News" and "General News." The entries are listed alphabetically, with a chronological listing within each topic. An abstract of each article is followed by the date, page, and column of the article. It is issued monthly and then published in an annual cumulation.

Evaluation: A necessity for libraries that maintain back files of the *Journal;* smaller libraries that do not subscribe or do not keep the *Journal* for any length of time can probably do without.

148. Ward's Directory of 50,000 Leading U.S. Corporations. Petaluma, CA: Ward Publications. Annual. $60.00.

Authority and scope: Published by the editors of *News Front,* this is a computerized list of the largest corporations in all manufacturing and nonmanufacturing industry categories of the Standard Industrial Classification System (SIC). They are ranked by annual sales and by 25 indexes, including profits, sales, assets, number of employees, cash flow, current ratios, stock holder equity, and totals—by industries—that determine individual company percentage of sales and share of the market. The 4 sections are public companies, public and private companies, geographical-zip code, and an alphabetical listing.

Evaluation: This is one of the few directories that ranks public and private companies together by SIC number. It is recommended for all special, academic, and medium to larger public libraries.

149. Where to Find Information About Companies. 2nd ed. Washington, DC: Washington Researchers, 1981. $79.00.

Authority and scope: Written to "show researchers sources of information about public and private companies, both foreign and domestic," this reference details sources in federal, state, and local government as well as in the private sector. Information is provided for finding the appropriate office at state and federal levels for information on such subjects as air pollution, banking, economic development, insurance, etc. Also listed are U.S. district courts and Freedom of Information Act offices in each federal agency. Resources such as trade unions, investigative services, credit reporting and bond rating services, and databases are noted for the private sector.

Evaluation: This relatively simple, straightforward, and convenient access to resources on companies is recommended for all business and academic libraries.

150. Who's Who in America. Chicago: Marquis Who's Who, 1899–. Biennial. $109.50.

Authority and scope: Produced by one of the best-known publishers of biographical material, the 42nd edition provides thumbnail sketches of approximately 73,500 individuals. Included are details obtained from the biographees, whose eligibility for inclusion is by virtue of position and/or significant contribution to society. The following information is provided: name, position, vital statistics, parents, educational background, marital status, career and related activities, professional and other memberships, writings, and home and office address. A necrology of biographees listed in the previous edition but since deceased is incorporated, as is a listing of more than 74,500 persons whose sketches have appeared in one of the regional directories (many of whom are not listed in the national edition).

Evaluation: This is recommended as an essential reference for all libraries.

151. Who's Who in Finance and Industry. Chicago: Marquis Who's Who, 1936–. $62.50.

Authority and scope: Now in its 22nd edition, this directory provides career sketches of leaders in the field of business and finance. Information provided includes: name, position, vital statistics, parents, educational background, marital status, career and related activities, professional and other memberships, writings, and home and office address. The "Standards of Admissions" statement indicates that executives were selected because of special prominence in their particular branch of business or because of positions held in financial and industrial concerns of certain sizes or ratings. The selected index of principal businesses was deleted with the 1975 volume.

Evaluation: Marquis's long tradition of quality in preparing biographical directories is borne out here. All libraries with a business collection of any size should hold this directory.

152. Wiesenberger Investment Companies Service. New York: Wiesenberger Financial Services, 1941–. Annual with supplements. $145.00.

Authority and scope: Wiesenberger Financial Services, a respected publisher in the financial field, has provided a guide to mutual funds and investment companies. The information is taken from annual reports to stockholders and other statistical sources and gives "background, management policy & financial record for all leading companies in the U.S. and Canada." It is divided into 4 parts: general information about investment companies, the use of investment companies, mutual funds and other types of investment companies, and closed-end investment companies and mutual fund management companies. Also provided are a list of investment company managers/advisers and an index. Two newsletters with up-to-date information appear quarterly.

Evaluation: Considered to be the best single source for basic information on mutual funds and investment companies, this service is recommended for all business libraries, and for smaller and medium-sized public libraries that can justify the price. Smaller libraries should consider sharing the purchase or simply identifying availability at libraries in the area.

153. World Almanac and Book of Facts. New York: Newspaper Enterprise Association, 1868–. Annual. $8.95.

Authority and scope: First published in 1868 and annually since 1886, this compilation of information and statistics covers almost every subject of interest to Americans. It contains statistics on social, industrial, political, financial, religious, and educational topics, lists of associations and societies, biographies of famous personalities, and important current events of the previous year. Sources for many of the statistics are given, and a good general index appears at the front of the volume.

Evaluation: No library should be without this indispensable ready-reference tool.

154. World Directory of Multinational Enterprises. John M. Stopford, John H. Dunning, and Klaus O. Haberich. New York: Facts on File, 1980. $195.00.

Authority and scope: Compiled by professors, authors, and consultants on international finance, this reference presents "profiles of 430 major multinational enterprises, accounting for over 80% of the world's stock of foreign direct investment." The information for each company has been taken from annual reports, general publicity releases, and reports submitted to the government as required by law. Each profile includes a summary, description of structure, products, history, current situation, 5-year financial summary, major stockholders, and principal subsidiaries. Useful summary statistical tables are included as an appendix.

Evaluation: This reference provides access to an increasingly important segment of business, and, while expensive, it nevertheless is an extremely useful source and is recommended for all except the smallest public libraries.

155. World Wide Chamber of Commerce Directory. Loveland, CO: Johnson Publishing, 1967–. Annual. $12.00.

Authority and scope: This directory provides a compact listing of Chambers of Commerce in the United States, with information including the manager or president of the chamber, its address, its telephone number, and the population it serves. There are also lists of American Chambers of Commerce abroad, Canadian Chambers of Commerce, Foreign Chambers in principal cities of the world, and embassies and consulates.

Evaluation: The usefulness of data, convenience, and low price make this a recommended purchase for all but the smallest libraries.

156. Yearbook of International Trade Statistics. United Nations. Statistical Office. New York: International Publications Service, 1950–. Annual. $65.00.

Authority and scope: Published by the Statistical Office of the United Nations, this yearbook provides basic information for 139 countries' external trade performances in terms of the overall trends in current values as well as volume and price. Also gives information on the significance of individual commodities imported and exported. Volume 1 contains data arranged by country for 5 to 10 years, and Volume 2 has data by commodity for the year preceding the volume year. The Standard International Trade Classification is used for commodities for most countries.

Evaluation: Comprehensive in coverage and detail, this reference is recommended for larger collections or special libraries whose companies have extensive international business.

Subject Index to Part I

Author/Editor/Publisher Index to Part I

Part II
The Literature of Business Reference and Business Libraries 1976-1981

Introduction

by Bernard S. Schlessinger

In several of the essays published as Part III of this book, statements are made indicating that the literature of business reference and business libraries is not as extensive as one might have expected. Several persons[1] cooperated to compile the following bibliography—searching the literature, analyzing individual items for applicability,.and abstracting those items that were pertinent. The author then produced edited versions of the abstracts and organized them alphabetically into the list that follows. The compilation of abstracts is indexed by subject and journal (or publisher) in the 2 indexes that complete Part II of the book.

Several descriptive comments should be made about the compilation of literature of 1976–1981.[2]

1. The total amount of literature is indeed small (109 items over the 6-year period). Within the total output is a heavy preponderance of journal articles (95), and the trend in volume of publication seems to have been downward in the past 3 years, as evidenced in Table 1.

Table 1. Volume of Publication

	1976	1977	1978	1979	1980	1981	Totals
Journal material	18	17	21	15	14	10	95
Other material	5	3	2	0	3	1	14
Totals	23	20	23	15	17	11	109

2. The interest in business reference and business libraries, as measured by the publishing record, seems higher in the United States than elsewhere. Of the 109 items, only 21 (19.2 percent) are attributable to other than U.S. sources.
3. Table 2 presents the breakdown of major subject interests in the literature.

Table 2. Major Subject Interests in the Business Literature 1976–81

Subject	# Articles
Availability of business information	2
Business/Company libraries	24
Specific	16
General	8
Business reference sources	57
Banking	2
Companies/Industries	1
Data processing	1
Economics	3
Financial services	1
Foreign trade	4
Franchises	1
General	27
Marketing	3
Money management	1
Serials	7
Small business	2
Statistical studies	4
Education in business reference	3
Fees	3
Indexing	1
Information brokers	1
Information needs of patrons	2
Organization of materials	4
Public relations	2
Publishing	2
Reference/Information services	8

As may be seen, business reference is the overwhelming subject interest. Of the 109 items, 57 treat business reference sources (27 of these general reference sources, 7 serials). Another 8 are concerned with reference/ information service itself, and an additional 14 are devoted to peripheral reference interests (availability 2, education 3, fees 3, indexing 1, information brokers 1, information needs 2, publishing 2). In all, 79 (72.5 percent) have a reference focus. The other significant subject interest is business/ company libraries, both specific and general. Twenty-four items (22.0 percent) are included in this category. These two large groupings account for 103 (94.5 percent) of the published items in the 6-year period.

4. It would seem that persons writing in business literature do so, for the most part, alone. Of the 96 items with identified author(s), 80 are a result of single authorship, 12 the work of 2 authors, and 4 were written by 3 authors.
5. Over the 6-year period, only 2 authors contributed more than 3 papers to the literature: M. Balachandran with 8 and S. DiMattia with 6. Six others contributed more than one paper: C. Popovich and B. Brown with 3 each and R. Behles, J. Pask, M. Leggett, and G. Smith with 2 each. In all, 93 authors are represented.
6. Of the 44 journals that published items on the list, only 9 published more than one. *Special Libraries* published the most (15), followed by *Library Journal* (14), *Reference Services Review* (9), *ASLIB Proceedings* (6), *Canadian Library Journal* (3), *Library Association Record* (3), *Publishers Weekly* (3), *Reference Quarterly* (3), *Serials Review* (3), and *College and Research Libraries* (2).
7. Finally, the length of items placed in these journals averages 8.1 pages, with a median of 6 pages. This would be even less, if the longer New Books articles in *Library Journal* were not counted.

REFERENCES

1. The persons involved were Kathleen Bessette, Pomfret Library, Pomfret, CT; Constance Cameron, Bryant College Library, Smithfield, RI; Margaret Thomas, Johnson and Wales College Library, Providence, RI; Virginia Vocelli, West Hartford Public Library, West Hartford, CT; and Jane Zande, Research Assistant. Jane Zande was responsible as well for the final compilation and the indexing of Part II of the book.
2. One item from 1982 is included in the 1981 tabulation.

Bibliography

1. Abraham, Deborah, and Pelcher, Annette. "Information for Tennessee Economic and Community Development." *Tennessee Librarian* 30 (Spring 1978): 24–26.
   The special library of the Tennessee Department of Economic and Community Development acts as a resource to department staff, state and local officials, and the public. In addition to the primary functions of acquiring, organizing, and disseminating information, the library staff has developed informational brochures and statistical studies and has conducted research projects. The library houses materials on all aspects of the Tennessee economy, from the local scene to topics of national interest. One of its special collections is the Office of Minority Business Collection, which includes information on the economic status of women in the work force.

2. Allott, A. M. "Confusion and Fragmentation in Service to Business." *Library Association Record* 79 (December 1977): 678.
   The 1970s have focused attention on the information needs of the business world. It is surprising therefore that England still has no centralized national business library, a situation that has resulted in confusion and fragmentation for those seeking information. The same state exists in many companies where it may take an internal crisis for different departments to share information. Paradoxically, the same information is often readily shared with outside agencies and even with rival companies. On the national level, an improvement in the availability of statistical serials has been achieved through the cooperative efforts of librarians and statisticians. The hope is that this example will serve as a model for a national business library in the near future, perhaps with an interim facility being designated soon.

3. "At Chase Manhattan Bank: Library Service For A Fee." *Library Journal* 103 (August 1978): 1456.
   Research and library services available to the business public on a one-shot fee basis or by yearly retainer are identified.

4. Baade, Harley D. "The Corporate Environment and the Librarian." In *Special Librarianship: A New Reader,* edited by Eugene B. Jackson, pp. 298–304. Metuchen, NJ: Scarecrow, 1980.

Every corporation reflects a distinct attitude toward information which affects the total library environment. Areas that may vary are the company's treatment of information professionals, placement of the library within the organization, and the degree of development of policies and procedures. Generally, corporations offer unique opportunities for individualism and career growth in a competitive, dynamic atmosphere.

5. Bailey, Martha J. "Functions of Selected Company Libraries/Information Services." *Special Libraries* 72 (January 1981): 18–30.
A survey of 108 industries established functions characteristic of company libraries or information services. Analysis is presented by function, (acquisitions, cataloging and indexing, circulation, distribution of information, publications, and references), and by 9 industry categories: advertising, aircraft and missiles, chemicals, foods, law firms, newspapers, office machines, petroleum, and pharmaceuticals.

6. Bakewell, K. G. B. "The London Classification of Business Studies." *International Classification* 6 (1979): 29–35.
The London Classification of Business Studies (LCBS) was initiated in London, England, in 1970 as an alternative to the Harvard Classification. Illustrative examples of the classification system and of the differences between the first and second editions are presented. An increasing number of libraries throughout the world are adopting LCBS.

7. Balachandran, M. *Basic Economic Statistics*. Exchange Bibliography No. 971. Monticello, IL: Council of Planning Libraries, 1976.
This descriptive bibliographic essay covers 112 economic statistics references in 3 broad categories: (1) historical, (2) current economic indicators, and (3) economic forecasts and projections.

8. Balachandran, M. "Foreign Trade Statistics." *Reference Services Review* 4 (October 1976): 870–90.
Statistical data on international trade are available from numerous reference sources. Some provide purely statistical data on import and export trade; others are analytical in nature and provide insights to current trends. Over 30 of the more important titles in this area are mentioned briefly in terms of scope and emphasis. The majority of the titles discussed are published by the U.S. Bureau of the Census.

9. Balachandran, M. "International Economic Statistics: A Selected List of Documents." *Reference Services Review* 5 (October/December 1977): 53–57.
Seventy-three statistically oriented publications selected from materials available from the U.S. federal government, foreign governments, and regional and international organizations are covered in this bibliographic essay.

10. Balachandran, M. ''Marketing Information Sources.'' *Reference Services Review* 4 (July 1976): 87–91.

A variety of demographic and socioeconomic information is available to professionals in marketing and product management, sales merchandising, advertising, and market research, covering both quantitative and qualitative market indicators. The majority of the sources are from the federal government, but private sources such as trade associations, trade journals, and commercial publishers also contribute. Over 50 titles in this field are discussed briefly in terms of emphasis and scope.

11. Balachandran, M. ''Research Guide to Economics.'' *Reference Services Review* 5 (July 1977): 33–37.

This guide to business reference sources is divided into the following categories: guidebooks and manuals; journal selection tools; comprehensive sources of historical statistics; publications on current economic indicators; and survey-type publications. Sources of information are noted for economic data, forecasts and projections, receipts and expenditures of governmental organizations, and government finance.

12. Balachandran, M. ''State of the Art Survey of Reference Materials in Business.'' *Reference Services Review* 4 (October 1976): 7–16.

An annotated survey of significant sources of information in business published in 1975 and 1976. Content and scope of databases, indexes, dictionaries and directories, and microforms are discussed. Some 58 evaluative reviews of titles in the fields of economics, marketing, accounting, real estate, women and minorities, and energy are included. Federal government publications are given special emphasis.

13. Balachandran, M. ''State of the Art Survey of Reference Sources in Business and Economics.'' *Reference Services Review* 6 (January 1978): 21–40.

An annotated survey of outstanding reference sources in business and economics which became available in 1976 and 1977 is presented. Online databases, indexes, and micropublications are discussed in terms of content and scope, and evaluative reviews of over 100 titles are included in the following categories: accounting, advertising, business information and management, business and technical writing, currency and banking, economics, finance and investment, labor and industrial relations, marketing, minorities and women, and real estate. Special mention is given to recent trends in publications on current research in economics and business.

14. Balachandran, Madhava. *A Subject Approach to Business Reference Sources*. Occasional Paper No. 128. Champaign, IL: University of Illinois Graduate School of Library Science, June 1977.

The information contained in almost 200 business reference sources is discussed in terms of scope and content. The first section examines both primary and secondary sources of information on specific companies, regardless of industry category. Sources that provide a broader perspective of the entire area are categorized in the second section into the following headings: multi-industries studies, single-industry studies, and consumer market analysis.

15. Bauer, Charles K. *"Managing Management." Special Libraries* 71 (April 1980) 204–16.

At the Lockheed Georgia Company, a continuous interaction between the information center and the administration earns the center recognition as a dynamic, integral partner in the management team. The information specialist must possess attitudes and behaviors that will clearly demonstrate the value and usefulness of information. Knowledge about the company, its products, and its information resources, as well as skills in salesmanship, supervision, and establishment of rapport with clients are essential. Support for the information center must come from all levels of management, starting from the top administrator.

16. Behles, Richard J. *"Business America." Serials Review* 6 (April/June 1980): 7–8.

Although it has undergone several title changes, *Business America* remains a primary serial title for current information on international trade and commerce. It includes 2 or 3 short articles per issue as well as regular departments, such as "Domestic Business Report," "Economic Highlights," "Business Outlook Abroad," and "Worldwide Business Opportunities." It is indexed in *Index to U.S. Government Periodicals* and *Business Periodicals Index* (entry 20 in Part I of this volume).

17. Behles, Richard J. *"Business Periodicals." Serials Review* 6 (April/June 1980): 9–16.

An annotated list of 24 business periodicals is provided under the categories of general periodicals, management, finance, marketing, industrial psychology, international business, and retail business. Discussion of each periodical includes scope and content and gives evaluative guidelines for making acquisition decisions.

18. Bernhard, Genore H. *"The Business Firm Library."* In her *How to Organize and Operate a Small Library*, p. 39. Fort Atkinson, WI: Highsmith, 1976.

A chapter is included on setting up a small business library. A brief profile of the staff, collection, cataloging system, and purchasing policies of a library in a large utility company is presented.

19. Blake, F. M., and Irby, J. *"The Selling of the Public Library." Drexel Library Quarterly* 12 (January/April 1976): 149–58.

A close partnership between public libraries and the information industry in the supply of information is suggested. Librarians must be willing to take already developed systems of storage and retrieval and apply them imaginatively rather than passively depending on commercial sources. An example is provided by a project in San Mateo, California, where the public library is building its own online database within an already existing information retrieval system.

20. Block, Bernard A. *"Fortune."* *Serials Review* 4 (January/March 1978): 7–12.
The origins and development of *Fortune* are discussed. *Fortune* has major index coverage in *Industrial Arts Index, Business Periodicals Index,* (entry 20 in Part I of this volume), *Readers Guide to Periodical Literature, Social Science Citation Index,* and *Public Affairs Information Service—Bulletin* (entry 110 in Part I of this volume). Subscription information is included.

21. Brown, B. E., ed. *Canadian Business and Economics: A Guide to Sources of Information.* Ottawa, ON: Canadian Library Association, 1976.
A comprehensive list of publications for Canadian business is presented in this reference tool. Brief annotations are included for many, and French as well as English front and back matter are incorporated. The entries are arranged first by province and within each province under more than 60 subject and form headings (bibliographies, atlases, business finance, ethnic groups, etc.). Entries are indexed by author, title, former title, publisher, and series.

22. Brown, Barbara E. "Update to *Canadian Business and Economics: A Guide to Sources of Information.*" *Canadian Library Journal* 33 (December 1976): 493–99.
This supplement to the 1976 book (entry 21) includes more titles annotated in both English and French. Subject headings similar to those utilized in the book appear here.

23. Brown, Barbara E. "Update to *Canadian Business and Economics: A Guide to Sources of Information.*" *Canadian Library Journal* 35 (February 1978): 5–15.
A listing of 105 titles which supplements the 1976 book (entry 21) is presented in both English and French. The annotations are divided into 40 categories and include titles specific to each province.

24. *Business Books and Serials in Print.* New York: Bowker, 1977.
Over 37,500 titles in the area of business—over 6,000 of which are serials—from some 1,580 publishers are included in the latest volume. Information includes author, title, and subject. Coverage emphasizes administrative and commercial (rather than industrial) aspects and extends to the areas of economics, agriculture, industry, finance, investment, insurance, taxation, prices, employment, wages, production, income spending and forecasting, and managerial functions.

25. Campbell, M. J. "Running Dogs in the Reference?" *New Library World* 77 (December 1976): 232–33.
Business, as a major taxpayer, is entitled to access to information through "free" public libraries. It is noted that 48 percent of public business library patrons come for personal and not company business. Online information retrieval services that eliminate the need for some expensive periodicals are suggested as one way of lowering the costs of maintaining library collections.

26. Clausen, Nancy M. "Your R&D Library Can Help You More Than You Think as You Take Advantage of Your Records and Information Center." *Industrial Research/Development* 20 (September 1978): 164–67.

The information specialist in a research and development library can provide professional services to support the research activities of the company. For example, (1) current publications evaluated as relevant to patrons' interests could be disseminated to appropriate staff, or (2) the specialist's expertise in searching online databases might increase access to corporate and research literature and to data not readily available.

27. Cojeen, R. H. "International Business Publications in the Seventies." *Choice* 15 (March 1978): 21–27.

Increased interest in multinational business dealings will result in greater demand for information on international business. This bibliographic essay covers around 80 sources, including government publications, popular works, and corporate literature, that would be useful in understanding international business in fields like accounting and area studies. Items recommended for basic collections are indicated.

28. Cooney, Jane; Gervino, Joan; and Hendsey, Susanne. "United States and Canadian Business and Banking Information Sources." *Law Library Journal* 70 (November 1977): 561–69.

An annotated bibliography, with an emphasis on banking sources, is presented. The list comprises over 60 American sources and over 40 Canadian sources. The categories include bibliographies, dictionaries, indexes, biographies, directories, bank directories, corporate information, statistics, and periodicals. Items the authors believe should be part of a core collection are also indicated.

29. Cox, Eli P. III; Hamelman, Paul W.; and Wilcox, James B. "Relational Characteristics of the Business Literature." *Journal of Business* 49 (April 1976): 252–65.

Scholarly business literature can communicate new information to the professional community. Systematic analysis of content, authorship, and relational characteristics of research journals gives insights into the development of the field as a research-oriented discipline. Citation indexes are an especially important tool in this regard. Nonmetric multidisciplinary scaling is a more refined technique for investigation of the relationships among journals and evaluation of their research characteristics.

30. Culley, J. D., et al. "Business Students and the University Library: An Overlooked Element in the Business Curriculum." *Journal of Academic Librarianship* 2 (January 1977): 293–96.

Whether university colleges of business are training students adequately in the use of business information sources is questioned on the basis of research on student knowledge and use of major business-related information sources, student use of business periodicals, and student attitudes toward use of the university library.

31. Cupoli, Patricia. "Reference Tools for Data Processing, Office Automation and Data Communications: An Introductory Guide." *Special Libraries* 72 (July 1981): 233–42.

Information from current reference tools in the areas of data processing, office automation, and communications is available either through loose-leaf services and catalogs or through online retrieval systems and printed indexes. A discussion of the content of these various reference sources is presented. A list of almost 70 of these tools also includes vendor information.

32. Cveljo, Katherine. "Business Librarianship: Information Services and Research." *Special Libraries* 70 (August 1979): 320–27.

Library services in business should respond to the clientele's changing and growing information needs. Successful librarians should be aware of the current information requirements and have a thorough knowledge of the organization, its staff, and its subject areas. Adequate education and training is essential. A model business information course is discussed, utilizing a variety of instructional methods and combining theoretical and practical aspects.

33. Dahlin, Robert, and Maryles, Daisy. "Books on Money Matters: A Current Checklist." *Publishers Weekly* 215 (16 April 1979): 53–55+.

The inflationary economy has led to an increase in the number of financial self-help books. This checklist includes over 125 current or forthcoming titles on money management for the consumer from 55 publishers. Categories include general money management, consumer advice, personal/family finances, women, stock market, real estate, taxes, estate planning, retirement, antiques and collectibles, and first person accounts.

34. Delaney, Oliver. "Selling to the Government." *Oklahoma Librarian* 28 (January 1978): 15–16.

Information on how businesses can sell their goods and services to the federal government can be obtained from several sources. The *Supply Catalog* and *Sources of Supply and Service*, both published by the General Services Administration (GSA), the *U.S. Government Purchasing and Sales Directory* (entry 142 in Part I of this volume) published by the Small Business Administration (SBA), and the *Commerce Business Daily* of the Department of Commerce, provide a variety of information on the kinds of goods and services used by government agencies. The purpose and use of specifications and ordering procedures can be obtained through SBA's *Guide to Federal Specifications and Standards*, GSA's *Index to Federal Specification and Standards*, and the *Index to Specifications and Standards*, published by the Department of Defense. Information on how to obtain each publication is included.

35. Dermyer, Angela. "Try on a Company Library." *Industry Week* 194 (1 August 1977): 56–57.

A company library is necessary if informational chaos is perceived by management. A librarian not only can bring order to that chaos, but also can provide professional services that can further the company's goals. Key issues to be considered before establishing a library include: where the library will stand within the organizational hierarchy; provision of an adequate budget, space, and clerical staff; and determination of the library's anticipated scope and subject coverage. The qualified librarian should have management skills as well as a background in all aspects of library work. Ideally, the librarian also should be viewed both as a part of the management support structure and as a full-fledged member of the professional staff.

36. DiMattia, S. *"Business Books 1976."* Library Journal 102 (1 March 1977): 554–59.

An annotated list of the best or most significant business books published during 1976 is presented. The more than 60 selected titles are classified under the following headings: "Business Library Newsletters," "Reference," "Advertising and Marketing," Business Crime," Business and Society," "Capitalists and Financiers," "Corporations," "Economic Conditions," "Employment," "Executives," "Human Capital," "Management," "Personal Finance and Investments," and "Women—Employment."

37. DiMattia, Susan. *"Business Books 1977."* Library Journal 103 (1 March 1978): 513–19.

This annotated listing is preceded by an introductory essay. The items listed are primarily intended to form a selection guide for public and academic libraries. Sixty-eight titles are included in subject areas entitled "Business and Management Strategy," 'Small Business," "Labor Unions," "People at Work," "Women in the Labor Force," "Economics," "Personal Finance," "Investments," "International Issues," and "Potpourri."

38. DiMattia, Susan. *"Business Books 1978."* Library Journal 104 (1 March 1979): 552–58.

Fifty-nine titles are included in this annotated listing, which is preceded by an introductory essay. Primarily intended as a selection guide for public and academic libraries, this bibliography includes items in subject areas entitled "National and International Economics;" "Corporations;" "Management, Operation, Growth, and Mergers;" "Business Opportunities;" "Advertising, Marketing, and Salesmanship;" "Employment, Labor Force, and Work Ethic;" "Personal Wealth and Money Management;" "Investments;" "Consumerism;" and "Miscellaneous."

39. DiMattia, Susan. *"Business Books 1979."* Library Journal 105 (1 March 1980): 578–84.

Primarily intended as a selection guide for public and academic libraries, this annotated listing is preceded by an introductory essay. Subject areas covered by the 67 titles included are entitled "Management Tactics," "Human Resources Management," "Workplace Environment," "Personal Strategies," "Women at Work," "Business Law," "International Business," "Taxation," "Personal Money Management," "Business Opportunities," and "Not Elsewhere Classified."

40. DiMattia, Susan. "Business Books 1980." *Library Journal* 106 (1 March 1981): 530–53.

This annual annotated compilation of selected business books is preceded by an introductory essay and is designed to serve primarily as a selection guide for public and academic libraries. Subject areas covered by the 77 titles included are entitled "Economics, Investment, and Financial Planning"; "Corporate Management"; "Industries and Corporations"; "Small Business"; "The Non-profit Sector"; "International Concerns"; "Worker and Workplace"; "Women in Transition"; "Business Miscellany"; "Reference;" and "New Periodicals: Small Business, Strategy."

41. DiMattia, Susan S. "Business Books of 1981." *Library Journal* 107 (1 March 1982): 519–25.

Trends in the publication of business titles of 1981 reflected concerns for the uncertain economic times. A selected list of 86 of these titles is presented. The annotated citations cover the following categories entitled "Economics, Financial Planning, and Taxation"; "Real Estate"; "Management Style and Function"; "Human Resources"; "Motivation"; "Productivity"; "Corporate Finance"; "Advertising"; "Marketing"; "PR and Sales"; "Entrepreneurs"; "Corporations and Executives"; "Business Abroad"; "Career Strategy"; and "Et Cetera."

42. Dodd, James B. "Information Brokers." *Special Libraries* 67 (May/ June 1976): 243–50.

A discussion is presented of the appearance in the 1970s of information brokers who obtain information (for a fee) for their users (many from industrial and business libraries) using their own collections as well as the collections of large libraries. Thirty-two information brokers were contacted. The variety of services those brokers offered includes document delivery, literature searching with different outputs, translation, library management, writing and editing, and indexing. Issues addressed briefly include conflict of interest, fees, ethics, and relationships with libraries used.

43. Feingold, Karen, and Ward, Jane. "A Survey of Library User Demands in an Industrial Corporate Library." In *Quantitative Measurement and Dynamic Library Service,* edited by Ching-Chih Chen, pp. 103–12. Phoenix, AZ: Oryx Press, 1978.

Projections of future library services in the branch locations of Digital Equipment Corporation were based on the analysis of a 60-hour user study. The frequency distribution of current services and the type of user group were cross-tabulated with job location. Patrons most likely to make use of library services were those located near the library. The findings of this study helped substantiate a successful request for the purchase of a bookmobile and the expansion of library services to outlying locations.

44. Figueroa, Oscar, and Winkler, Charles. *A Business Information Guidebook.* New York: AMACOM, 1980.

Sources of information in business and economics are presented in 3 sections. Part I considers the broad aspects of information retrieval, including geographic considerations, and discusses the Standard Industrial Classification (SIC) and the Establishment Standard Industrial Classification (ESIC) coding systems, as well as the federal government Documents Depository System. Part II is an annotated list of sources of information in 82 subject categories particularly applicable to planning and managing a business. The final section contains sources on personal investing, embracing the following categories: securities, mutual funds, security dealers, the New York and American Stock Exchanges, investment companies, and securities research.

45. Flower, Clara K. *Guide to Sources: Business Administration and Guide to Sources: Economics.* Orono, ME: University of Maine, 1980.

The major sources of information in business administration and economics, available at the Raymond H. Fogler Library at the University of Maine at Orono are listed in these 2 introductory resource guides. Over 90 titles are included in the following categories, entitled "Abstracts and Indexes," "Bibliographic Guides," "Biographies," "Dictionaries," "Directories," "Encyclopedias," "Government Publications," "Handbooks," and "Statistical Sources." The *Guide to Sources: Business Administration* also identifies the library's holdings in loose-leaf business services.

46. Forest, Robert B. "Let's Go to the Library." *Infosystems* 24 (December 1977): 78.

The products of batch computer systems can be organized into a programing support library. The person in charge of the library not only can provide supportive clerical tasks but can also act as the link between the programers and the stored information. Some of the benefits of an organized library include improved efficiency, more consistent communications among staff members, and better control over the computer programs.

47. Goeldner, C. R., and Dirks, Laura M. "Business Facts: Where to Find Them." *MSU [Michigan State University] Business Topics* 24 (Summer 1976): 23–36.

An annotated list of information sources for material on analyzing and controlling business operations is presented, including references both to prime data sources and to bibliographical publications. The information is organized in two broad categories: (1) "Sources of Primary Data and Statistical Information," including the subheadings of "Government Publications," "Trade Publication Statistical Issues," and "Business Guides and Services," and (2) "General Reference Sources," including the following subcategories: "Indexes," "Periodicals," "Bibliographies and Special Guides," "Trade Associations," and "Other Basic Sources." Over 80 publications are included.

48. Haines, Michael. "Company Correspondence: An Important Information Resource." *ASLIB Proceedings* 31 (August 1979): 401–11.

First discussed are the problems of making business correspondence accessible as an information resource, including multiple generation, indexing, subject and security classification, and multiple storage locations. The Charter Consolidates Ltd. system for correspondence files is then treated, with special attention given the indexing access points of company, country, commodity, and hierarchical subject classification. Finally, the fine points of computerization are presented.

49. Hatzfeld, Lois A. "*Business.*" In *Periodical Indexes in the Social Sciences and Humanities: A Subject Guide,* pp. 22–26. Metuchen, NJ: Scarecrow, 1978.

A listing of key indexing sources that provide access to periodical literature in business is presented. The annotations define the scope and explain the arrangement and indexing of each source. The publications listed are: *Accountants' Index* (entry 1 in Part I of this volume), *Accounting Articles, Anbar Management Services, Business Periodicals Index* (entry 20 in Part I), *Consumers Index to Product Evaluations and Information Sources, F & S Index International, F & S Index of Corporation and Industries,* and *Personnel Management Abstracts.*

50. *Illinois Libraries.* 62 (March 1980). Entire issue.

Articles relating to libraries in business and industry are included in this issue devoted to special libraries. The role of the business library and information center and its relation to the national information network are considered in "Library and Information Services for Business and the Professions," by David E. King (pp. 228–31). The services and collections of specific Illinois business libraries are discussed in "Clark, Dietz Engineers, Inc: A Library Profile," by Felicia Rodriguez Bagby (pp. 231–33); "Profile of a Library Serving a Corporate Headquarters," by Betty S. Hagberg (pp. 239–42); "Portland Cement Association Research and Development/Construction Technology Laboratories Library," by Marilyn Macku LaSalle (pp. 242–45); "Technical Information Center: Caterpillar Tractor Company," by Carol E. Mulvaney (pp. 256–58); and "An Advertising and Public Relations Agency Library," by Ellen Steininger (pp. 272–74).

51. "Information for Business: Problems of Availability and Access." *ASLIB Proceedings* 30 (September 1978): 316–41.

Papers presented at a 1977 ASLIB conference dealt with problems in gaining access to business information. The papers collected here include: "Business Information: A Review of User Difficulties," by Judith Collins, a discussion of a survey that identified problems inherent in the information being sought as well as on the part of the information seeker; "Government Statistical Information," by Brian Mower, which considers the organization and role of the Government Statistical Service of the United Kingdom; "Some Problems in the Provision of Market Research Information," by Harry Henry, a comment not only on problems but also on the identification of primary market research information sources; and "Public Libraries," by Malcolm J. Campbell, which gives suggestions for strengthening the provision of business information, primarily by British public libraries.

52. "Instant Data from the New York Times." *Canadian Business* 50 (October 1977): 13+.

The *Information Bank* of the *New York Times,* which makes available to business subscribers items from 81 different publications, includes information from 12 U.S. daily newspapers; 12 daily, weekly, and monthly business publications; 12 foreign affairs publications; 5 scientific publications; and 40 news weeklies, monthlies, and quarterlies. Nearly 1.5 million items are available, with 20,000 items added monthly.

53. Jensen, Rebecca J.; Asbury, Herbert O.; and King, Radford G. "Costs and Benefits to Industry of Online Literature Searches." *Special Libraries* 71 (July 1980): 291–99.

A telephone survey of clients of the NASA Industrial Application Center, University of Southern California, and the NASA-Small Business Administration Technology Assistance Program examined the dollar costs and benefits of an online literature search. Over 50 percent of those interviewed reported dollar benefits, especially in acquiring technical information with more efficiency. The survey indicates that when more dollars are invested in the service, more dollar benefits are realized. Interactive searches were found to be the most expensive type of search, but also the most cost effective. Overall, the rates of dollar benefit to investment averaged 2.9 to 1.

54. Jones, H. "Why the Bookmen Turn to Business." *Director* 29 (December 1976): 33–34.

In England, prior to 1930, books and magazines about business were almost all American in origin. Only the Finsbury public library in London had a business collection. The Second World War, with its emphasis on production management, and the creation, by Henry Luce's *Fortune,* of an international audience for business management changed the situation, and, in 1949, *Director* became the forum for discussion of British business. The *Director's* "Bookshelf" feature, with reviews of books, remains important. Significant publishing firms that emerged included Allen and Unwin, Hutchinson, Harrap, Longman, Macdonald and Evans, Macmillan, McGraw-Hill, Routledge and Kegan Paul, Penguin, and Pan. The Economist's Bookshop in London remains a place to consider.

55. Junge, Alfred R. "Business Information Sources on Asia." *Special Libraries* 70 (February 1979): 82–90.

Although the diverse economic practices in Asia make business trade and investment more difficult than in other parts of the world, Asia has significant potential as an economic market. Information on potential markets is available in standard business tools, such as the publications of the United Nations and the Department of Commerce. However, these sources need to be supplemented. Banks, trade organizations, and corporations provide a wide variety of useful periodicals, often available on a complimentary basis. A discussion of these documents is accompanied by an annotated list of almost 30 free publications.

56. Katz, Toni. *Guide to Sources: Company/Industry Information*. Orono, ME: University of Maine, 1981.

Listed are over 65 reference sources that provide information on companies and industries and that are available at the Raymond H. Fogler Library, University of Maine at Orono. The coverage includes general, regional, state, and Canadian corporate directories as well as directories of industries in 18 specific areas. The final section is composed of sources for financial information and guides, investment services, and statistical sources for industry analysis.

57. Keating, Michael. "Taking Stock of Two Services: Moody's *Investors Fact Sheets* and Standard and Poor's *Stock Reports.*" *Reference Services Review* 7 (April/June 1980): 37–46.

Two major stock reporting services, Moody's *Investors Fact Sheets* and Standard and Poor's *Stock Reports* are compared, noting differences and similarities in format, price, photocopying policies, history, circulation, coverage, revision policies, and industry review. A point-by-point comparison is further made of the services' treatment of elected companies. Some of the major differences noted are price, the "Industry Review" feature in *Investors Fact Sheets,* and the greater familiarity of Standard and Poor's *Stock Reports.*

58. King, Richard L., ed. *Business Serials of the U.S. Government*. Chicago: American Library Association, 1978.

This annotated list of 105 U.S. serial publications includes information on pagination, kind of illustrations typically included, where the serial is indexed, sources for the data reported, and a description of each serial's purpose, coverage, and utility. The volume's 10 chapters cover the following categories, entitled "National Economic Conditions," "Domestic Commerce," "International Commerce," "Industry," "Agriculture," "Labor," "Small Business," "Consumerism," "Patents and Trademarks," and "Environment."

59. Kingman, Nancy M., and Vantine, Carol. "Commentary on the Special Librarian/Fee-Based Service Interface." *Special Libraries* 68 (September 1977): 320–22.

Fee-based information services such as INFORM can efficiently provide corporate librarians with accurate and pertinent business information. However, a high-quality service requires professional commitment to participate in the system and to support its goals. An improved interface between the librarian and the information broker will provide higher-quality information to the business community, and will ultimately improve the professional caliber of librarianship.

60. Koch, Jean E., and Pask, Judith M. "Working Papers in Academic Business Libraries." *College and Research Libraries* 41 (November 1980): 517–23.

Working papers provide a means for circulating current research results in the fields of business and economics. The acquisition, collection, maintenance, and use of these documents vary among libraries. A survey of 119 academic business libraries indicated that a minority (33 percent) actively collect working papers, usually selecting on the basis of the institution's reputation and on specific requests from library patrons. The majority of libraries surveyed do not catalog or bind working papers. A parallel user study of the business libraries of Purdue University and the University of Illinois indicated that faculty are the main users of working papers and consider them an essential research tool.

61. Legett, M. "Bank Letters, Bulletins, and Reviews." *Special Libraries* 68 (December 1977): 425–29.

Several commercial banks and all 12 Federal Reserve System district banks publish letters, bulletins, and reviews that deal with facets of the national and international economy. The publications vary in cost, frequency, format, content, and scope. In sum, they provide coverage of past, current, and future economic events. A bibliography of 26 commercial bank publications, the 12 federal reserve system titles, and 10 indexing tools is included.

62. Leggett, Mark. "Employment Announcements in Business, Science and Technology Periodicals—A Checklist." *Southeastern Librarian* 29 (Fall 1979): 158–60.

Periodicals in business, science, and technology have generally been overlooked as potential sources for advertisements of employment and career opportunities. A list of 205 periodicals (including over 50 relating to business) that carry job announcements is presented. A key that indicates the average number of listings per journal is also provided.

63. McDermott, D. "Hallmark of Publishing for Professionals." *Publishers Weekly* 210 (11 October 1976): 35–36.

The business of publishing books for business is seen as one in which direct mail advertising and sales is still overwhelmingly strong, and in which authors quickly become professional consultants, spending much of their time on speaking engagements or on writing for journals.

64. McDonald, David R., and Maxfield, Margaret W. "The Reference Library: Resource for the Small Business." *Journal of Small Business Management* 17 (January 1979): 51–56.

Information essential to the small business manager is readily accessible through an understanding of basic reference tools and with the help of a reference librarian and interlibrary loan. Some examples of tools commonly used by the small business manager include: *The Business Owner's Advertising Handbook, U.S. Industrial Outlook* . . . (entry 143 in Part I of this volume), *Census of Population,* and *County Business Patterns* (entry 30 in Part I).

65. McKee, David H. "Business Reference Review." *Reference Services Review* 4 (July 1976): 93–95.

The following business reference sources are reviewed: *Trade Names Dictionary* (entry 139 in Part I of this volume), *Dictionary of Development Terminology, Executive and Management Development for Business and Government: A Guide to Information Sources, The Institutional Investor, Business People In the News, Consultants and Consulting Organizations Directory: A Reference Guide to Concerns and Individuals Engaged in Consulting for Business and Industry* (entry 28 in Part I), and *New Consultants: A Periodic Supplement to Consultants and Consulting Organizations Directory.*

66. McKinnon, Linda M. B. "Technology Transfer from the Corporate Library." *Management Review* 68 (May 1979): 47–49.

The Sanders Associates library is an example of a high technology library that complements and maximizes the company's research and development budget. Information provided by the library can modify or improve the company's research programs and can preclude costly duplication of research efforts. The total program includes a well-trained staff, experienced in the scientific and engineering disciplines, and tailored library services, such as current awareness profiles, computer and manual literature searches, and telephone reference. Special techniques are used at Sanders to encourage library use, including orientation sessions for new staff, announcements of future conferences, the "roaming bookmobile," and encouragement of recommendations for new purchases.

67. "Marketing Literature: How to Find it with a Computer." *Journal of Marketing* 42 (April 1978): 12–13+.

Researchers at the University of Oregon examined the efficiency of computer-assisted literature searches for the marketing scholar by determining which databases most thoroughly index the "core" journals in the field. The major journals were judged to be: *Academy of Marketing Science Journal, Journal of Advertising Research, Journal of Consumer Research, Journal of Marketing, Journal of Marketing Research, Proceedings of American Marketing Association,* and *Proceedings, Association of Consumer Research.* Marketing literature from these journals is more likely to be found in the *Management Contents* and *Social Scisearch* databases.

68. Marshall, Peter. "Guiding Business—Via Prestel." *Library Association Record* 83 (February 1981): 78–79.

Prestel, a British computerized viewdata system, provides the business community with the best sources of information on a topic, identifies which sources are available at reference libraries, provides a directory of libraries, gives guidance on what publicly available records contain information not available from published sources, and recommends contact points for some categories of unpublished information. "Business London" is one component of Prestel which consists of data appropriate to the London area. Although potentials of this system have not been fully realized, it is pointed out that, while Prestel can provide immediate access to some information, the public library will still be valuable for the comprehensiveness of its resources.

69. "Meeting the Need of GM Research Laboratories." *Information Manager* 2 (Spring 1980): 21–25.

The General Motors Research Laboratories Library is profiled: its collection, clientele, staffing, and services. The library's 26 professionals meet the information needs of more than 700 scientists and engineers with a collection of over 50,000 book titles and 1,300 journal titles, and with substantial use of interlibrary loan. Mechanized services include computerized literature searches and computerized circulation and acquisition. A unique feature is the System on Automotive Safety Information (SASI), a special collection containing all published information relating to automotive safety.

70. Melanson, Robert A. "Using the SIC in Business Reference." *Reference Quarterly* 18 (Fall 1978): 16–18.

The Standard Industrial Classification (SIC) categorizes establishments by type of business activity. This numerical code is used in government statistical documents and in commercially published resources to provide a standard access point to information on particular industries, products, and services. Examples of publications using this system are: government documents published by the Bureau of the Census, Dun and Bradstreet's *Million Dollar Directory* (entry 97 in Part I of this volume), and *Middle Market Directory, Standard and Poor's Register of Corporations* . . . (entry 124 in Part I), and *Predicasts*.

71. Moyer, R. Charles, and Crockett, John H. "Academic Journals: Policies, Trends and Issues." *Academy of Management Journal* 19 (September 1976): 489–95.

Trends in the submission of manuscripts to over 100 management, business, and economic journals were examined for the period of 1970–74 in terms of rate of acceptance, review time, and effect of submission fees. The acceptance rates from both major and secondary journals declined significantly in the time period studied, while the lag time between submission and publication for these journals grew substantially. It was further found that journals requiring submission fees provide more substantial manuscript critiques than those that do not. There is evidence that fees have not been a hindrance to submission of quality research.

72. Mueller, B. "MBA Library—An Unmined Wealth of Information." *Mortgage Banker* 37 (October 1976): 119–20.

The services of the Mortgage Bankers Association Library (100 requests per month for specific books, information requests on specific subjects, more than 7,000 books, journals, brochures, and periodicals used by 350 people on a regular basis) are reviewed. Several cases of effective use by good users are presented.

73. Mulford, Thomas W. "Discipline Resource Package: Business and Economics." In *Reference Resources: A Systematic Approach,* by James M. Doyle and George H. Grimes, pp. 120–41. Metuchen, NJ: Scarecrow, 1976.

Almost 150 citations of business reference works are presented in the systematic manner devised by Doyle and Grimes. The categories in this guide for the beginning researcher are arranged according to the "bibliographic chain": works in progress, unpublished studies, periodicals, reports and monographs, indexes and abstracting services, bibliographic lists and essays, annual review and state-of-the art reports, books, and encyclopedia summaries.

74. O'Donnell, William S. " The Vulnerable Corporate Special Library/ Information Center: Minimizing the Risks." *Special Libraries* 67 (April 1976): 179–87.

The corporate information center, usually operated as a staff function and thus representing cost overhead, is particularly vulnerable in times like the present one of corporate belt-tightening, especially since its elimination would not be interpreted as affecting profits in the short term. To avoid being targeted as a budget reduction, it is suggested that librarians (1) establish strong ties with middle management executive users, (2) demonstrate an understanding of the library's role and a thorough knowledge of the industry and the corporation, (3) aggressively pursue the appropriate resources, (4) maintain a trained and effective staff and administration, (5) keep management informed, and (6) relate to the users and their needs. Methods for self-assessment are also included.

75. Ohlson, June, and Tabuteau, Christine. "Microfiche Project on Australian Companies' Annual Reports." *Australian Academic and Research Libraries* 9 (December 1978): 215–18.

The project to microfiche 12,200 annual reports of 605 Australian companies by the Australian Graduate School of Management Library is described. Attention is paid to the subjects of usage, company selection, fiche features, quality control, and availability.

76. Pask, Judith M. "Bibliographic Instruction in Business Libraries." *Special Libraries* 72 (October 1981): 370–78.

The most popular methods of bibliographic instruction for graduate and undergraduate business students were identified by the responses to a survey of 61 academic libraries, including 33 separate business libraries. Although a variety of methods are employed, the most useful approach appears to be a combination of lecture and printed material, used in conjunction with regular coursework. However, this type of instruction requires a cooperative relationship between the business librarian and the faculty. The librarian can provide bibliographies, give lectures, or prepare a slide tape presentation for the class.

77. Paterson, G. D. L. "Designing A Business Information Service for Top Management." *ASLIB Proceedings* 30 (April 1978): 142–44.

The library of a corporation should be its primary source for information. A properly designed business library can inform a company of its outside image as well as provide information for corporate decisions. This information must be accurate, of high quality, and readily available at any time. It is suggested that the flow of information between management and the library can be facilitated by structuring the library as part of the public relations department.

78. Pertell, Grace M. "Selling the Business Library." *Special Libraries* 72 (October 1981): 328–37.

An effective public relations program is more than just a "job well done." It is an assertive promotion of the library's services and functions, a marketing campaign that will recognize the library as a vital component of the corporation.

Selling the library's services means pursuing goals and objectives that correspond with those of the organization, establishing open channels of communication with management, library staff, and the clientele, and adopting policies and activities that will encourage increased use of the library. With the present concerns about the tight economy, a definitive public relations program is a critical factor in ensuring the survival of the business library.

79. Popovich, C. J. "Characteristics of a Collection for Research in Business/Management." *College and Research Libraries* 39 (March 1978): 110–17.

Citation analysis of 2,805 citations from 31 dissertations in business management was carried out. The characteristics considered were: publication form, periodical title, subject, time span, language, and publisher. The analysis revealed that 49.1 percent of the citations were to periodicals and 31.9 percent to monographs, with 78 percent of the citations to periodicals appearing in 62 titles. Monograph citations were dispersed as follows (LC classifications): 14.7 percent in Business, 11.5 percent in Economics—Labor, 10.8 percent in Economics—Production, with no other percentage higher than 10. More than 70 percent of all cited materials was 10 years old or less, and nearly 85 percent was 15 years old or less. Only 4 (0.1 percent) of the citations were to non-English-language titles. Commercial publishers were the most frequently cited (33.8 percent), followed by association publishers (29.6 percent), university publishers (24.4 percent), and government publishers (5.8 percent).

80. Popovich, Charles J. "A Bibliographic Guide to Small and Minority Business Management." *Reference Quarterly* 18 (Summer 1979): 369–75.

Relevant resource materials are identified in this annotated list, an update of an earlier pamphlet, *Helping Minority Business: A List of Selected Materials.* The publications are grouped under the following categories: "Starting a Small Business," "Financing the Operation," "Managing the Business," and "Other Requirements." Addresses of associations and agencies that can provide further information are also included.

81. Popovich, Charles J., ed. "Business Data Bases: The Policies and Practices of Indexing." *Reference Quarterly* 18 (Fall 1978): 5–18.

The state of the art of indexing in business databases was discussed at a 1977 American Library Association conference by representatives of 3 database businesses. Persons from *Management Contents, ABI/INFORM,* and *Predicasts* summarized the features of their databases with respect to scope, purpose, content, publications index, dates covered, and accessibility. The reactions of a panel of business librarians from special, academic, and public libraries are also included.

82. Rowley, J. E. "Local Current Awareness Services in Industrial Libraries." *ASLIB Proceedings* 31 (October 1979): 476–84.

A survey of 147 British industrial libraries and information centers indicated that a wide range of current awareness services are offered, including circulation of bulletins and publications, scanning, and distribution of current contents of appropriate journals. The majority of libraries engage in in-house services rather than those commercially produced. Only 21 percent of the libraries used automation in current awareness activities.

83. Ruokonen, K. "Survey of Economic and Business Libraries in Scandanavia." *UNESCO Bulletin for Libraries* 31 (September 1977): 277–85.

Information about economic and business libraries in Finland, Denmark, Norway, and Sweden is presented, including hours, collections, microforms, periodicals, newspapers, special depositories, subject fields, services, publications, automated operations, and personnel. Collectively, this information not only provides profiles of individual countries but also forms a picture of general conditions.

84. Russell, Ann N. "Tri-County Regional Library Serves Special Needs of Business Community." *Georgia Librarian* 17 (February 1980): 10.

The Business Library of the Tri-County Regional Library of Rome, Georgia, helps meet the specific information needs of business and industry in its service area. The library has several promotional programs, including a series of workshops on business topics and a video production entitled "Minding Your Business."

85. Russell, J. Thomas, and Martin, Charles H. "Sources of Scholarly Publications in Marketing, Advertising, and Public Relations." *Journal of Advertising* 5 (Summer 1976): 29–34.

Articles published in the fields of advertising and marketing from January 1970 to December 1974 in *Journal of Marketing Research, Journal of Marketing, Journal of Advertising, Journal of Advertising Research, Public Relations Journal,* and *Journalism Quarterly* were examined in terms of vocation of author, specific universities and departments represented, content of articles, and citation sources used by each publication. The majority of authors were from departments of marketing, almost 60 percent were academicians, and 7 of the 165 universities represented in the study accounted for 15 percent of the articles.

86. Salter, B. T. "Economics Libraries in the United States." *INSPEL* 12 (1977): 113–24.

Strong economics collections are often held by 5 types of libraries: company; college and university; public; government agencies; and non-profit organizations, institutions, and associations. Brief background information is given for each group, and some of the stronger collections are discussed. A solid growth in economic libraries has been fostered by a growing economy, and library cooperation has become a highlight of special collections. A lack of development in the area of information retrieval may have to be remedied by international efforts.

87. Sardella, Mark. "A Bull Market Library." *Bay State Librarian* 68 (Fall 1979): 7–9.

The Stock Advisory Information Library, developed by Donald Bye, is a special library geared to the interests of stock investors. It is a subscription endeavor whose patrons share the cost of acquiring very expensive and esoteric investment services publications. The collection, which includes stock advisory aids such as *The Wall Street Transcript* and *Forbes Special Situation Service,* serves as a supplement to public library resources.

88. "Scientific, Technical, Business and Professional Books." *Publishers Weekly* 209 (19 April 1976): 53–69.

An annotated listing of over 100 business-related titles published between February and late summer of 1976.

89. "Scientific, Technical, Medical and Business Books." *Library Journal* 103 (1 March 1978): 533–48.

A listing of forthcoming books is provided with each entry including publisher, author, title, and publication date. Twenty-seven business titles are included in the following subject areas, entitled "Reference"; "General"; "Accounting"; "Banking"; "Finance and Investment"; "Communications and Education"; "Computers for Business"; "Economics for Business"; "Law for Business"; "Management"; "Marketing"; and "Taxes."

90. "Scientific Technical, Medical and Business Books." *Library Journal* 103 (1 November 1978): 2183–223.

A listing of forthcoming books is provided with each entry including publisher, author, title, and publication date. In all, 329 business titles are included in the following categories: "Reference"; "General"; "Accounting"; "Advertising and Public Relations"; "Banking"; "Finance and Investment"; "Communications and Education"; "Computers for Business"; "Economics for Business"; "Law for Business"; "Management"; "Marketing"; "Mathematics and Statistics for Business"; "Real Estate"; and "Taxes."

91. "Scientific, Technical, Medical and Business Books." *Library Journal* 104 (1 March 1979): 574–613.

This bibliographic entry listing of new titles in the field of business includes 243 titles in the following subject areas: "Reference"; "General"; "Accounting"; "Advertising and Public Relations"; "Banking"; "Finance and Investment"; "Communications and Education"; "Computers for Business"; "Economics for Business"; "Law for Business"; "Management"; "Marketing"; "Mathematics and Statistics for Business"; "Real Estate"; and "Taxes."

92. "Scientific, Technical, Medical and Business Books." *Library Journal* 104 (1 November 1979): 2297–326.

Forthcoming business titles (333) are included in this listing, with each entry identifying publisher, author, title, and publication date. Arrangement is by categories: "Reference"; "General"; "Accounting"; "Advertising and Public Relations"; "Banking"; "Finance and Investment"; "Communications and Education"; "Computers for Business"; "Economics for Business"; "Law for

Business''; ''Management''; ''Marketing''; ''Mathematics and Statistics for Business''; ''Real Estate''; and ''Taxes.''

93. *''Scientific, Technical, Medical and Business Books.'' Library Journal* 105 (1 November 1980): 2227–312.
This list of forthcoming books includes 337 business titles. Each entry provides publisher, author, title, and publication date. Categories used are ''Reference''; ''General''; Accounting''; ''Advertising and Public Relations''; ''Banking''; ''Finance and Investment''; ''Communications and Education''; ''Computers for Business''; ''Economics for Business''; ''Law for Business''; ''Management''; ''Marketing''; ''Mathematics and Statistics for Business''; ''Real Estate''; and ''Taxes.''

94. *''Scientific, Technical, Medical and Business Books.'' Library Journal* 106 (1 November 1981): 2109–24.
Publisher, author, title, and publication date are provided for 201 forthcoming business titles. They are grouped in the following categories: ''Reference''; ''General Accounting''; ''Advertising and Public Relations''; ''Banking''; ''Finance and Investment''; ''Communications and Education''; ''Computers for Business''; ''Economics for Business''; ''Law for Business''; ''Management''; ''Marketing''; ''Mathematics and Statistics for Business''; ''Real Estate''; and ''Taxes.''

95. Seabrooks, N. *''Detroit Library Network.'' Library Journal* 102 (15 May 1977): 1123–27.
The dimensions of cooperation in Detroit's library community are reviewed, with business one of the noted participants. Mentioned in the area of business are the Detroit Public Library's collections and its information service to business and industry (over 400 ''company card'' holders), the Wayne State University Library, the Campbell-Ewald Reference Center Advertising Agency Library, and the General Motors Public Relations Library.

96. Seng, Mary. *''Reference Service Upgraded Using Patrons' Reference Questions.'' Special Libraries* 69 (January 1978): 21–28.
Reference questions evaluated over a 3-year period by the staff in the Business Administration Economics Library at the University of Texas at Austin fell into 3 broad categories: directional, information-related, and general reference. Typical questions in each category are described. Analysis of the data identified improvements that could be made in such areas as graphics, publicity, and staff training to reducing the number of directional and information questions and maximize staff availability for answering reference questions.

97. Sharp, Geoffrey. *''Online Business Information.'' Online* 2 (January 1978): 33–40.
Information is an essential resource to support business decision making, and it can be successfully retrieved through the use of online business databases. The

13 principal online business databases—surveyed for identification of subject coverage, the essential characteristics, time periods available, and vendors—are: ABI/INFORM; MANAGEMENT CONTENTS; the PREDICASTS TERMINAL SYSTEM (MARKET ABSTRACTS, F & S INDEXES, U.S. STATISTICAL ABSTRACTS, INTERNATIONAL STATISTICAL ABSTRACTS, U.S. TIME SERIES, U.S. REGIONAL SERIES, INTERNATIONAL TIME SERIES, and EIS PLANTS); CHEMICAL INDUSTRY NOTES (CIN); P/E NEWS; and the PHARMACEUTICAL NEWS INDEX (PNI).

98. Shaver, Nancy B. "Suggested Bibliography for Prospective Franchisees—1979." *Unabashed Librarian* 30 (1979): 14.

The following titles on franchising are listed: *International Franchise Association Classified Directory of Members, Investigate Before Investing, Facts on Selecting a Franchise, Federal Trade Commission Consumer Bulletin No. 4—Franchise Business Risks, Franchise/Index Profile, Franchise Opportunities Handbook* (entry 66 in Part I of this volume), *Franchised Distribution, Franchising in the Economy,* and *Securities and Exchange Commission "10K" Reports.* Information on how to obtain the publications and brief descriptions of their contents are included.

99. Smith, Gerry M. "The Demand for Business Information in an Academic Library: An Analysis of the Library Inquiry Service of the City University Business School." *ASLIB Proceedings* 28 (November/December 1976): 392–99.

The nature of the reference service and the suitability of the collection in the City University Business School Library in London was studied by analyzing reference requests according to subject, originator, source, and frequency of requests. The need for a staff with extensive knowledge of the subject was indicated by the preponderance of requests centered on management and business functions, practices, and techniques. Patrons are equally divided among students, faculty, alumni, and outsiders and are more likely to ask for information in person than by telephone or mail. It was found that only a small proportion of reference sources, primarily bibliographical tools, are consulted and that a low number of requests are recorded. Results should help in formulation of future collection development policies.

100. Smith, Gerry M. "Keybooks in Business and Management Studies: A Bibliometric Analysis." *ASLIB Proceedings* 29 (May 1977): 174–87.

Heavily used monographs from British business school libraries were bibliometrically analyzed in terms of authorship, type of book, subject, nationality, publisher, language, and date of publication. Results showed that the books are written primarily by academics, are predominately textbooks and monographs, and cover a wide range of subjects. Approximately 150 publishers are active in this field, although 70 percent of the material is published by only 30 publishers. Use is evenly split between British and American materials, and 90 percent of the material used is 10 years old or less.

101. Spencer, J. *Business Information In London: A Study of the Demand and Supply of Business Information In Thirteen London Business Libraries.* London: ASLIB, 1976.

This 3-part study covers the use of London business libraries, subject coverage at each library, and staff views at 2 of the libraries. A summary, as well as an attempt to place the conclusions into some type of theoretical structure, is provided.

102. Stoakley, R. J. "Why Should Our Users Pay Twice?" *Library Association Record* 79 (April 1977): 170+.

Continuation of free library service in Great Britain is advocated, with consideration of major arguments such as whether we already pay for library service through taxes, whether fees charged would go into general coffers, what services could be charged for, and whether fees might be charged for entertainment or business.

103. Tufts, Aileen. "Vancouver Public Library's Business and Economic Division." *Canadian Library Journal* 34 (April 1977): 87–89.

Important considerations of policies and practices employed by the Business Information Service at the Vancouver Public Library are presented to provide information on a successful special library service in a public library setting.

104. Venett, Anthony J. "Technology Transfer for Industry and Business through the University Library." *Special Libraries* 72 (January 1981): 44–50.

PENNTAP, the Pennsylvania Technical Assistance Program, provides free information assistance to business, industry, and local governments. Originally funded by the State Technical Service Act (PA 89-182), it is now supported by the Department of Commerce of the Commonwealth of Pennsylvania and Pennsylvania State University. A wide variety of technical questions are answered for clients. Access to the comprehensive library collection of the Pennsylvania State Libraries and the corporation of the university, faculty, library staff, and federal private sources have been instrumental in the center's success.

105. Vernon, K. D. C. "Classification of Business and the Business of Classification." *Catalog and Index* 57 (Summer 1980): 8–12.

The beginnings, use, and revision of the *London Classification of Business Studies* are discussed. The classification's continuing popularity is indicated by sales of 300 copies of the 2nd edition and use by 50 libraries in the United Kingdom and 30 libraries elsewhere. Attention is paid to the idea of reclassification, to the future of the system, and to the major changes in the 2nd edition (abandonment of completely hierarchical notation, provision of some alternate locations, incorporation of a thesaurus in the schedules, introduction of 5 classes, restructuring of 4 classes, addition of 500 terms).

106. Warden, Carolyn L. "Use or Evaluation of a Corporate Library Online Search Service." *Special Libraries* 72 (April 1981): 113–17.

An evaluative questionnaire, given to 233 first-time users of the online search service available at General Electric Corporation's Research and Development Library, requested information on the relevancy and benefits of the service. It was found that, overall, a high percentage of useful citations are retrieved. Interactions between the searcher and the patron yield a greater number of relevant titles than does a search done solely by the librarian. Significant benefits in time savings and cost effectiveness were identified.

107. Wood, Elizabeth J. "How the International Business Directories Compete: A Comparative Review." *Reference Services Review* 8 (July/September 1980): 54–58.

Four reference sources on international or multinational businesses are compared: *Kelly's Manufacturers and Merchants Directory* (entry 86 in Part I of this volume), *The Who Owns Whom (WOW) Directory*, *Bottin International: International Business Register*, and *Principal International Businesses*. While the purpose and content of each are similar, the scope and ease of use differ. Suggested audience and price are also discussed.

108. Wood, Frances K. "Business and Industrial Needs: Special Libraries Are Willing to Share Resources." *Wisconsin Library Bulletin* 76 (May/June 1980): 109–10.

The state of Wisconsin has from 50 to 60 business and industrial libraries, located throughout the state, but particularly in the Milwaukee area. The major subject areas covered by these libraries are: banking, paper making, packaging, plastics technology, motor machinery of all types, insurance, pension planning, pollution control, electric power generation, food technology, household products, batteries, and law. The staff members in these libraries are receptive to public requests for information and welcome library tours.

109. Zimmerman, Anne R. "Library Services for Members: How the FHL Banks Can Help." *Federal Home Loan Bank Board Journal* 11 (September 1978): 13–16.

The Federal Home Loan Bank System Library of Seattle was initiated by management to provide efficient access to research and reference materials. The collection consists of a wide range of information on financial institutions and the savings and loan industry. Staffed by a professional librarian and a clerical assistant, the library provides patrons with an appraisal of current activities in the field, assists in research and planning projects, and provides access to information otherwise unavailable. The Seattle library is also open to the public by appointment.

Subject Index to Part II

Journal and Publisher Index to Part II

Entered below are the names of the journals in which the articles in Part II appeared and the publishers of the books entered in this section. Titles reviewed by the articles in this Part II are entered in the subject index. Numbers refer to entries.

Part III
Business Reference Sources and Services: Essays

Education for Information Service to Business*

by Katherine Cveljo

INTRODUCTION

American society since the turn of the century has progressed from a basically agrarian to a dynamic, industrial society with a higher level and greater diversity of education and the highest standard of living in the world. This has been accompanied by massive scientific and technological developments as well as extreme changes in social structure and a heightened consciousness of international relationships. Each change, whether political or social in nature, each environmental threat, each business collapse has affected and has been affected by the need for readily available and relevant information. Information is required to deal with these changes and developments; that is, knowledge from many disciplines must be focused on the specific problem situations that have substantially altered the operations and managerial aspects of organizations, including libraries and related institutions. Access to relevant and up-to-date information has become vital to every human endeavor.[1]

In the special library field, particularly in business and industrial libraries and information centers, change has been extreme and information has become recognized as an imperative to intelligent decision making and choice of applications. As suppliers of relevant and timely information, business librarians have lasting influence on their parent institutions' structure and an equally great impact on the community as a whole. And as business librarians improve the information flow and quality to their respective user communities, their status improves.

Although the above concepts are well-recognized, there are still librarians who do not meet the expected standards of service to business and

*The author wishes to express her appreciation to the schools of library and information sciences that have responded to the questionnaire and provided her with information for the above exposition.

related user communities. One might ask "Why have they not developed the skills, the understanding, and the means with which to provide timely, relevant, and comprehensive information as needed?" It is this question that we address here, as well as the question of how best to train future business librarians to understand the nature of the information needs in business, industry, and the related community.

BUSINESS-RELATED INFORMATION NEEDS

The needs for specific information of businesspersons and business-oriented community citizens range from the very simple to the complex— from information on company addresses, assets, sales, products, etc. to information on questions, such as whether to pursue conventional or alternative energy sources, what the role of the USSR as the world's largest producer of oil is and what its potential status as a producer of gas might be, or whether oil is scarce because the proved annual quantity acts as a constraint on the annual rate of production. The need for up-to-date information is paramount and further includes a great dependence on "non-book" materials (newspapers, periodicals, loose-leaf services, bankletters, reports), and within the past few years, an increasing dependence on computerized services. Any course for training business librarians must thus be based on a recognition of the needs of business personnel and business-oriented community users for up-to-date and relevant information as well as for help in its proper assimilation and application to ensure the excellence rather than mediocrity of the organization in which the library resides and the satisfaction of the business-oriented user community served in a public or academic library.

THE BUSINESS LIBRARIAN IN CONTEMPORARY SOCIETY

The philosophy that underlies business librarianship and the training for its practice should be based on that expressed in the Special Libraries Association motto—"Putting knowledge to work"—or stated more specifically in its bylaws—". . . to encourage and promote the utilization of knowledge through the collection, organization and dissemination of information; to develop the usefulness and efficiency of special libraries as information centers. . . ." In addition to preparing librarians to work in libraries at traditional library tasks, library education should emphasize the responsibility to work intensively with users. This is particularly true in our new society, in which information for decision making has increased in importance and in which delivering information in electronic form has become a reality.

The new modes of access to information that have become available, especially with the use of the computer, provide a basis for new approaches to the generation, manipulation, and exchange of quantified data and qualitative ideas. Simultaneously, the entire communication process has undergone a radical transformation. In training for positions in business libraries, it is obvious that one must include the new technologies of information handling as well as an emphasis on managerial skills. Technological and information handling skills must be accompanied by the development of organizational ability, leadership, initiative, and adaptability. Much of the latter is based on certain personal traits that should be present, including an analytical intelligence and a creative mind, self-confidence, flexibility, a highly developed sense of humor, patience, and a high frustration threshold.[2] As brought out in numerous writings and emphasized by Echelman in 1974, "the secret of a successful manager is that he is able to employ intelligence, self-confidence, patience, and good humor to minimize the frustration of corporate reality and to maximize the satisfaction of his job and those of the staff members."[3]

Business librarians must know the organization and the user community and understand the subject areas involved. Structure of the corporation or the community, public interests, personnel, products, plants, and policies all are important. The business librarian in a corporate setting must strive to situate the library "high enough in the corporation's organization chart so that it is perceived as a part of the 'management support structure,' especially in terms of receiving information about the company and its plans."[4] In an analogous way, the business librarian in a public or academic setting must see that the library is perceived as a center of activity that recognizes user needs.

The author should also note that the business library is not recommended to anyone who is not prepared to work under pressure. Demands on the business librarian tend to be complex, almost overwhelming. The work requires excellence and high standards of performance. Only students who want to experiment, to innovate, and who look forward to challenges as spelled out above, should be encouraged to prepare for work in business libraries. And they should also be prepared to accept continuing education as a constant part of their thinking to ensure future ability to meet current information needs and adjust to change.

CONSIDERATION OF COURSE CONTENT IN LIBRARY EDUCATION FOR BUSINESS LIBRARIANS

In addition to what has been said earlier, it should be noted that the practice of business librarianship is difficult to fit into a general mold because of the many types of business libraries—libraries attached to public, academic, or governmental agencies, libraries within corporations, and freelance information brokerages. Contemporary library education must, as a result, take into consideration the training of a new information specialist—a person who might work in any of the above-mentioned libraries or operate in a freelance brokerage situation. This new information specialist, in addition to performing the ordinary tasks of acquisition, cataloging, and providing access to information, will probably be called upon to repackage information. The job will require knowledge, responsiveness to specific user needs and to their information-seeking behavior, aggressive marketing, and an ongoing feedback.

While courses covering special libraries and information centers and courses treating specialized bibliography and literatures prepare graduates to work successfully in any type of special library, the author believes that business librarianship is different enough to justify a separate course devoted to it. This is further justified by the interdisciplinary aspects of the subject areas and the great diversity in the information needs of the business and business-oriented user community.

While education for business librarianship has received far less attention in the literature than other fields of special librarianship, the general trend seems to be toward special training for specific types of special libraries, including business libraries. The trend carries with it a greater emphasis on areas introduced in the general library education program, such as the foundations of information science, library automation, networking, systems analysis, and online searching.[5]

The author conducted a survey of the accredited library schools in the United States to determine the status of courses for business/librarianship and found that the area of business and economics is covered as a separate course in some schools, as a part of the social sciences bibliography course in other schools, and as a part of the special libraries course in still others.

RESULTS OF THE SURVEY

The results of the survey of accredited schools of library and information sciences are interesting, and particularly so in comparison to the results of a survey conducted 6 years ago by a student of the author. In the earlier survey (1976), it was found that only 6 graduate schools of library and information sciences offered a separate course for business librarianship and that most of the schools providing a section on business in an advanced reference course or a social sciences literature course covered only the basic information sources in business. The recent survey (42 returns) indicated that (1) at least 20 schools (49 percent of returns) now offer a course in business librarianship, while 7 others (16 percent) indicate plans for a separate course in Summer or Fall 1982, and (2) 21 schools (51 percent) have no separate course but provide extensive coverage of the subject under a variety of course titles, such as Advanced Reference Work, Introduction to Management, Library Management, Socioeconomic Data Resources, and Special Libraries and Information Centers, and further, that 19 schools (44 percent) now offer an extensive section in their social sciences literature course. The general trend toward greater recognition of the importance of a course offering in business librarianship is gratifying.

The present survey further showed that information resources in the broad categories basic to any business library (such as those for information on companies, organizations, and individuals, statistical sources, including industry statistics, sources for information on business and economic trends, and investment sources) are well covered whether the coverage is in a separate course or not. Subject areas—with emphasis on corporate finance and banking, management, marketing, computers, and management information systems—also seem to be well represented, no matter what approach is used.

An analysis of the methodology revealed the use of a variety of methods, including problem analysis, online searching, take-home examinations, and individual projects, with a number of programs requiring a bibliographic essay. Inclusion of a variety of databases is common, with some schools offering extensive hands-on experience while other schools use demonstrations of online systems. Additional attention is given to user needs, journal literature, abstracting/indexing services, and familiarity with terminology, and special emphasis is placed on loose-leaf services.

The most significant finding is that preparation for business librarianship is on the increase, both quantitatively and qualitatively. This is reflective of the evidence in recent library and information sciences literature, which testifies to the increasing number of alternative specialties offered by schools of library and information sciences. In light of existent opportunities and those developing in business, industrial, and related libraries, including libraries in banks, advertising agencies, and other similar environments, provision of specific preparation for such careers is logical, and students should carefully consider the direction of their future careers to take advantage of the educational opportunities available.

A COURSE PROFILE

In a previously published article (1979)[6] the author analyzed the nature of business information needs and described a course in business librarianship. The article described the course content, instructional objectives, structure, and methodology. Only the course content has changed in the interim. Course content, quite naturally, is subject to change dependent upon continuously published information and the rapid development of computerized sources of business-type data. (See Appendix 1: Course Outline.)

As presently organized, the primary thrust of the course is toward access to and usage of sources of information, with special attention focused on computerized information systems. The analysis of user needs and the procedures in planning a business library or similar information agency are also stressed. The course design acknowledges both the shifting nature of the boundaries of the literature relevant to business and the diversity in student backgrounds and interest. In this respect, the selection of the subject areas differs from semester to semester with some subject areas continuously offered and others included based on the nature of the student body. Appendix 2 includes a list of the subjects, giving an indication of those considered basic and covered in every course.

The course is taught in seminar fashion with the teacher serving as the facilitator who sets the climate for both individual and group experiences. Relevance and freedom form the basis of the course. A wide range of learning resources is made available, and the student pursues his/her learning process through an independent attitude and self-perception. An extensive syllabus is provided, including a variety of instructional aids and a set of problem-analysis exercises and projects from which to select. Appendix 3 outlines options in the course methodology.

In offering the students a certain degree of independence and responsibility for the learning process, it is hoped that they will develop (1) a sense of self-sufficiency and direction, (2) the ability to think critically and creatively, (3) an awareness and an understanding of a variety of information resources, and (4) the ability to use these resources effectively.[7] It is not only the knowledge of material and technical resources that will make the entrant to business libraries better prepared for the complex functions in these libraries but also the development of sensitivity and communication skills along with information services skills and the proper utilization of technologies as information facilitators.

SPECIALIZED TRAINING OTHER THAN FORMAL LIBRARY SCIENCE COURSES

Since most library students have little or no background in business, finance, or related subject areas, they should recognize that basic competencies will be achieved only through hard work, a dedicated attitude, and personal commitment. The commitment is made easier when the person recognizes the potential for rewarding careers in this area, but there is still a tendency to avoid the effort and advance planning required by enrollment in formal library science courses. It should be emphasized therefore that specialized training other than formal library science courses is available and should be exploited. Some of the available opportunities that should be considered include:

1. A program of basic business courses covering the areas of economics, marketing, accounting, and management. This would be especially pertinent for the academic business librarian who might have such basic courses available on site.
2. Workshops and institutes of various lengths covering both the areas of business and business librarianship. The business librarian should be alert to those available through library schools, state library agencies, public libraries, and commercial firms.
3. Brief sessions held during the annual conferences of library associations. Both the American Library Association and the Special Libraries Association meetings are helpful in this regard.
4. Training sessions in computerized searching advertised by business database producers and vendors, including Lockheed, Systems Development Corporation, Bibliographic Retrieval Services, ABI Inform, Predicasts, etc.

The neophyte business librarian and the practiced business librarian alike must consider, in addition to formal long-term and short-term training sessions that constitute a life-long commitment to continuing education of all sorts, the same commitment to self-education. This will require a concerted effort to contact the world of business, both its literature and its people. In the case of the literature, the business librarian should make it a practice to read the daily financial information in a variety of newspapers, to study the introductory material in standard reference tools (especially revised versions), and to peruse the wealth of information provided by associations, publishers, and database producers and vendors. As for the business community, the business librarian should participate in its workshops, meetings, breakfasts, etc., and make every effort to interact on its social, educational, and work levels.

APPENDIX 1

Course Outline

Unit I: Introduction to:
(1) The specialized nature of business, finance, management and other related fields;
(2) Business and other related libraries—their organization and activities;
(3) Characteristics of business literature, with references to:
     Methods of Locating Facts
     Basic Time-Saving Sources.

Unit II: Introduction to:
(1) Government as Information Source;
(2) Legislation and Regulation.

Unit III: Introduction to specialized services in business and public affairs, with emphasis on loose-leaf services and their usefulness in providing information in a variety of libraries.

Unit IV: Serials and their use in business and related fields.

Unit V: Locating facts on people, companies, organizations, agencies, etc.

Unit VI: Guides to information sources:
(1) Bibliographies;
(2) Periodical Indexing and Abstracting Services;
     (Special emphasis given to current awareness tools).

Unit VII: Research organizations as data sources.

Unit VIII: Basic information sources in subject fields selected in accordance with student background and interests.

Unit IX: Selection and acquisition resources in business and related fields (with an introduction to leading publishers).

Unit X: Databases (Lecture and guest lecturers).

Unit XI: }
Unit XII: }   Overview sessions with student discussion of broad problems and applications identified during the semester.

APPENDIX 2

Consideration of Subject Areas
(Based on survey returns)

SUBJECT AREAS*	Coverage Basic / Heavy	Medium
Accounting/Control and taxation	X	
Corporate finance and banking	X	
Insurance		X
Real estate		X
Management	X	
Marketing	X	
Personnel management		X
Industrial relations		X
Production and operations management		X
Computers and management information systems	X	

Economics, in most business courses, is considered as a basic subject area underlying all other subject areas but in many cases is not covered per se, as are other more practically business-oriented topics. Other subject areas covered by some schools represent a great variety, including industrial relations, international business, public relations, business law, and employment and training, to name a few.

APPENDIX 3

Options Offered In Course Exercises*

(To be selected in accordance with student backgrounds and needs and the length of the semester—Winter, Spring versus Summer)

I.   LABORATORY WORK (On a weekly basis regularly assigned)
      (1) Queries
          Involves work on queries that are typical of any library.
      (2) Problem-analysis
          Involves the various aspects of subjects encountered in business, finance, and management, and includes the usage of statistical, economic, and financial information sources.

II.   EXERCISE I: Defining
      Defining some of the most frequently encountered terms and concepts, with emphasis on terms in business, finance, and management.

III.   EXERCISE II: Loose-leaf Services
      Provides students with an opportunity to gain a better understanding of the nature and usefulness of a variety of loose-leaf services through critical analysis and evaluation.

IV.   PROJECT I: Identification and Analysis of a Variety of Information Sources for Data on a Manufacturing Firm (or other)
      Evaluation of a variety of information sources on the various aspects of a selected organization (manufacturing or other). The discussion involves a description of the extent to which different sources of information provide the same, similar, or different data and the manner in which they complement each other.

V.   PROJECT II: Semester project
      (1) Selection, Analysis, and Description of Information Sources in a Specialized Area of Business, Finance, and Management.

---

*First described in Cveljo, "Business Librarianship" (Ref. 6).

(2) Development of a Special Collection to Serve as a Hypothetical "Model" (Core) for a Company Library Within a Selected Type of Industry.

VI.   GROUP PROJECTS: Case studies
Offer students opportunities to serve in the capacity of "professional librarians" in the solution(s) of the problems described in a variety of situations.

VII.   ONLINE RETROSPECTIVE SEARCHES
The selection of online retrospective searching, providing students with hands-on experience in computer searching, is based on the continuous increase since the early 1970s in the usage of online training for online information retrieval systems.

REFERENCES AND BACKGROUND NOTES

1. To illustrate the changes in contemporary society and their impact on organizations of all types, including libraries and related institutions, the following articles were selected: Ralph J. Coffman and M. Hope Coffman, "Trends in Industrial Information Resource Centers," *Science & Technology Libraries* 1 (3) (Spring 1981): 42–54; Cyrus F. Gibson and Ava A. Schnidman, "Information Technology and Organizational Change," *Information Reports and Bibliographies* 11 (2) (1982): 3–10; Mildred S. Myers and William C. Frederick, "Business Libraries: Role and Function in Industrial America," *Journal of Education for Librarianship* 15 (1) (Summer 1974): 41–52; David Rowe, "Information Transfer in the Industrial Environment—The Requirements of Industry," *ASLIB Proceedings* 25 (11) (November 1973): 425–29; and Louis Vagianos, "Education for Scientific and Technical Information Work," *Journal of Education for Librarianship* 14 (2) (Fall 1973): 83–95.
2. Shirley Echelman, "Libraries are Businesses, Too!" *Special Libraries* 65 (10/11) (October/November 1974): 410–11.
3. Echelman, pp. 410–11.
4. Echelman, p. 409.
5. The following articles are selected to illustrate the changes in education for library and information services: M. Balachandran, "Advanced Subject Bibliography in Business and Economics: A Course Out-

line," *Journal of Education for Librarianship* 17 (4) (Spring 1977): 247–51; Lloyd J. Houser and Gerald J. Lazorick, "Introducing a Significant Statistics Component into a Library Science Research Methods Course," *Journal of Education for Librarianship* 18 (3) (Winter 1978): 175–92; Irving M. Klempner, "The New Imperatives: Decisions for Library School Curricula," *Special Libraries* 67 (9) (September 1976): 409–14; Antje B. Lemke, "Alternative Specialties in Library Education," *Journal of Education for Librarianship* 18 (4) (Spring 1978): 285–94; Whitten, Benjamin, Jr., "Social Sciences Bibliography Course: A Client-Oriented Approach," *Journal of Education for Librarianship* 16 (1) (Summer 1975): 25–32.

6. Katherine Cveljo, "Business Librarianship: Information Services and Research," *Special Libraries* 70 (8) (August 1979): 320–27. Note should also be made of the author's previous paper: "On-line Retrospective Searching as a Method in Teaching Information Sources, Services and Research in Business, Finance and Management," (Paper presented at American Society for Information Science 5th Mid-year Meeting, Vanderbilt University, Nashville, TN, May 2–22, 1976).

7. Cveljo, "Business Librarianship," p. 325.

Acquisitions and Collection Development in Business Libraries

by Constance Cameron, Kathleen H. Fencil, and
Bernard S. Schlessinger

THE LITERATURE

Although the literature 1975–1982 contains little written about either acquisitions or collection development in business libraries, there is some material worthy of mention.

In the area of acquisitions, a paper by Martha Bailey notes that acquiring all library materials is a function performed by 106 of the 108 responding libraries operating in the areas of aircraft and missiles, chemicals, foods, law, newspapers, office machines, petroleum, and pharmaceuticals.[1] She also notes that 34 of the 108 librarians order personal books and subscriptions for employees. In addition, a brief note on purchasing policies is found in a pamphlet by Bernhard,[2] and Koch and Pask[3] report on the acquisition of working papers.

Collection development policy is related to an analysis of reference requests in a paper by Smith,[4] and the general importance of the collection is noted in the pamphlet by Bernhard[5] and a paper by Dermyer.[6] Aids to collection development, for both general and special collections, are discussed in papers by Haines,[7] Jones,[8] Koch and Pask,[9] and Ohlson and Tabuteau.[10] The other papers that relate to collection are concerned with descriptions of various collections.[11–18]

Integral to the development of a strong collection is the availability of evaluative materials on individual components of the collection. Of special interest in this regard are 3 authors' series only the latest of each of which is noted below: Balachandran,[19] DiMattia,[20] and the *Library Journal series*.[21] Also worthy of note are the Behles treatment of business periodicals,[22] the

Brown material on Canadian sources,[23] the Bowker volume,[24] the King presentation on U.S. serial publications,[25] and the Hatzfeld material on indexes.[26] For more specific areas of interest, the reader is referred to the collection of abstracts of the literature included as Part 2 of this book.

PRACTICE IN SELECTED LIBRARIES

To develop data about practices in acquisitions and collection development for business libraries entering the 1980s, data were collected from 6 New England libraries. The 6 included:

1. A major state university research library, granting both graduate and undergraduate degrees in its business school.
2. A small, private 4-year business college granting undergraduate and some master's level degrees.
3. A small to medium-sized, private 4-year college with undergraduate and master's level programs which focus primarily on business areas.
4. A small to medium-sized public library serving an active business community.
5. A small to medium-sized public library serving a small business community.
6. A small corporate library serving a specialized business clientele.

The data collected were secured from each library through a personal visit with the professional(s) directly responsible for the selection/acquisition of business materials within each facility. The visit was preceded by an advance mailing of an explanatory cover letter and a list of core questions to be covered. The visits averaged 2 hours in length.

Although the business library environments differed, and funding and general procedures often deviated, some general conclusions can be drawn. These conclusions are summarized below in reference to each question, with additional material added by the authors.

Summaries of Replies

1. *How is the selection of business materials handled? Who initiates the requests for purchase?* The general trend for selection is for one person to be responsible for business reference and a second person responsible for circulating business materials. For the universities, the larger the library the less direct the involvement of the librarians in selection. For the largest

library visited (an academic library), selection was reported as handled by the business faculty in conjunction with total purchasing of the offerings of major business publishers. On the other hand, the smallest academic library showed the most specific attempt to coordinate business selection in a library/teaching faculty environment. By assigning each professional librarian certain faculty members and their subject areas, a liaison system for communicating and coordinating selection was successfully carried out. Although in all cases requests for purchase of materials were encouraged from all active business library users and professionals (including students), the largest number of requests were initiated by the library professionals.

The authors have found it useful, in selecting new business materials, to vary the selection procedures according to the price of the item, as described below.

    a. For expensive items (those priced at more than $100.00): Many of these are identified to the selector by a sales representative or by a brochure containing an introductory offer. Even in the largest libraries, in light of limited budgets, one must carefully consider the purchase by:

    (1) obtaining full information and, if possible, a copy.

    (2) comparing the tool against comparable tools held by the library or by other libraries in the area. The tool should also be compared with the earlier edition, if there is one, to see if substantive (and valuable) changes have been made. A useful technique is to look up the same entries in earlier editions and in comparable tools.

    (3) weighing the price against the value evidenced by the comparison in (2).

    (4) consulting with colleagues in the library.

    (5) investigating the holdings of neighboring libraries.

    (6) considering current client demand.

Expensive items of this sort may be candidates for resource sharing or for "trial" purchase.

    b. For items of medium expense ($50.00–$100.00): These are usually identified through use of the tools listed later in this essay. It is helpful to send a simple inquiry form to the publisher, expressing interest in acquiring a copy, and asking for information on price and for a sample copy. If, on the basis of the preliminary information, the title looks promising, its value should be confirmed by checking for a review, or, if no review is found, by consultation with a colleague, preferably with the tool in hand.

c. For the item of "average" expense (under $50.00): "Inexpensive" items may be identified from the ordinary tools or major publishers listed later in this essay. It is important to stay current with the brochures of specialized publishers to make sure client demand is satisfied in specialty areas. The client is often helpful here, too, in that s/he may be on mailing lists not available to the librarian or may notice advertisements in specialty journals. Close liaison with the patron is always recommended in any case.

Once an item has been identified, a decision for or against purchase can generally be made easily. Where available, reviews are helpful. And, of course, the decision always must be made on the basis of the value to the collection and to the user.

It should also be noted that, in addition to selecting new business materials, the business librarian must remember the process of ongoing business acquisitions, which requires a semiannual review of serials, annuals, and standing orders, all done in some regular, organized form that utilizes all the available staff expertise. The authors strongly recommend that a regular annual review of interlibrary loan requests be made as input for collection development decisions.

2. *What are the major selection tools used? Which are used most frequently in actual practice?* Reviewing media were the tools for selection most prominently mentioned. Advertisements and publishers' brochures, especially from publishers of established quality, were also noted as heavily used. Currency and easy availability of recent material is the prime need of most business users. The stability in a general sense of the smaller academic environment releases this time pressure to some extent. In the more public and the corporate environment, the focus is on the ability to mesh funds and on knowledge of both subject and patron to keep selection one jump ahead of the need. In these environments, a more concerted effort is made to order directly from publishers, to ensure currency.

Generally, the greater the availability of funds, the more likely librarians are to use advertising materials of established publishers in conjunction with reviewing media. The more specialized the library environment, the less likely that general library reviewing media will fill the need; greater dependence will be placed on specialized journal reviews and user requests.

The major general materials selection and review tools used by the authors for business materials are:

Book Review Digest. New York: H.W. Wilson, 1905–.
Booklist. Chicago: American Library Association, 1905–.
Choice. Middletown, CT: Choice, 1964–.

College and Research Libraries. Chicago: Association of College and Research Libraries, 1934–.

Current Book Review Citations. New York: H.W. Wilson, 1976–.

Directory of Directories: An Annotated Guide to Business and Industrial Directories, Professional and Scientific Rosters and Other Lists and Guides of All Kinds. James M. Ethridge, ed. Detroit: Gale, 1980.

Encyclopedia of Associations. Margaret Fisk, ed. 16th ed. Detroit: Gale, 1981.

Harvard Business Review. Boston: Harvard University, 1922–.

Library Journal. New York: R. R. Bowker Co., 1876–.

Management Review. New York: American Management Association, 1923–.

Marketing Information Guide. Garden City, NY: The Trade Marketing Information Guide, Inc. (monthly).

New Books in Business and Economics: Recent Additions to Baker Library. Boston: Harvard University (10/year).

New York Times Book Review. New York: New York Times, 1896–.

Wall Street Journal. New York: Dow-Jones, 1889–.

3. *What major standard catalogs or lists are used as checks for the strength and balance of your collection?* Two major sources were mentioned in almost all cases: *New Books in Business and Economics: Recent Additions to Baker Library, Harvard University* and Lorna M. Daniells's *Business Reference Sources: An Annotated Guide for Harvard Business School Students*. Daniells was also noted as most useful when basic purchases in a ''new'' business area are being considered. In addition to these, the authors recommend regular review of:

Library Journal. New York: R.R. Bowker Co., 1876–.

Reference Services Review. Ann Arbor, MI: Pierian Press, 1973–.

Sheehy, Eugene P. *Guide to Reference Books*. 9th ed. Chicago: American Library Association, 1976. *Supplement*, 1980.

Wynar, Bohdan S. *Best Reference Books*. Littleton, CO: Libraries Unlimited, 1981.

and a selected list of business journals as appropriate to the particular library.

4. *Are purchases made through a jobber or directly from the publisher? Who are the major jobbers and publishers?* In all cases, the majority of purchases were made through a jobber, with Baker & Taylor listed most frequently as the source. A variety of publishers were listed. Publisher's

brochures recommended for routine screening by the authors include those of:

American Enterprise Institute for Public Policy Research. 1150 17th St., N.W., Washington, DC 20036.

American Management Association, Inc. 135 W. 50th St., New York, NY 10020.

Brookings Institution. 1775 Massachusetts Ave., N.W., Washington, DC 20036.

Bureau of National Affairs, Inc. 1231 25th St., N.W., Washington, DC 20037.

Commerce Clearing House, Inc. 4025 W. Peterson Ave., Chicago, IL 60646.

Dow Jones-Irwin. 1818 Ridge Rd., Homewood, IL 60430.

Dun and Bradstreet, Inc. C/O Technical Publishing, 666 Fifth Ave., New York, NY 10019.

Lexington Books. 125 Spring St., Lexington, MA 02173.

Matthew Bender and Co., Inc. 235 E. 45th St., New York, NY 10017.

Moody's Investors Service, Inc. 99 Church St., New York, NY 10007.

National Retail Merchants Association. 100 W. 31st St., New York, NY 10001.

Prentice-Hall, Inc. Englewood Cliffs, NJ 07632.

Progressive Grocer. 708 Third Ave., New York, NY 10017.

Standard and Poor's Corporation. 25 Broadway, New York, NY 10004.

5. *Is there a written selection policy?* Selection policies, although generally in existence, are not a major focus. The principal selection criterion is meeting a curriculum need or current demand.

6. *Are there financial limitations on the purchase of single books?* Generally there are not financial limitations on the purchase of single books, as long as need is demonstrated and funds are available. The authors' additional comments on question one above should also be noted as applicable here.

7. *Is the emphasis in your business collection on the purchase of monographs, serials, or periodicals?* The general aim in the majority of the libraries visited is to strive for a balance between monographs and serials in the allocation of business material funds. Minimal funding upsets the ratio significantly. The heavy costs involved in maintaining serials (e.g., investment sources and value lines) on occasion does not permit minimal purchases outside of these areas. The smaller business library environments

reduce this pressure somewhat and reduce costs by alternate-year updating of services.

8. *How many journals/serials are currently received?* Numbers of current periodical subscriptions range from a low of approximately 80 in the public library to highs of approximately 880 in the larger academic environments. Back issues are held in direct relation to available space for storage and funds for binding. The purchase of back issues on microforms is directly related to funding, and academic libraries are more likely to purchase microforms.

REFERENCES

1. Martha J. Bailey, "Functions of Selected Company Libraries/ Information Services," *Special Libraries* 72 (January 1981): 18–30.

2. Genore H. Bernhard, "The Business Firm Library," in her *How to Organize and Operate a Small Library* (Fort Atkinson, WI: Highsmith, 1976), p. 39.

3. Jean E. Koch and Judith M. Pask, "Working Papers in Academic Business Libraries," *College and Research Libraries* 41 (November 1980): 517–23.

4. Gerry M. Smith, "The Demand for Business Information in an Academic Library: An Analysis of the Library Inquiry Service of the City University Business School," *ASLIB Proceedings* 28 (November/December 1976): 392–99.

5. Bernhard, p. 39.

6. Angela Dermyer, "Try on a Company Library," *Industry Week* 194 (1 August 1977): 56–57.

7. Michael Haines, "Company Correspondence: An Important Information Resource," *ASLIB Proceedings* 31 (August 1979): 401–11.

8. H. Jones, "Why the Bookmen Turn to Business," *Director* 22 (December 1976): 33–34.

9. Koch and Pask, pp. 517–23.

10. June Ohlson and Christine Tabuteau, "Microfiche Project on Australian Companies' Annual Reports," *Australian Academic and Research Libraries* 9 (December 1978): 215–18.

11. Deborah Abraham and Annette Pelcher, "Information for Tennessee Economic and Community Development," *Tennessee Librarian* 30 (Spring 1978): 24–26.

12. *Illinois Libraries* 62 (March 1980). Entire issue.

13. "Meeting the Need of GM Research Laboratories," *Information Manager* 2 (Spring 1980): 21–25.

14. K. Ruokonen, "Survey of Economic and Business Libraries in Scandinavia," *UNESCO Bulletin for Libraries* 31 (September 1977): 277–85.

15. B.T. Salter, "Economics Libraries in the United States," *INS-PEL* 12 (1977): 113–24.

16. J. Spencer, *Business Information in London: A Study of the Demand and Supply of Business Information in the Thirteen London Business Libraries* (London: ASLIB, 1976).

17. Frances K. Wood, "Business and Industrial Needs: Special Libraries are Willing to Share Resources," *Wisconsin Library Bulletin* 76 (May/June 1980): 109–10.

18. Anne R. Zimmerman, "Library Services for Members: How the FHL Banks Can Help," *Federal Home Loan Bank Board Journal* 11 (September 1978): 13–16.

19. M. Balachandran, "State of the Art Survey of Reference Sources in Business and Economics," *References Services Review* 6 (January 1978): 21–40.

20. Susan S. DiMattia, "Business Books of 1981," *Library Journal* 107 (March 1982): 519–25.

21. "Scientific, Technical, Medical and Business Books," *Library Journal* 106 (1 November 1981): 2109–24 (Business 2122–24).

22. Richard J. Behles, "Business America," *Serials Review* 6 (April/June 1980): 7–8.

23. B.E. Brown, ed., *Canadian Business and Economics: A Guide to Sources of Information* (Ottawa, Ontario: Canadian Library Association, 1976).

24. *Business Books and Serials in Print* (New York: Bowker, 1977).

25. Richard L. King, ed., *Business Serials of the U.S. Government* (Chicago: American Library Association, 1978).

26. Lois A. Hatzfeld, "Business," in her *Periodical Indexes in the Social Sciences and Humanities: A Subject Guide* (Metuchen, NJ: Scarecrow, 1978), pp. 22–26.

Organization of Materials in Business Libraries

by Carol Hryciw with the aid of Ann Dugan

INTRODUCTION

In 1919 Stanley Jast created a definition of a business library which emphasized both the provision of commercial information *and* "the collection, arrangement, and cataloguing of such printed matter so as to render it quickly and conveniently available for enquirers and readers."[1] Perhaps it is because organization of materials has always been recognized as the heart of librarianship that the literature of business librarianship does not include much on the organization of business materials specifically. It is as if the process of organization is taken for granted, based on library school education and the reading of the literature. But this general knowledge leads to a false sense of security; service in a business library is unique, which affects the way material is organized in a business library collection.

Types of Business Libraries

Myers and Frederick describe 3 kinds of business libraries: the library of a private organization, the business department or branch of a public library, and the university business library.[2] Lorna Daniells notes these same categories of business libraries but adds trade and professional association libraries.[3] While neither of these sources speaks of organization of business materials, their views on the differences among the types of business libraries provide valuable background information necessary for an understanding of organizational principles and methods in these libraries. These views may be summarized as follows. (1) Corporate and trade business libraries exist to serve the information needs of their patrons, and they collect material to reflect those needs. Emphasis is not on maintenance and organization but on getting information for individuals. The librarian is expected in many cases to locate the information needed by the client and to "spoon-feed it, if necessary, to the person who needs it."[4] (2) The public business library must serve "anyone who needs it, from large corporations and universities with their own libraries to the lone small business man who has nowhere to turn but to the public library."[5] The users' need is still mainly for information, but more often a client is pointed to sources when extended research is needed. Therefore, logical organization of materials in a manner comprehensible to both the business professional and the layperson is a firm requirement. (3) Both the university business library and the business school library must support the academic programs, and sometimes the faculty research, of the institution and must develop the collection to meet these needs. Library staff members must instruct students in how to locate materials and should therefore provide a variety of access points in their catalogs and other aids which are understandable to these students, as well as to business users.

The Literature of Organization

In-depth coverage of the topic of organization may be found in 3 publications. In the first, Malcolm Campbell discusses principles of organization and acquisition of a variety of business materials, including special treatment of all types of directories, periodicals and newspapers, and corporate reports.[6] In a second, A. Leslie Smyth proposes some general principles of arrangement, compares the City Business Library and the Manchester Commercial Library in their arrangement of directories, periodicals, market product and industrial data, statistics, and vertical file material, and includes special subject classifications provided by these libraries.[7] In the third, Smyth presents opinions about the objectives and use of business libraries, how such libraries should be designed, and how they should be fitted out with furniture and shelving for different types of material (directories, company card services, vertical file materials, maps, etc.).[8] As with much of the other material located, all 3 treatments are by British authors and show a British bias.

One recent paper by Carol Tenopir is American in focus and content and emphasizes the need for utilizing effective, computerized systems for organization and retrieval of materials.[9] She endorses the establishment of comprehensive information centers in small and medium-sized companies, presents a comparison of a computerized and a manual card catalog, and elaborates on the flexibility and adaptability of storage space, cataloging procedures, classification schemes and thesauri, subject headings, and maintenance procedures within the company library setting, and concerns herself with the design of all of these features in view of "the unique needs of each individual company."[10]

Eva Lou Fisher's checklist of questions for planning and evaluating company libraries, although now dated, still has some value when one considers cataloging and classification.[11]

Still other articles authored by non-American persons are worth noting. (1) K. D. C. Vernon writes about using the literature of business and management, explains in detail what catalogs are and how they are arranged, discusses classification in general, provides a clear outline of the *London Classification of Business Studies*, and notes the importance of interlibrary cooperation.[12] (2) Ronald Stavely and K. G. B. Bakewell both include business libraries in their chapters on special libraries in Lock's *Manual of Library Economy*.[13] Stavely delineates some of the organizational features of the special library at Borden UK and that of the IBM United Kingdom laboratories. Bakewell includes treatments of classification, cataloging, and indexing of materials in special libraries, notes the increase of indexing in preference to classification, and stresses the advantages of maintaining a catalog. (3) In the results of a survey taken by the Special Libraries Association of Tokyo, the preference of Japanese business libraries for the Nippon Decimal Classification system and for access to materials through card indexes is noted.[14] (4) G. D. L. Peterson, in an article on establishment of business information services within companies, states the need to access and organize such nontraditional materials as newswire printouts, radio and TV transcripts, microforms, and cassette tapes.[15] (5) George Henderson, in Campbell's *Manual* on directories and company information sources, addresses the optimal arrangement of telephone and city directories and briefly describes the special 2-digit classification scheme for specialized directories used by the City Business Library in London and by other business libraries in England.[16] (6) Michael Haines details the objectives and actual classification breakdowns of the company-wide correspondence filing scheme used at the Data Retrieval Unit of the mining company, Charter Consolidated, Ltd. in England.[17] (7) Ohlson and Tabuteau describe a microfilming project for approximately 12,200 annual reports of Australian companies, carried out at the Australian Graduate School of Management Library, including an explanation of the layout of the fiche and the plan for organizing the file and for updating and filing a particular company's reports.[18]

On the topic of cataloging rules specifically geared to business materials, some literature also exists. In an early article, Suzanna Lengyel describes a classification system developed for materials in the Union Carbide Corporation Business Library, based on a modified Dewey classification, which allowed for the application of the full Dewey range of numbers (0–999) to the materials and which resulted in a more detailed breakdown of subjects without use of long numbers.[19] A classification and indexing scheme utilized by the American Society for Quality Control (ASQC) for its publications is outlined by Ray Wachniak.[20] This literature classification system was originally adopted by the ASQC in 1959 and was revised in 1975. The coding includes the methodology or techniques of quality control described, the normal functions using the method or techniques, and the specific business or industry involved. Additions to the numbers identify the journal and issue numbers of the articles. Still of interest is the first major specialized classification for business literature, the *Classification of Business Literature*, first published at Baker Library of the Harvard University Graduate School of Business Administration in 1937 and appearing in a revised edition in 1960.[21] Although not used at Baker since 1976, it is probably still being used by some private business libraries in this country. The introduction to the revised edition (pp. xiii–xviii) provides the best explanation of the scheme. The classification was intended to accommodate books, periodicals, manuscripts, maps, prints, broadsides, and reports and used 3 main elements: (1) subject analysis of business organization and activity, divided into many main sections with capital letter notations; (2) an "Industries List," which is a classified arrangement of industries and occupations with numerical notations; and (3) a "Local List," which is a classified arrangement of geographical and political divisions with numerical notations.

The best known classification for business materials, however, is the *London Classification of Business Studies* (LCBS), compiled by K. D. C. Vernon and Valerie Lang, and published first in 1970 by the London Business School with a revised version appearing in 1979.[22] There is no record of libraries in the United States using the LCBS, but at least 50 libraries in the United Kingdom and 30 in other countries use it.[23] Two articles provide excellent background information on LCBS. The earlier of the 2, by K. G. B. Bakewell, describes the origins, scope, and principles of LCBS, outlines the reasons for a revision, and examines the revision process and the major differences between the first and second editions with illustrative examples.[24] Bakewell notes that the scheme can also be used as a thesaurus or authority list of terms or "as a source of headings for an alphabetical subject catalogue (precoordinate mode) or a postcoordinate index."[25]

In the second article, K. D. C. Vernon concentrates on the necessity for, revision of, and use of LCBS. He includes evidence concerning the usefulness of the second edition and its increasing popularity among business libraries.[26] Bakewell's introduction to the second edition of LCBS not only best explains the background, principles, and revision of the scheme, but indicates the notation and order of the classes and auxiliary schedules of the system.[27] He presents hints on reclassifying from LCBS 1 to LCBS 2 and gives a complete list of libraries that are using the system. Differing from the Harvard *Classification* in that it uses facet analysis, LCBS is broken down into 3 main categories, which, in turn, are divided into a number of main classes and concepts given capital letter notations. Auxiliary tables can be used to specify form of presentation (e.g., dictionary) or country, and these are given numerical notations.

Turning to another topic, subject headings for business materials are treated in the literature of the 1950s and 1960s, but interest seems to have waned since then.[28] The related topic of indexing of materials is treated in several articles and books. The first, by Bakewell, treats the indexing used in ANBAR, a documentation service for management which provides access to selected articles in over 200 journals through abstracts (monthly) and an index (quarterly).[29] The index is classified with its own alphabetical subject index. In a book-length presentation, John Blagden describes his Management Information Retrieval System (MIRS), which is designed to answer inquiries of companies about their files of management information.[30] MIRS employs postcoordinate indexing and has a thesaurus. Finally, F. A. Graham's article advocates subject indexing of all materials in industrial libraries and coordination of individual efforts as means of attaining true universal bibliographic control.[31]

One other related topic found in the literature is computer-produced catalogs. In a recent article, G. de Saedeleer explains how the acquisitions, bibliographic retrieval, and loans departments at the Central Library of the Belgian Ministry of Economic Affairs (the ''Fonds Quetelet'') were all integrated into an automated system.[32] The Library has a microfiche catalog of books and articles divided into 3 sections (author, key word in title, and Universal Decimal Classification number) and updated on a bimonthly basis. Copies of this catalog are distributed to interested libraries and are encased in a special cassette-microfiche reader. Representative of other articles is one on a COM (microfiche) catalog that Autographics developed for the Johns Manville Company, a mining company in Colorado, and that covers 1,300 items in the subject areas of mining and geology.[33]

THE PRACTICE OF ORGANIZATION IN BUSINESS LIBRARIES

Information for this section was derived from a status survey of 11 business libraries representative of the 4 general categories of such libraries listed by Myers and Frederick and by Daniells, and noted earlier in this paper. Table 1 is a chart of information compiled from this status survey. The libraries are not identified by name and are instead both identified and referred to below by their alphanumeric code.

The data from the survey reported here are compared, where applicable, with data from a 1968 survey by Maura Klingen of 5 different types of special libraries in business and industry.[34] Klingen visited libraries representative of 5 of the 6 types of business libraries identified by the Special Libraries Association in their published profiles.[35] Table 2 indicates the types of libraries she studied and charts information related to the organization of materials in these libraries. The data are discussed below in 4 major categories: collections/files maintained, treatment of material in the library's main catalog, other locally developed aids/methods to accessing collections or files, and aids to information access.

Collections/Files Maintained

All of the libraries studied have general (circulating) book collections, and most have reference collections composed largely of books. Yet, other collections and files of material abound, most containing nonbook material. In fact, more of the collections and files in the company libraries surveyed are made up of nonbook materials than are made up of book materials. Pamphlets, annual corporate reports, periodicals, telephone directories, and clippings are the most frequently found items organized in separate collections or files. Archives are found in only 4 of the libraries, although 2 others have access to archives that are not associated with the library at all. These 2 are company archives, arranged by archival methods. Moreover, 2 of the archive collections set up in the libraries surveyed are not organized in any fashion. Clearly, contemporary issues are more important to the users and staffs of these libraries.

Treatment of Material in the Library's Main Catalog

Type and form of catalog. The card catalog is the predominant type used in the libraries surveyed, although one library has initiated a COM catalog (Library D.1). The online approach is not being developed by any of the libraries at present, although 2 corporate libraries are thinking of this type of catalog for the not-too-distant future (Libraries A.1 and A.5). Interestingly enough, Klingen's Research Library in a Chemical Manufacturing Company (Library 4 in Table 2) provided a machine-produced book catalog—a progressive move for the time. Most libraries also seem to favor the dictionary form over the divided catalog, with the divided approach found mainly in the academic libraries with larger book collections and thus larger main catalogs.

Materials accessed through the catalog. Only in a few instances are materials other than books included in the main catalog, which endorses the general view that full or even partial descriptive and subject cataloging are not as appropriate for other materials as they are for book materials. Indeed, Libraries A.1 and A.3 are unique in providing access to vertical file materials in the main catalog.

Classification systems. Both surveys indicate that the majority of the libraries surveyed employ the Library of Congress (LC) or the Dewey Decimal Classification system, the former being more common in the public and academic libraries and the latter in the company libraries. The lone exception is Library B.1, a professional library in the area of insurance, which developed its own classification system with highly specific insurance categories and notations for these categories in the early 1970s. Staff members at this library are still confident of the usefulness of this system, since very few categories have been outdated, and the schedule is accommodating to insertion of new categories. On the other hand, Library D.2 changed in 1976 from its own elaborate and effective system to LC in order to take advantage of the MARC cataloging opportunities.

While those libraries using the LC system modify the numbers only slightly, if at all, rigid use of the Dewey system is rare. Sometimes Dewey numbers are modified to avoid the lengthy extensions beyond the decimal point which would otherwise result. At other times, new sequences of numbers are developed to accommodate special or new subjects, especially when a library is committed to an older edition of Dewey. Although some might criticize the practice, it seems reasonable if the library's staff is trained in proper application of the changes and if provision is made for proper input of Dewey numbers into the databases with which the library is involved. For OCLC, for example, this means utilization of the 19th edition of Dewey at the present time. Dewey 19 is being used for current cataloging in most of the surveyed libraries, although several are greatly concerned about major changes in the schedules. Reclassification to conform to these changes has been accomplished only on a limited basis.

Aids to and codes for cataloging. Joining a bibliographic utility to aid in cataloging was not seen as a practical option for most of the libraries surveyed because of the expense and the relatively small use they thought they would make of the databases these utilities offer. As a result, these libraries rely on other manual and computer-produced aids such as the *National Union Catalog,* Cataloging-in-Publication (CIP) information, MARC printed products, Library of Congress cataloging tools, *Book Pub-*

lishing Record, and the GPO's *Monthly Catalog.* They also take advantage of commercial services or use their own technological processes which provide multiple copies of cards or card sets ready for filing. Libraries C.2 and C.3 have computerized aids not related to a bibliographic utility, which brings them one step above the traditional, more time-consuming methods without incurring the expense of membership in a regional or national bibliographic utility.

Nonusers of the bibliographic utilities and of MARC tapes (4 libraries) still generally follow the first edition of the *Anglo-American Cataloging Rules* or use no standard code at all and feel that changing to *Anglo-American Cataloguing Rules, 2nd edition (AACR2)* would be far too costly a venture. However, those libraries that have access to and contribute to a bibliographic utility or that make extensive use of MARC records have found it necessary to use *AACR2.* OCLC, for instance, requires input of records in *AACR2* form, and thus, all of its cataloging products that represent current cataloging appear in this form. Library of Congress MARC records also appear in *AACR2* format, which affects the libraries that subscribe to MARC products (Libraries C.2 and C.3). Nearly all of the libraries that have made the switch to *AACR2* are distressed at the expense incurred thereby; on the other hand, Library D.1, having begun its COM catalog just when *AACR2* was implemented, is not experiencing much difficulty with the new code.

Subject headings. Both surveys indicate that business libraries favor Library of Congress subject headings over Sears headings, although specialized headings from other sources (*Business Periodicals Index,* journal literature, corporate reports) are often included as well. The company libraries surveyed tend to make greater use of non-LC subject headings, employing them in the catalogs and other tools for accessing whatever collections and files they maintain (*see* Libraries A.1 and A.4). It was also noted that those libraries that use LC subject headings for their main catalog do not necessarily use them for their other files. For instance, *Business Periodicals Index* headings are applied to materials in the vertical file at Library A.3. The conclusion is that, generally, the company libraries want more specific headings, especially for accessing special materials, and, therefore, use non-LC headings. On the other hand, other libraries feel bound by their use of MARC records to use the Library of Congress headings found in those records, but still see the utility of other, more specific, non-LC headings for special collections and files.

Authority files. Only 3 of the libraries in the survey do not maintain at least one authority file documenting the use of certain name, subject, or series headings. These 3 are corporate libraries with smaller main collections, which are just as easily searched for previously used headings as any authority file would be. Most common are files of subject headings taken from non-LC sources (Libraries A.3, A.5, B.1, and C.2) and those representing forms of series used in bibliographic records (Libraries A.5, B.1, C.1–C.3, D.1, and D.2). Name authority files are maintained by 4 of the 5 public and academic libraries surveyed, which bears witness to their large main catalog files and the need to discover discrepancies between forms of the same name and name changes quickly and efficiently.

Filing rules. Current practice leans toward the use of locally developed sets of rules, mostly undocumented. Library D.2 is the only one among these to have a printed set of rules that is given to new filers. The other libraries use standard sets of rules, but only 3 are using the *ALA Filing Rules,* published in 1968. None appears to be ready to institute the newest ALA rules of 1980. Filing does not seem to be a major concern among any of the libraries. They want to use whatever makes most sense and is easily understood. This is commendable. Yet, the more complex filing and retrieval problems in large dictionary files might argue for more attention being paid to this area.

Other Locally Developed Aids/Methods to Accessing Collections or Files

The business libraries surveyed employ cross-references in the various catalogs to notify the user of material available elsewhere in the library on the same or similar topics or to guide the user to other subject headings or entries that may be more appropriate or just as useful as the ones consulted. In addition, collections or files of material not represented in the main catalog are often accessed by many tools developed in-house. These range from Kardex files and more elaborate book catalogs for periodicals collections to simple card files arranged in the same order as the collections/files themselves. Where such tools do not exist, either the collections are organized so as to be self-indexing, or they require no indexing mechanism for ease of access.

Pamphlets and clippings generally are kept in a vertical file arrangement, free-standing or in folders arranged alphabetically by topic. Other materials ordinarily arranged in simple alphabetical order are: (1) periodicals, which appear alphabetically by title (in all of the libraries except D.2); (2) corporate annual reports, which are arranged by company name or in some cases by product, state, or country (Libraries A.1–A.4, C.3, and D.1–D.2); and (3) telephone directories, which are kept in order alphabetically by state, then by city or town (Libraries A.1, A.2, A.5, D.1, and

D.2). Only Library D.2 classifies its periodicals by Library of Congress numbers, while Library C.2 assigns its telephone directories (and city directories) locally developed classification numbers.

Appearing less frequently in the libraries, maps tend to be placed in vertical files (Libraries C.1 and C.2) or are not organized to any extent for public use. An example of the latter is at Library B.1, whose collection of Sanborn maps lacks any strict shelf arrangement and has only a simple card file as an access tool. However, libraries using *AACR2* and those having access to OCLC catalog maps more fully and apply LC or Dewey numbers to them (Library D.2, for example). Finally, accessions lists are printed by 3 of the libraries (A.1, A.3, and D.1) to help the user find materials, as well as to identify what has been added to the collections or files.

Aids to Information Access

A large number of business libraries furnish access to information in their collections/files or in the literature of business at large. The Klingen survey noted the indexing of material by the staff at the Research Library in an Industrial Corporation (Library 3 in Table 2) and the daily clipping service at the Library for a Public Utilities Firm (Library 5 in Table 2). Similar indexing projects are still pursued by more than half of the libraries in the recent survey (A.2, A.3, A.5, B.1, C.1, C.3, D.1, and D.2).

As a supplement to indexing, the business libraries surveyed are learning how best to use technology, both through subscription to a variety of online bibliographical retrieval systems and through creation of their own systems, such as the system developed by Library D.2. Alone in its lack of desire for such a retrieval system is the professional library (B.1), whose needs are so specific (insurance) that anything but an insurance database appears unnecessary.

In summary, organization in business libraries remains exciting, innovative, varied, and still dedicated to providing information for users quickly and efficiently.

TABLE 1. Survey of Business Libraries (1980-82)

TYPE OF LIBRARY	COLLECTIONS/ FILES MAINTAINED	TYPE AND FORM OF CATALOG	TREATMENT OF MATERIAL IN MAIN CATALOG						OTHER LOCALLY DEVELOPED AIDS/ METHODS TO ACCESS COLLECTIONS/FILES	AIDS TO INFORMATION ACCESS
			MATERIALS ACCESS THROUGH CATALOG	CLASSIFICATION SYSTEM	AIDS TO AND CODES FOR CATALOGING	SUBJECT HEADINGS SOURCE(S)	AUTHORITY FILES MAINTAINED	FILING RULES		
A. CORPORATE										
1. Insurance Company Library FOUNDED: 1912 SIZE OF MAIN COLLECTION: 13,000 vols. (Books) SPECIALTIES: Accounting, Auditing, Banking, Life insurance	* Books (General) Archives Corporate annual reports (alpha. arr. by co.) Old Scottish actuarial files Old international actuarial files Periodicals (alpha. arr. by title) Rate books (other companies) (uncat.) Reference collection Telephone directories (alpha. arr.) Old Moody's Vertical file Videotapes	TYPE: Card FORM: Dictionary	Books (General) Archives Old Moody's Old Scottish actuarial files Old international actuarial files Reference collection Vertical file Corporate annual reports (corporate name card only)	Dewey Decimal (16 ed.; nos. only extended to 4th digit after the decimal point.)	CODE: AACR1 Purchased LC card sets	Locally developed from journals and corporate reports	None	ALA (1968)	Card catalog (divided) for videotapes Kardex for periodicals Telephone directory index (alpha. arr. by state, then city and town) Accessions list (monthly)	None locally developed ONLINE: None
2. Insurance Company Library FOUNDED: 1949 SIZE OF MAIN COLLECTION: 15,000 vols. (Books) SPECIALTIES: Business & Mgt., Health & Life insurance, Pensions	* Books (General) Archives (uncat.) Corporate annual reports (alpha. arr. by co.) Insurance histories file (alpha. arr. by co.) Newsletters (alpha. arr. by title) Periodicals (alpha. arr. by title) Reference collection Telephone directories (alpha. arr.) Vertical (marketing) file (alpha. arr. by geo. location)	TYPE: Card FORM: Dictionary	Books (General) Reference collection	Dewey Decimal (19th ed.; 200s developed into "Company Library Insurance Classification.")	CODE: AACR2 (with some modifications) Card sets reproduced internally	Library of Congress (Locally developed list for other collections/files/aids)	None	ALA (1968)	Catalog of pamphlets & articles (card; subject arr.) Investment services index (card) Periodicals list (book; generated by word processor; title & subject arr.) Telephone directory index (Kardex; arr. by towns & cities)	Catalog of pamphlets & articles (card; subject arr.) ONLINE: BRS DIALOG NY Times Information Bank

*Signifies Main Collection

TABLE 1. Survey of Business Libraries (1980-82) (continued)

TYPE OF LIBRARY	COLLECTIONS/ FILES MAINTAINED	TYPE AND FORM OF CATALOG	MATERIALS ACCESS THROUGH CATALOG	TREATMENT OF MATERIAL IN MAIN CATALOG					OTHER LOCALLY DEVELOPED AIDS/ METHODS TO ACCESS COLLECTIONS/FILES	AIDS TO INFORMATION ACCESS
				CLASSIFICATION SYSTEM	AIDS TO AND CODES FOR CATALOGING	SUBJECT HEADINGS SOURCE(S)	AUTHORITY FILES MAINTAINED	FILING RULES		
CORPORATE cont'd										
3. Insurance Company Library FOUNDED: 1945 SIZE OF MAIN COLLECTION: 22,000 vols. (Books) SPECIALTIES: Big business, Fire & liability insurance, Occupational safety, Special hazards	* Books (General) Historical collection Periodicals Reference collection Vertical file (includes Corporate annual reports; alpha. arr. by title)	TYPE: Card FORM: Dictionary	Books (General) Historical collection Reference collection Vertical file (except corporate annual reports)	Dewey Decimal (19th ed.)	CODE: AACR1 CIP Card sets reproduced internally	Library of Congress & others locally developed (*Business Periodicals Index* headings for vertical file)	Subject, for locally developed headings	Akers filing rules	Kardex for periodicals Acquisitions list (quarterly; books)	None locally developed ONLINE: BRS DIALOG NY Times Information Bank ORBIT
4. Chemical Company Library FOUNDED: 1965 SIZE OF MAIN COLLECTION: 5,500 vols. (Books & bound periodicals) SPECIALTIES: Chemicals, Plastics	* Books (General) Corporate annual reports (alpha. arr. by co.) Marketing research reports Periodicals (alpha. arr. by title) Reference collection Vertical file (alpha. arr. by subj.)	TYPE: Card (union, of materials in main catalog of company's 3 libraries) FORM: Dictionary	Books (General) Reference collection	Dewey Decimal (17th ed.)	CODE: AACR2 OCLC (Cataloging not performed at this library but at the main company library)	Library of Congress (Locally developed headings for vertical file)	None		Locally developed	Computer-printed list (author and title sections) of holdings Marketing research reports catalog (card) Periodicals list (book; subject arr.; generated by computer) Kardex for periodicals	None locally developed ONLINE: BRS DIALOG Dow Jones News/ Retrieval NEXIS ORBIT
5. Bank Library FOUNDED: 1921 SIZE OF MAIN COLLECTION: 45,000 vols. (Books & serials) SPECIALTIES: Banking, Finance, Economics	* Books (General) Telephone directories (alpha. by title) Census materials Federal Reserve pubs. (Subsection: Statistical releases) Microforms Periodicals (alpha. arr. in oblique files by title) Reference collection Vertical file (uncat.)	TYPE: Card (union, of materials in all depts. which are cataloged) FORM: Dictionary	Books (General) Census materials Federal Reserve publications Reference collection	Library of Congress	CODE: AACR2 OCLC	Library of Congress (And others locally developed & developed by Federal Reserve banks)	Series Subject	ALA (1968)	Kardex for periodicals CIS index annotated for microform holdings from 1979 on	Reference Sources Index (card; arr. by subject- simplified LC) ONLINE: BRS DIALOG DRI Federal Reserve System database

*Signifies Main Collection

TABLE 1. Survey of Business Libraries (1980-82) (continued)

TYPE OF LIBRARY	COLLECTIONS/ FILES MAINTAINED	TYPE AND FORM OF CATALOG	TREATMENT OF MATERIAL IN MAIN CATALOG						OTHER LOCALLY DEVELOPED AIDS/ METHODS TO ACCESS COLLECTIONS/FILES	AIDS TO INFORMATION ACCESS
			MATERIALS ACCESS THROUGH CATALOG	CLASSIFICATION SYSTEM	AIDS TO AND CODES FOR CATALOGING	SUBJECT HEADINGS SOURCE(S)	AUTHORITY FILES MAINTAINED	FILING RULES		
B. PROFESSIONAL										
1. Insurance Library FOUNDED: 1887 SIZE OF MAIN COLLECTION: 6,000 vols. (Books)	* Books (General) Corporate annual reports (uncat.; alpha. arr. by co.) Old pamphlet file Periodicals (alpha. arr. by title) Reference collection Sanborn maps (uncat.) Vertical file: pamphlets & clippings (uncat.; alpha. arr. by subj.)	TYPE: Card FORM: Dictionary	Books (General) Reference collection (Old pamphlet file gradually being added)	Locally developed (Uses very specific divisions for various aspects of insurance)	CODE: None: Locally developed practice Card sets reproduced by commercial jobber	Locally developed (combining LC, those of 1974 *Business Periodicals Index* headings, list of insurance headings from SLA, & those used at business branch of the local library)	Subject (for main cat.) Subject (for vertical file) Cross-refs. file (subj.)	Locally developed	Old pamphlet file catalog (card) Sanborn map file (card)	Clippings inserted into vertical file (alph. arr. by subj.) Subject lists of important articles, pamphlets (arr. numerically in lists) ONLINE: None
C. PUBLIC										
1. Branch Specializing in Business FOUNDED: 1944 SIZE OF MAIN COLLECTION: 46,326 vols. (Books)	* Books (General) Corporate annual reports (hardback & fiche) (Arranged according to Standard & Poors' *Security Owner's Stock Guide* Import-Export Books Investment services Periodicals (alpha. arr. by title) Reference collection Law collection Taxation collection Telephone directories Trade & business directories Vertical file: maps & pamphlets (alpha. arr. by subj.)	TYPE: Book (to 1896): Card (from 1897 on) FORM: Dictionary	Books (General) Import-export books Investment services Reference collection Law collection Taxation collection Telephone directories Trade & business directories	Dewey Decimal (19th ed.; modifications for business focus)	CODE: AACR2 OCLC (Cataloging performed at main library) NUC BNB other LC tools	Library of Congress (Vertical file has own set of subject headings, locally developed)	Author (personal) Added entry (personal author/title) Series Subject (includes corporate names)	Locally developed (based on ALA (1968)	Trade & business directory catalog (main entry, title, subject access points) Statistics catalog (main entry, title, subject access points) Periodicals file (check-in; card) Serials printout (at main library only; book; union list of all branches)	Statistics catalog includes citations to statistics in articles, pams., etc., as well as in books ONLINE: DIALOG

*Signifies Main Collection

TABLE 1. Survey of Business Libraries (1980-82) (continued)

TYPE OF LIBRARY	COLLECTIONS/ FILES MAINTAINED	TREATMENT OF MATERIAL IN MAIN CATALOG							OTHER LOCALLY DEVELOPED AIDS/ METHODS TO ACCESS COLLECTIONS/FILES	AIDS TO INFORMATION ACCESS
		TYPE AND FORM OF CATALOG	MATERIALS ACCESS THROUGH CATALOG	CLASSIFICATION SYSTEM	AIDS TO AND CODES FOR CATALOGING	SUBJECT HEADINGS SOURCE(S)	AUTHORITY FILES MAINTAINED	FILING RULES		
C. PUBLIC (continued)										
2. Branch Specializing in Business FOUNDED: 1930 SIZE OF MAIN COLLECTION: 41,000+ vols. (Books)	* Books (General); City directories; Corporate annual reports (fiche); Gov't statistical annuals; Periodicals (alpha. arr. by title); Periodical indexes; Reference collection; Telephone directories; Investment services; Vertical file (maps, pamphlets)	TYPE: Card FORM: Dictionary	Books (General) (Non-public catalog accesses); Reference collection	Library of Congress (City, telephone directories & investment services have special locally developed classification; Reference collection also has locally developed shelf numbering system)	CODE: AACR2 Locally developed cooperative database, based on MARC tape use; LC proof-sheets (for non-Roman); ROM index to MARC database; NUC; LC tools (Cataloging performed at main library)	Library of Congress (some modifications made at the branch) ("Fast find" file uses locally developed headings)	Series Name Subject (Name & subject files only for locally developed headings)	Locally developed (based originally on LC Filing Rules)	City & telephone directory index (strip listings; alpha. arr.); Kardex for periodicals	"Fast Find" file (card) for important facts and figures frequently sought (arr. by subject) ONLINE: None
3. Department Specializing in Business FOUNDED: 1954 SIZE OF MAIN COLLECTION: 60,000+ vols. (Books)	* Books (General); Corporate annual reports (alpha. arr.); Fed. & military specs. (chron. arr.); Gov't pubs. (classed by SuDocs. system); Newsletters (alpha. arr.); Periodicals (alpha. arr.); Photofact folders; Reference collection; Trade directories (alpha. arr.); Vertical file: pams. & photocopies (alpha. arr.); Trade catalogs	TYPE: Card FORM: Dictionary	Books (General); Reference collection	Dewey Decimal ("B" placed before number designates location in this Dept.; 800s for business, rather than 300s) (19th ed.)	CODE: AACR2 MiniMARC CIP NUC Book Pub. Record (Cataloging performed centrally for all depts.)	Library of Congress (with some additional "popular term" headings) (Vertical file uses locally developed headings)	Series Name Subject	Carnegie Filing Rules with some local modifications	Trade catalog and directory file (Rolodex; title & subject access); Selected gov't publs. file (Rolodex; subj. approach; frequently sought items); Corporate annual report file (card; alpha. approach by company); Newsletter list; Periodicals list & Rolodex file; Vertical file card index (alpha. arr. by subject)	Index local Sunday newspaper for major articles on business ONLINE: None

*Signifies Main Collection

TABLE 1. Survey of Business Libraries (1980-82) (continued)

TYPE OF LIBRARY	COLLECTIONS/FILES MAINTAINED	TREATMENT OF MATERIAL IN MAIN CATALOG							OTHER LOCALLY DEVELOPED AIDS/METHODS TO ACCESS COLLECTIONS/FILES	AIDS TO INFORMATION ACCESS
		TYPE AND FORM OF CATALOG	MATERIALS ACCESS THROUGH CATALOG	CLASSIFICATION SYSTEM	AIDS TO AND CODES FOR CATALOGING	SUBJECT HEADINGS SOURCE(S)	AUTHORITY FILES MAINTAINED	FILING RULES		
D. BUSINESS SCHOOL										
1. College (4-yr. undergraduate & graduate programs) FOUNDED: 1919 SIZE OF MAIN COLLECTION: 81,000+ vols. (Books)	* Books (General) Archives (uncat.) Corporate annual reports (hardback & fiche) Company information file (alpha. arr. by company) Investment collection Sir Isaac Newton collection Special collection for founder of college Pamphlet file (alpha. arr. by subject) Periodicals (alpha. arr. by title) Reference collection Telephone directories (alpha. arr. by title) Stock reports	TYPE: COM (film) FORM: Divided (author/title/subject)	Books (General) Archives (10%) Sir Isaac Newton collection (partial) Reference collection	Library of Congress	Code: AACR1 OCLC	Library of Congress	Series (Subject, for pamphlet file)	GRC filing rules for COM catalogs (based on *ALA Filing Rules*)	Corporate annual reports check-in file Periodicals listing (includes investment collection and stock reports) Kardex for periodicals Accessions list (monthly) Company information file authority file (card; alpha. arr. by company)	Local company information file (card; info. taken from selected unindexed journals) ONLINE: DIALOG
2. Graduate School FOUNDED: 1908 SIZE OF MAIN COLLECTION: 526,000+ vols. (Books)	* Books (General) Career Resources Center Core collection (3,500 recent titles in business & related fields) Corporate annual reports (hardbound & fiche; alpha. arr. by co.) Manuscripts & archives Recreational reading collection Reference collection Periodicals & serials (classified by LC) Special collection Telephone directories (alpha. arr. by place) *Current Industry Reports* file (alpha. arr. by subj.)	TYPE: Card: Old (pre-1971)- New (1971-) (Also book catalog for pre-1971 holdings) FORM: Divided (author/title/subject)	Books (General) Core collection Periodicals & serials (discontinued titles only) Reference collection	Library of Congress (until 1976 used locally developed system)	Code: AACR2 OCLC NUC Other LC tools	Library of Congress (Industry & statistics index uses *Business Periodicals Index* headings)	Series (monographic) Name	Locally developed system	Core collection catalog (book) Corporate annual reports catalog (card) Periodicals & serials catalog (book, with computer updates) Recreational heading catalog (card) Special collection catalog (book)	Industry & statistics index (card; arr. by subj); indexes articles from a variety of journals) ONLINE: Locally developed system (accesses about 20 different databases)

*Signifies Main Collection

TABLE 2. Survey of Business Libraries (1968)*

TYPE OF LIBRARY	COLLECTIONS/ FILES MAINTAINED	TYPE AND FORM OF CATALOG	TREATMENT OF MATERIAL IN MAIN CATALOG						OTHER LOCALLY DEVELOPED AIDS/ METHODS TO ACCESS COLLECTIONS/FILES	AIDS TO INFORMATION ACCESS
			MATERIALS ACCESS THROUGH CATALOG	CLASSIFICATION SYSTEM	AIDS TO AND CODES FOR CATALOGING	SUBJECT HEADINGS SOURCE(S)	AUTHORITY FILES MAINTAINED	FILING RULES		
1. Research Library in a Manufacturing Company FOUNDED: 1950 SIZE OF MAIN COL-LECTION: 2,000 items (company reports) SPECIALTIES: Aerodynamics, Business mgt., Electronics, Optics, Physics, Space science	†Company reports Books (General) Pamphlets Periodicals Reference collection Research reports	TYPE: Card FORM: ?	Books (General) Reference collection	Library of Congress	CODE: AACR1? Purchased LC card sets	Library of Congress (*Thesaurus of ASTIA Descriptors* for company & research reports)	?	?	Indexes to Company & research reports	None
2. Bank Library FOUNDED: 1922 SIZE OF MAIN COL-LECTION: 10,000 vols. (Books) SPECIALTIES: Central banking, Economics, Federal Reserve System, Finance	†Books (General) Pamphlets Periodicals	TYPE: Card FORM: ?	Books (General)	Dewey Decimal	CODE: AACR1?	? (Headings for pamphlets based on *PAIS* and *Business Periodicals Index*)	?	?	?	None
3. Research Library in an Industrial Corporation FOUNDED: 1947 SIZE OF MAIN COL-LECTION: 100,000 items (Pamphlets) SPECIALTIES: Aeronautical and aerospace engi-neering, Military science	†Pamphlets (includes gov. pubs., technical reports, annual reports, reprints, specifications) Books (General) Periodicals Reference collection	TYPE: Card FORM: Divided: author, title, specific model	Books (General) Reference collection	Library of Congress	CODE: AACR1? Purchased LC card sets	Library of Congress (Locally developed headings for reports & other non-book materials)	?	?	Marginal punched card applications for many materials	Abstracts & indexes made for technical content of signif-icant data (Planning for mechanized retrieval system for technical subject content)

*Source: Maura Downey Klingen. *A Study of Special Libraries in Business and Industry* (M.L.S. thesis, University of Mississippi, 1968).
†Signifies main collection.

TABLE 2. Survey of Business Libraries (1968)* (continued)

TYPE OF LIBRARY	COLLECTIONS/ FILES MAINTAINED	TYPE AND FORM OF CATALOG	MATERIALS ACCESS THROUGH CATALOG	TREATMENT OF MATERIAL IN MAIN CATALOG					OTHER LOCALLY DEVELOPED AIDS/ METHODS TO ACCESS COLLECTIONS/FILES	AIDS TO INFORMATION ACCESS
				CLASSIFICATION SYSTEM	AIDS TO AND CODES FOR CATALOGING	SUBJECT HEADINGS SOURCE(S)	AUTHORITY FILES MAINTAINED	FILING RULES		
4. Research Library in a Chemical Manufacturing Co. FOUNDED: 1961 SIZE OF MAIN COLLECTION: 26,350 vols. (Books) SPECIALTIES: Fibers, Chemicals, Plastics, Electronics, Engineering, Agriculture	†Books (General) Chemical samples & records; Directories; Company reports & reprints; Patents; Internal reports; Pamphlets; Periodicals; Reference collection; Trade catalogs; Translations	TYPE: Book (Union) FORM: Divided: author, title, subject	Books (General) Reference collection	Dewey Decimal	CODE: AACR1?	?	?	?	Serials list Variety of finding lists & indexes produced through IBM Dokument Writer use	Subject bibliographies (through use of IBM Dokument Writer)
5. Library for a Public Utilities Firm FOUNDED: 1941 SIZE OF MAIN COLLECTION: 7,367 vols. (Books) SPECIALTIES: Engineering, Financing, Public & private power, Public utility regulations, Public utilities	†Books (General) Company reports Pamphlets (including maps, gov. pubs., public utilities regulations, items of local interest, scientific reports) Periodicals	TYPE: Card? FORM: ?	Books (General)	Dewey Decimal	CODE: AACR1?	Library of Congress Also, SLA's *Subject Headings Suggested for Use in Public Utilities Libraries*	?	?	Special bibliographies (prepared upon request) List of acquisitions (monthly)	Library clipping service (citations from area newspapers, *NY Times*, *Wall St. Journal*, about company, power industry, electrical service) performed daily & distributed company-wide

*Source: Maura Downey Klingen, *A Study of Special Libraries in Business and Industry* (M.L.S. thesis, Univrsity of Mississippi, 1968)

†Signifies main collection.

REFERENCES

1. A. Leslie Smyth, "Organisation and Administration: Objectives Planning and Staffing," in *Manual of Business Library Practice,* ed. by Malcolm J. Campbell (London: Clive Bingley, 1975), p. 31.

2. Mildred S. Myers and William C. Frederick, "Business Libraries: Role and Function in Industrial America," *Journal of Education for Librarianship* 15 (Summer 1974): 41–52.

3. Lorna M. Daniells, *Business Information Sources* (Berkeley, CA: University of California Press; Paris: Center for Business Information, 1976), pp. 1–4.

4. Myers and Frederick, p. 49.

5. Myers and Frederick, p. 49.

6. Malcolm J. Campbell, *Business Information Services: Some Aspects of Structure, Organization and Problems* (London: Clive Bingley, 1974), pp. 62–83.

7. A. Leslie Smyth, "Organisation and Administration: Classification, Cataloguing and Arrangement," in *Manual of Business Library Practice,* ed. by Malcolm J. Campbell (London: Clive Bingley, 1975), pp. 47–55.

8. Smyth, "Organisation and Administration: Objectives Planning and Staff," pp. 31–46.

9. Carol Tenopir, *Total Information Centers* (Arlington, VA: Educational Resources Information Center, 1978) (ERIC Report Ed 165-738).

10. Tenopir, p. 9.

11. Eva Lou Fisher, *A Checklist for the Organization, Operation, and Evaluation of a Company Library,* 2nd rev. ed. (New York: Special Libraries Association, 1966), p. 21.

12. K. D. C. Vernon, "Using Libraries as Information Resources," in his *Use of Management and Business Literature* (London: Butterworths, 1975), pp. 61–80.

13. Ronald Stavely, "Special Libraries," in *Manual of Library Economy: A Conspectus of Professional Librarianship for Students and Practitioners,* ed. by Reginald Northwood Lock (London: Clive Bingley, 1977), pp. 74–95; K. G. B. Bakewell, "The Special Library," in *Manual of Library Economy: A Conspectus of Professional Librarianship for Students and Practitioners,* ed. by Reginald Northwood Lock (London: Clive Bingley, 1977), pp. 320–43.

14. SENTOKYO (Special Libraries Association), Tokyo, Japan. Committee for the Survey of Small Special Libraries, "The Status of Small

Special Libraries in Business in Japan,'' *Special Libraries* 66 (September 1975): 416–20.

15. G. D. L. Peterson, ''Designing a Business Information Service for Top Management,'' *ASLIB Proceedings* 30 (April 1978): 142–44.

16. George P. Henderson, ''Directories and Company Information Sources,'' in *Manual of Business Library Practice,* ed. by Malcolm J. Campbell (London: Clive Bingley, 1975), pp. 63–78.

17. Michael Haines, ''Company Correspondence: An Important Resource,'' *ASLIB Proceedings* 31 (August 1979): 401–11.

18. June Ohlson and Christine Tabuteau, ''Microfiche Project on Australian Companies' Annual Reports,'' *Australian Academic and Research Libraries* 9 (December 1978): 215–18.

19. Suzanna Lengyel, ''Modification of Dewey for a Business Library,'' *Special Libraries* 52 (May 1961): 245.

20. Ray Wachniak, ''To Find It, File It Right,'' *Quality Progress* 8 (July 1975): 8–9.

21. Harvard University. Graduate School of Business Administration. Library, *Classification of Business Literature,* rev. ed. (Hamden, CT: Shoe String Press, 1960).

22. Kenneth Denis Cecil Vernon and Valerie Lang, *The London Classification of Business Studies,* 2nd ed., rev. by K. G. B. Bakewell and David A. Cotton (London: ASLIB Publications, 1979).

23. Vernon and Lang, p. 9.

24. K. G. B. Bakewell, ''London Classification of Business Studies,'' *International Classification* 6 (March 1979): 29–35.

25. Bakewell ''London Classification of Business Studies,'' p. 32.

26. K. D. C. Vernon, ''Classification of Business and the Business of Classification,'' *Catalogue & Index* 57 (Summer 1980): 8–12.

27. Vernon and Lang, pp. 6–24.

28. Special Libraries Association. Financial Division, *Subject Headings for Business and Financial Libraries* (New York: Special Libraries Association, 1952); Special Libraries Association. Financial Division, *Subject Headings for Financial Libraries* (New York: Special Libraries Association, 1954); and Elin B. Christianson and Edward G. Strable, comp., *Subject Headings in Advertising, Marketing, and Communications Media* (New York: Special Libraries Association, 1964).

29. K. G. B. Bakewell, ''ANBAR Indexing,'' *Catalogue & Index* 21 (January 1971): 14–15.

30. John Blagden, *Management Information Retrieval: A New Indexing Language,* 2nd ed. (London: Management Publications, 1971).

31. F. A. Graham, "The Industrial Librarian and Universal Bibliographic Control," *International Journal of Special Libraries* (INSPE) 9 (1–2) (1974): 16–21.

32. G. de Saedeleer, "Automation of the Library, 'Fonds Quetelet,' " *Network* 3 (4) (1976): 9–17.

33. Gretchen Redfield, "Automation and Networking," *Colorado Librarian* 6 (June 1980): 29.

34. Maura Downey Klingen, "A Study of Special Libraries in Business and Industry (MLS thesis, University of Mississippi, 1968).

35. "Profile of a Library for the GHI Public Utilities Firm," *Special Libraries* 57 (April 1966): 227–29; "Profile of a Library for the JKL Bank," *Special Libraries* 57 (April 1968): 229–31; "Profile of a Library for the Research and Development Division of the DEF Industrial Corporation," *Special Libraries* 57 (March 1966): 182–84; "Profile of a Library for the Research and Development Division of the QRS Chemical Manufacturing Company," *Special Libraries* 57 (May/June 1966): 329–31; and "Profile of a Research Library in the ABC Manufacturing Corporation," *Special Libraries* 57 (March 1966): 180–81.

Reference Service in the Business Area

by John Etchingham

Key to the provision of good reference service to business clientele is the business reference librarian, who must begin (1) by understanding the subject area of the library collection (business and its related fields), (2) by appreciating the necessity for a collection that meets the needs of clientele and by working toward such a collection, and (3) by providing good reference through application of his/her skills and talents and through the effective use of the reference interview.

TRAINING OF THE BUSINESS LIBRARIAN

In order to accomplish these objectives, the business reference librarian should ideally hold academic credentials related to business and should have several years of experience in the field. This is not, however, generally the case. More often, the beginning business librarian is without either significant academic training or experience. Acquiring the necessary experiences requires, first and foremost, a personal commitment *over time* to pursue them. Once this commitment is present, there are several alternatives to on-the-job experience that should be explored.[1]

1. Business courses being offered at local institutions can be invaluable to the beginner. Although business reference courses in library schools are helpful, even more important are introductory courses in the business school. A package of the basic courses in accounting, management, and finance will provide a sound base for the business librarian. One should, however, give careful consideration to the money and time spent in such classes. At least part of the costs will likely be covered for academic librarians in institutions where business school coursework is offered, but the public library business librarian will probably have to absorb the costs alone. Time, however, will be a critical factor for both. Three basic courses would probably take 3 semesters for a working librarian. Such an extended (and costly) educational package leads many to consider the other 2 alternatives.

2. Beginning librarians might explore the availability of training sessions in business and in business librarianship. These are usually no longer than 2 or 3 days and take a variety of forms, such as business reference workshops offered by library schools or state library agencies, presentations given by the information vendors such as DIALOG and Predicasts in computerized database searching, and short-term noncredit courses given by the continuing education agencies in academic institutions.[2] Keeping abreast of all these activities is not difficult. Information vendors are usually very willing to add the librarian's name to their mailing lists, and a call to the local continuing education agency will accomplish the same for its announcements. Watching the state library journals will help as well, since many carry continuing education listings as a regular feature.

3. Self-education should not be overlooked. In its broadest sense, this is an all embracing life-long activity in many subject areas. The narrow context used here refers to becoming as familiar as one can—and as quickly as possible—with the bibliographic materials at hand. This may be done by reading the introductory matter of a set of the popular and high demand business reference sources *word for word*. As an example, if the librarian had never heard of a financial ratio, a thorough reading of about 6 pages of the introductory matter in the *RMA Annual Statement Studies*[3] would quickly turn ignorance into knowledge. In the same way, contacting the representatives of business publishers and investment services for their virtually unending flow of announcements of new and old wares—and critically reading the output—would efficiently make the librarian aware of what certain titles provide in relation to competitive materials. Still another method of self-education regarding the basic business sources is to consult the secondary sources. Although they usually provide only a brief overview of the listed materials, they represent an organized and classified collection of many diverse titles. This can afford the librarian a sense of the range of tools in specialized areas of the business spectrum. Three such secondary sources recommended by the author are M. J. Campbell's *Manual of Business Library Practise*, L. M. Daniells' *Business Information Sources*, and Oscar Figueroa's *A Business Information Guide Book*.[4]

It should be emphasized again, in advocating training, that there is no substitute for subject area knowledge. ''Winging it,'' for the business reference librarian, is not a viable method of operation.

APPRECIATION OF THE COLLECTION

The essence of reference work is to match the patron's question with the right answer. Central to this process is the availability of a reference collection that will provide the required information. Part I of this book has presented a core collection for the smaller or medium-sized library. The author has found that, especially in academic libraries, a very limited number of services/titles can provide answers to a very large number of the business reference questions received at the desk. These include the following.

Moody's Investors Service Materials

The 6 annual corporate manuals (*Bank and Finance, Industrial, International, OTC (Over the Counter) Industrial, Municipal and Government,* and *Public Utility and Transportation*) present descriptive and tabular data on approximately 20,000 corporations and institutions operating in the national and international sectors, including information on history, subsidiaries, business lines, and plants and properties, as well as management data, income accounts, and balance sheets.[5] Coverage ranges from the comprehensive to the narrowly selective, with retrospective analysis varying with each manual. Start-up of the manual ranges from 1920 for the *Industrial Manual* to 1970 for the *OTC Industrial Manual* and 1981 for the *International Manual*.

Arrangement in the set varies with each manual. The *Industrial Manual* is organized by coverage (i.e., complete, full, comprehensive, or standard) and then alphabetically by corporation/institution name; the *International Manual* is organized first by country then by name. Indexing provides, for example, alphabetical, geographical (state and city), and industry/product access in the *Industrial Manual*. All of the titles are kept current with loose-leaf issues (usually received twice a week) filed in matching *News Reports* binders. The user should be careful of incomplete or broken pagination, such as the gaps of 100 pages or more between some coverage sections in the *Industrial Manual*.

Other Moody titles of interest to the researcher, investor, or business student are the *Investors Fact Sheets—Industry Review, Bond Record,* and *Handbook of Common Stock.*[6] The *Industry Review* provides tabular and graphic presentation of over 150 industries and the chief companies in each. In addition, comparative industry statistics in company rank order are displayed. This loose-leaf service is in a constant state of revision; 10 to 12 industries are updated every 2 weeks. The monthly *Bond Record* covers over 30,000 issues and situations. The format allows quick assessment of market position and background statistics. The quarterly *Handbook of Common Stock* provides financial and business information on over 900 common stocks. The data on each company include a long-term price chart, capitalization, earnings, dividend information, company background, and recent developments.

Moody's Investors Service also offers other products that are worth investigating.

Standard and Poor's (S&P) Corporation Materials

Whether Moody's or S&P occupies first place as a source of business reference materials is a matter of personal preference. Both offer a comprehensive business collection, with many titles in such close parallel that it is difficult if not impossible to choose one over the other. Two S&P titles, however, deserve special consideration for the business reference collection.

The *Standard and Poor's Register of Corporations, Directors, and Executives* is an annual publication in 3 volumes, kept current with 3 cumulated supplements.[7] Volume 1 is an alphabetical arrangement of approximately 38,000 corporations, with information including addresses, names, and titles of officers and directors; primary bank, law firm, and accounting firm; stock exchange(s) on which the company's stock is traded; annual sales; number of employees; and Standard Industrial Classification (SIC) codes. Volume 2 is a listing of over 70,000 individual directors and executives, with brief biographical and company affiliation data. Volume 3 is the index volume, listing corporations geographically, by SIC code, and by corporate family. The corporate family index is a "Who Owns Whom" directory, identifying subsidiaries, divisions, and affiliates. In terms of quantity and quality, the *Register* is unique.

Industry Surveys offers a wide variety of data useful for analysis of an industry.[8] Sixty-nine major domestic industries are analyzed in 2 sections, a "Basic Analysis" and a "Current Analysis." The "Basic Analysis" examines the prospects for the industry and presents historical background data. The "Comparative Company Analysis," a regular part of the "Basic Analysis," provides tabular data on industry leaders. The "Current Analysis," revised 3 times a year, offers the latest developments and statistics along with an appraisal of the investment outlook. *Industry Surveys* is available in loose-leaf or bound quarterly format. For high-use environments, the author strongly recommends the bound format.

The Value Line Investment Survey.[9]

Approximately 90 industries embracing some 1,600 companies are covered in this important title for industry and company analysis. *Value Line* is published in 3 parts. Part I is *Summary and Index*. In addition to its index of companies, this publication contains a screens section that includes a listing of timely, conservative, and high-yielding stocks; best and poorest performing stocks; companies with high return on capital; low and high P/E (Price-Earnings) stocks; and option information. Part 1 is completely revised every week. Part 2, *Selection and Opinion*, is a weekly newsletter that offers investment recommendations. A regular feature of Part 2 is the stock highlight column in which an exceptionally high-performing stock is analyzed and strongly recommended to the reader. Part 3, *Ratings and Reports*, is organized into 13 editions, consecutively revised on a weekly schedule such that the entire body is revised quarterly. Each industry and its allied companies are given a one- or 2-page coverage, providing a statistical, narrative, and graphic overview of historical and projected performance. The author notes that the physical format of Part 3 (printed on newsprint) causes some problems in that, in a high-use setting, the editions rarely survive their 90-day life.

Accounting/Banking/Management Analysis Materials

Two highly specialized titles of interest to the accounting, banking, and management analyst are the *Almanac of Business and Industrial Ratios* and the *RMA Annual Statement Studies*.[10] Use of these titles presumes extensive prior knowledge of financial analysis. The *Almanac* supplies complete corporate performance facts and figures displayed on an industry basis. Twenty-two displayed percentages allow one to answer such questions as: how well is the company performing, when compared to the industry as a whole, in its ratio of profit to sales? What is its net worth? and What share of sales is going to amortization? *Statement Studies* provides composite financial data on manufacturing, wholesaling, retailing, and contracting lines of business. The comparative analytical data, shown for the current year and for the previous 4 years, are critical for making accurate financial judgements. Both the *Almanac* and *Statement Studies* are annuals, but the *Almanac* tends to be less timely in publication.

Statistics Materials

Recognizing that few business decisions are not influenced by statistics, a limited business reference collection must contain sources for answering questions in this area. Chief among these sources would be the *American Statistics Index (ASI)* and its companion the *Statistical Reference Index (SRI)*.[11] The *ASI* aims to be a master guide and index to all the statistical publications of the U.S. government. Since there is no single central source of statistical publications published by the federal government, the *ASI* satisfies a very important need by filling this void. Specifically, it identifies, catalogs, announces, describes, and indexes, on a monthly schedule, federal statistics, the range and depth of which are without parallel. The *SRI* provides access to statistical information from U.S. sources other than the federal government. It announces statistics published by trade and business organizations, commercial publishers, research centers, and state government agencies. It does *not* cover municipal and county publications (these are announced in the *Index to Current Urban Documents).*[12] Worthy of special note are the fine abstracts, the cumulation of all loose-leaf monthly issues into annual hardbound editions, and the availability of microfiche for virtually all of the documents cited in the *ASI* and of about 90% of the material cited in the *SRI,* which can be provided by subscription or on demand.

In addition to the *ASI* and *SRI,* the author must note 2 other indispensable publications in the area of statistics: the annual handbook, *Statistical Abstract of the United States,* and the yearly *U.S. Industrial Outlook.*[13] The *Abstract* is a 900-page document of tabular data, citing the primary source for each table and thus providing identification of the source of much federal statistical data. Published for over 100 years, it serves as an excellent tool for retrospective analysis for such diverse areas of interest as state and local government finances; banking, finance, and insurance; business enterprise; and mining and mineral production data. The section on comparative international statistics is especially valuable to those analyzing or considering foreign markets. The *Outlook* is a forecasting publication in which 200 industries are reviewed. Performance projections, extending in some cases to several years, are provided. Much of the data in the *Outlook* come from the U.S. Bureau of the Census.

In this area of statistics, the librarian should further consider acquiring certain specific census documents, viz., *Census of Retail Trade, Census of Wholesale Trade, Census of Service Industries, Census of Transportation, Census of Manufacturers,* and *County Business Patterns.*[14] These are available on a state-by-state basis, so that the librarian can select the titles for only his/her state and/or region. For the nondepository library, a subscription service is available from the Superintendent of Documents at a relatively modest price.

Directories

Occupying a prominent place in the business reference section are the directories. In addition to the Standard and Poor's *Register of Corporations, Directors and Executives,* several others should be considered.

Heading the list is the *Thomas Register of American Manufacturers*.[15] Its organization into the *Products and Services Volumes, The Company Volumes,* and the *Thomcat Catalog Volumes* gives the researcher access to "who makes what where." Over 100,000 companies—both publicly and privately held—are identified. A strong feature of the *Thomas Register* (and of other company directories as well) is that it provides the job seeker with an extensive listing of companies that may be sources of employment. It is also of importance to the market analyst and to sales force personnel.

The *Thomas Register* provides a comprehensive national tool. A number of local and regional directories should be made available as well. Examples are the *Directory of New England Manufacturers* and the *Connecticut-Rhode Island Directory of Manufacturers,*[16] both of which are organized into an alphabetical, geographical, banking, and product sections. The wide variety of such titles gives the librarian a certain degree of flexibility in selection, especially when operating under budget restrictions. In addition to the Polk City Directories and local publishers, the librarian should consult Commerce Register, Inc. of Hohokus, New Jersey, and George D. Hall Company of Boston, Massachusetts.

The user should be aware of the validity of the disclaimers found in many directories, that such works are inherently incomplete since much of the information is provided voluntarily and nonresponses are inevitable.

THE REFERENCE PROCESS

The patron—the information seeker—and the effectiveness of his/her interaction with the librarian and with the collection are the key elements in the reference process. If there were no patrons, all the available librarians' expertise and all the titles in the reference collection would serve no purpose. That the presence and needs of the patron are paramount in the process is accepted. That the communication of these needs and the understanding of them by the librarian is difficult to achieve in many cases is equally accepted. Human communication is frail; what we say is easily misunderstood, and what we hear is often only a part of the message. The importance of understanding the patron as well as the patron's needs cannot be overemphasized.

Types of Patrons

No neat scheme of categorizing patrons exists. Some patrons know exactly what information they want and where it is; others know what they want but don't know where to search; still others aren't really sure of the ''what'' and certainly are less sure of the ''where.'' The librarian has a role to play with each of these patrons. The involvement varies inversely with the patron's knowledge and self-organization.[17]

For the experienced user, such as the investor in the public library or the researcher in the academic or special library, the librarian's role is to make the link. The opportunity to do so presumes at least 2 preconditions: that the library holds the appropriate titles and that the librarian knows where they are and/or how to locate them quickly. Whether the titles are held is a function of collection development; whether they can be found is a function of the librarian's experience and skill. Collection development, practical experience, and skills development take time, but even if all have been diligently pursued, the success of the process is not assured. There may be other germane and available titles unknown to the librarian which may contain the information sought, or at least part of it. Determining whether the patron has found an answer in the available titles or whether the librarian should intervene and recommend other sources depends on the reference interview, which may be triggered by a formal request or by the briefest of verbal or nonverbal communication.

The author should parenthetically note that the in-house reference guides in his library, which are readily available and prominently announced, have been very helpful. The kinds and numbers of such guides that should be on hand will depend on the needs of the library clientele. In any case, they should be brief, annotated listings of subject-oriented materials that are in the library, probably no longer than 2 pages. Business librarians faced with the task of developing such guides will wish to consult sources available from other libraries with similar clientele, especially the guides used in the libraries of the well-known business schools and in the larger business-oriented public libraries.

For the user who knows what s/he wants but who doesn't know where to start, the role of the librarian goes beyond the basic directional reference encounter and involves careful and difficult judgements. As one example, let us look at the student who indicates interest in the historical development of a public U.S. company. The librarian would probably start with a *Moody's Manual* rather than *Value Line*. By the same measure, the ''Corporate Section'' of the *Wall Street Journal Index* rather than the companion ''General Section'' would probably be more appropriate.[18] Perhaps the student should be referred to the legions of books written on companies, especially the conglomerates and supranational corporations. Perhaps the periodical literature should be consulted, the *Business Periodicals Index (BPI)* or the *Public Affairs Information Service*, or even the *Social Sciences Citation Index*[19]

A second example of the user who doesn't know where to start may be found every day in the public library in the person of the beginning investor. The growth of investment clubs and the general interest in small-scale investing has produced a multitude of such patrons. The public library business desk specialist or reference librarian occupying that role has an obligation to instruct this type of user, first in the mysteries of the simpler tools such as *Moody's Handbook,* then on to more advanced financial services such as *Value Line,* and finally to the intricate world of technical considerations in investing and its associated literature.

One might assume that the user who doesn't know where to start is scarce. However, Pask notes that, in her study, 48 percent of the graduate business students surveyed could not list one index or abstract they knew how to use well. In the same source, Pask cites another survey, in which both undergraduate and graduate business students were queried, where 10 percent of the group had never even heard of the *BPI.*[20] If this is true of the college student who is specializing in the field, it is probably even more true of the general user of the public library, and the librarian should realize that this patron will need considerable help, not only in identifying the applicable primary and secondary sources, but also in hands-on use of the research tools.

For the patron who is uncomfortable with both the ''what'' and the ''where'' and who shyly approaches the reference desk (if indeed s/he is aware that the service exists), the reference librarian's role is crucial. The librarian will be called upon not only to render substantial assistance with the bibliographic sources but also to help define and refine the patron's objective: just what it is that is being sought. A typical question from this type of patron might be ''Where are the magazines?'' generally asked haltingly and apprehensively. The sensitive librarian, in different environments, may discover very different answers are necessary for this seemingly simple question.

The author is most familiar with this question from the college student and has not been surprised to find that the student has been assigned the first term paper of his/her college career, that one requirement is an 8-citation bibliography, half journal citations and half book citations, that s/he has been given a choice of several broad subjects, that the breadth of each choice requires refinement in order to make the paper manageable within the framework of the course, and that the student has selected legislation controlling the multinational corporation and has no idea what to do or where to go.

For this type of student, the librarian might start with an explanation of the library organization and the different bodies of literature within it (books, serials, microforms, etc.). This might be followed, ideally, by a session on the procedures involved in retrieval of the materials likely to provide the information needed for the paper. This would involve several tasks: an introduction to the card catalog, an overview of the subject classification scheme, a review of the selection process for the appropriate indexes for the subject periodicals, and the methods of searching those indexes.

For specific questions, such as those on multinational corporations, the author has found it effective to work with students first to see how the subject is treated in the *Sears List of Subject Headings* or the *Library of Congress Subject Headings*.[21] In the latter, for example, the searcher is referred to "International Business Enterprises" under which there are several topical subdivisions, one of which is "Law and Legislation." In the same way, a scan of the organization under "Multinational corporations" in the latest cumulative volume of the *Business Periodicals Index* shows 12 subdivisions, one of which is "Laws and Regulations." The editor of this volume tells of an experience with the same question in a corporate library. The patron, a respected Ph.D. chemical researcher, based his question on the necessity to develop information on products, services, and research interests of competitors in a specific product field. Although he was a good user of *Chemical Abstracts* and research journals, he had no idea where to begin his search for this unfamiliar type of information, or even what class of materials to approach; hence the use of the popular term "magazines." Patient and sympathetic treatment introduced this patron to a new world of the *Thomas Register*, the *Moody's Manuals*, the products of the Institute for Scientific Information, and even to a better understanding of the familiar *Chemical Abstracts* and scientific journals.

Finally, public librarians may find in the question, "Where are the magazines?" anything from a truly directional question to a request for instruction in the use of popular magazine literature by a town resident inventor seeking to maintain currency with the interests of the teenage buying public.

Issues in the Reference Process

1. No matter the level of the patron, the librarian must be careful not to overwhelm him/her. The guidance must be clear and precise, and an attitude of understanding and friendliness must prevail throughout. Any lengthy discourse on the finer points of the bibliographic world will surely fall on impatient if not deaf ears and jeopardize the success of the entire process.

2. How much time should a librarian be expected to devote to rendering individual assistance? Given the usual press on the librarian's time, isn't there a better way than a one-to-one encounter? If time and staffing permit, the librarian should render as much help as is required. Unfortunately, in very few business libraries is there time or staff adequate to meet completely all the demands placed upon reference service. The reasonable alternative is to enable and encourage the patron to exploit the library independently. The reference interview should reveal the level of independence with which the patron can and desires to operate. With the proper guidance, delivered in a suitably appropriate, warm and concerned manner, most patrons should welcome and seize upon the opportunities of independent research. Most users simply don't require or like a librarian breathing down their necks. It is incumbent upon the librarian to recognize when the job is done, and to appreciate the rewards to the student in the feeling of accomplishment and satisfaction stemming from self-reliance.

3. What about considering library instruction on a group basis, in light of the economies of such a procedure? The answer to this question depends on whether one is considering public, special, or academic libraries. The opportunities for group instruction in the public or special library are few. Any session would have to be widely announced, planned at a time convenient to the intended audience, and structured with considerable appeal. In the academic setting, the situation is quite different. The audience can be a captive one and generally is at least minimally motivated. The presentation can be carefully planned to show the clear sequence of steps necessary to retrieve the required information from the applicable bodies of literature. The author has found that a packet of illustrative material reflecting the subject at hand and given to each student at the beginning of the session can be helpful in relating the library resources to the course content and to the assignment. An added benefit of these hand-out packets is that they may be consulted by the students again and again as a library retrieval directory. The packets should be no more than 6 or 7 pages in length and able to be copied readily. The author also should note that, in setting up the presentation, the desirability of the course instructor's presence during instruction should be strongly emphasized.

4. Should computerized database searching be available? This form of reference is becoming increasingly popular. A full discussion of the various business-oriented databases is presented in the next essay. The point is often made that computerized searching is extremely timely and efficient. th the right array of terms used to make the enquiry, one can achieve in a matter of minutes what would take days or even weeks if done by a researcher working with print indexes and abstracts. Although these

points would seem to support the efficacy of online searching, one must consider its high price. Still, many public and academic business libraries have initiated computerized searching, usually in concert with a fee schedule for such service,[22] and special libraries have been notable and enthusiastic users of database searching since it became available.

REFERENCES

1. In addition to courses in local institutions, the reader should consult *Continuing Education for Business People* (Detroit, MI: Gale Research Co., 1981).

2. For a model business librarianship course, *see* the Katherine Cveljo essay in this book.

3. Robert Morris Associates, *Annual Statement Studies* (Philadelphia, PA: Robert Morris Associates, Annual).

4. Campbell, Malcolm J., *Manual of Business Library Practise* (London: C. Bingley, 1975); Daniells, Lorna M., *Business Information Sources* (Berkeley: University of California Press, 1976); and Figueroa, Oscar, *A Business Information Guidebook* (New York: Amacom, 1980).

5. *Moody's Manuals* (New York: Moody's Investors Service. Annuals and Supplements).

6. *Moody's Investors Fact Sheets: Industry Review* (New York: Moody's Investors Service, Biweekly revisions); *Moody's Bond Record Corporates, Convertibles, Governments, Municipals* (New York: Moody's Investors Service, Monthly); and *Moody's Handbook of Common Stocks* (New York: Moody's Investors Service, Quarterly).

7. *Standard and Poor's Register of Corporations, Directors and Executives* (New York: Standard and Poor's Corporation, Annual and Supplements).

8. *Industry Surveys* (New York: Standard and Poor's Corporation, Quarterly).

9. *Value Line Investment Survey* (New York: Bernard and Co., Weekly [Parts 1 and 2], and Quarterly [Part 3]).

10. Troy, Leo, *Almanac of Business and Industrial Financial Ratios* (Englewood Cliffs, NJ: Prentice-Hall, Annual); and Robert Morris Associates, *Annual Statement Studies* (Philadelphia, PA: Robert Morris Associates, Annual).

11. *American Statistics Index* (Washington, DC: Congressional Information Service, Annual and Monthly); and *Statistical Reference Index*

(Washington, DC: Congressional Information Service, Annual and Monthly).

12. *Index to Current Urban Documents* (Westport, CT: Greenwood Press, Quarterly).

13. U.S. Bureau of the Census, *Statistical Abstract of the United States* (Washington, DC: Government Printing Office, Annual); and U.S. Department of Commerce, *U.S. Industrial Outlook* (Washington, DC: Government Printing Office, Annual).

14. U.S. Bureau of the Census, *Census of Retail Trade* (Washington, DC: Government Printing Office); U.S. Bureau of the Census, *Census of Wholesale Trade* (Washington, DC: Government Printing Office); U.S. Bureau of the Census, *Census of Service Industries* (Washington, DC: Government Printing Office); U.S. Bureau of the Census, *Census of Transportation* (Washington, DC: Government Printing Office); U.S. Bureau of the Census, *Census of Manufacturers* (Washington, DC: Government Printing Office); and U.S. Bureau of the Census, *County Business Patterns* (Washington, DC: Government Printing Office).

15. *Thomas Register of American Manufacturers* (New York: Thomas Publishing Co., Annual).

16. *Directory of New England Manufacturers* (Boston: George D. Hall Co., Annual); and *Connecticut-Rhode Island Directory of Manufacturers* (Hohokus, NJ: Commerce Register, Inc., Annual).

17. See Katz, William A., *Introduction to Reference Work*, Vol. 2, (New York: McGraw-Hill, 1981), pp. 44–48, for a discussion of the reference interview.

18. *Wall Street Journal Index* (New York: Dow Jones and Co., Monthly).

19. *Business Periodicals Index* (New York: H.W. Wilson Co., Monthly except July); *Public Affairs Information Service Bulletin* (New York: PAIS, Semimonthly); and *Social Sciences Citation Index* (SSCI) (Philadelphia, PA: ISI, Triannual).

20. Pask, Judith M., *Special Libraries* 72 (10): 370–78.

21. *Sears List of Subject Headings* (New York: H.W. Wilson, 1977); and *Library of Congress Subject Headings* (Washington, DC: Library of Congress, 1980).

22. Drinan, Helen, *Online* 3 (4): 14–21.

Business Databases Online

by Janice F. Sieburth with the aid of Mary Latham

Online access to database files has become a regular part of business information service in the 1980s, and announcements during 1981 indicate that the field is still in the growth phase. The latest announcement of a government contract, a list of companies in the computer industry, several years of Producer Price Indexes for a particular commodity, or extensive financial and management data on an individual company can all be retrieved by going "online." The results obtained are citations to specific literature, the data themselves, or a directory listing.

INTRODUCTION

Databases are computerized files of information. Online access to them means an interactive arrangement, with the questioner receiving an immediate response of specific citations, data, or a listing. Access to these files may be arranged by going directly to a producer such as Predicasts or Dow Jones who may publish a print version, to a vendor such as DIALOG who supplies a variety of databases, or to an intermediary such as a library or information broker. Producers usually require minimum contracts or subscriptions for their services; vendors generally charge on a use basis, while libraries and information brokers provide the hardware and trained searchers and vary widely in charging practices.

Since 3 major vendors provide by far the greatest volume of search services, this discussion will concentrate primarily on the information available through these companies: Bibliographic Retrieval System (BRS), Dialog Information Systems (DIALOG), and System Development Corporation (SDC). While the 3 vendors are similar in many ways, there are some differences. Contracts with DIALOG and SDC result in charges only for services utilized. BRS requires a subscription but overall fees are lower. Direct costs, which are easily calculated, are based on computer connect time, printing and mailing of results offline, and use of a national communications network (usually Telenet or Tymshare) available through a local telephone number. Indirect costs should also be noted and added to the total, including terminal rental, personnel costs, training, purchase of manuals and resource materials, and telephone charges.

Remarkably, vendor charges have remained relatively stable even though files have grown both in size and in comprehensiveness. Fees for the 3 vendors are based on a charge for individual databases and range from $45.00 to $120.00 per connect hour. Royalty fees assessed by the database producers are an additional cost and have increased considerably in recent years. Reduced rates are offered by all 3 vendors for volume use.

A few specific details should be stressed here.

1. Each system requires a different computer language, but all allow for great depth of searching, procedural simplicity, flexibility, and precision of retrieval.

2. Access for up to 23 hours per day via various communication modes makes current information a vast resource for individuals located anywhere in the world.

3. Available databases are of 3 types: bibliographic files, which contain literature citations; numerical files containing composite data, time series, or forecasts; and directory files for listings of business firms, trade opportunities, or government contract information.

4. Searching may utilize words from a structured thesaurus listing, descriptive subject words, company or personal names, or geographic locations. Each file has different components and vocabulary, and the computer will search as desired any components of individual records to retrieve pertinent citations. Some databases also provide access by numerical codes for various categories of the record. For example, Predicasts, a business and marketing research organization, has developed uniform codes for their various databases with numbers (or numbers and letters) for products, events, and countries or geographic areas. In the Predicasts databases, a product code of 2082000 is used for beer and other malt beverages; a geographic code of 1906 for California; and an event code of 44 for facilities and equipment. A search of a bibliographic database with a combination of these 3 codes could result in citations on the subject of California beer industry facilities and equipment; use of a different Predicasts database could retrieve data or forecasts.

It is possible to:

• Combine the results of search terms by a preplanned search strategy providing both comprehensiveness and precision of results.

- Save the search strategy utilized in one database and reuse it in other databases. Knowledge of the subject matter of each and appropriate terminology are required for satisfactory results.
- Store a saved search for Selective Dissemination of Information (SDI). By arrangement with the vendor, the search will automatically be run against each file update and the results mailed for a continuing list of the most recent information on a topic. BRS charges $3.00 for each time the search is run plus royalty fees and printing charges. DIALOG's SDI fee varies with the database and includes up to 25 citations printed for each search. Approximate costs range from $6.00 to $17.00 per update and may include any number of search statements. SDC has a base charge of between $2.40 and $5.00 per update plus a $.10 statement fee and a citation fee at the regular database rate.
- Buy comprehensive manuals outlining content and procedures for accessing each database from all 3 vendors.
- Accomplish training in many locations both at the introductory and advanced or more specialized level.

THE DATABASES

DIALOG's list of more than 167 databases includes 24 files that are concerned primarily with business or economic resources. There is some overlap with SDC's 10 files and BRS's 6 in this field, but each vendor has some unique files. The total of 32 databases directly focused on business affairs is listed in Table 1 (*see* Appendix) with details of source, years available, size of database, costs, and the SDI service if available. Costs are calculated on the bases of minimum access rates.

The 32 major business/economic databases included are described in the following informational material arranged alphabetically. Table 1 in the appendix to this paper presents pertinent material in tabular form.

Bibliographic Databases

ABI/INFORM. Designed to meet the management and administrative information needs of executives for decision making, this database covers the years since 1971 and is available from all 3 vendors, including an SDI treatment. There is no print form of this file. Citations are selected from more than 540 business publications. During 1981, the coverage was expanded to include significant articles from 19 European business publications, which have abstracts translated from German, Netherlands, Swiss, and French journals. Approximately 2,400 citations are added to the file each month. Subject content of the database includes accounting, banking, labor relations, data processing, finance, insurance, marketing, taxes, and international trade. Articles selected usually define or describe a method, technique, tactic, or strategy that is of value to managers and administrators. All records include the full citation and an informative abstract. General subject searching will retrieve words or phrases from the title, abstract, and assigned descriptor terms.

ACCOUNTANTS. This file from SDC corresponds to the *Accountants Index*. Available back to 1974, it covers international literature that embraces English-language books, pamphlets, government documents, and journals on accounting and related fields. Approximately 3,000 citations are added per quarter. Subjects included are auditing, data processing, investments, financial management, and taxation. Information can be found on business and nonbusiness organizations and on accounting in many specific industries.

BANKER. SDC provides this computerized file which corresponds to the *Index to the American Banker,* retrospective through 1979. The *American Banker*, which is published 5 times a week, covers news about bank developments, marketing, automation and data processing, national and international monetary affairs, bank stocks, money markets, mergers, trust banking, and the mortgage industry. About 1,100 items are added to the file each month.

ADTRACK. This file from DIALOG indexes advertisements of ¼ page or larger appearing in 150 major U.S. consumer magazines since October 1980. It is estimated that these periodicals represent 98 percent of the consumer magazine advertising revenues. There is no printed equivalent. About 13,000 records are added per month. Designed primarily for advertising agencies, magazine publishers, product managers, and retailers, ADTRACK identifies advertisements by subject, company name, product name, content and characteristics of the advertisement, and names of individuals designing or appearing in the ads. The citation record includes company/organization, brand name, full source citation, color, named person, product name, and special features of the advertisement.

CHEMICAL INDUSTRY NOTES. DIALOG's file corresponds to the printed publication *Chemical Industry Notes* and is available back to 1974. Approximately 2,000 citations are added biweekly. Emphasis is on the business literature of the chemical processing industry, which includes the pharmaceutical, petroleum, paper and pulp, agriculture, and food areas. Eighty international journals of interest to the chemical industry are monitored. Subjects include production, pricing, sales, facilities, products and processes, corporation activities, government matters, and people. The records include abstracts and can be searched by country name or code, by type of event such as production, pricing, sales, facilities, and corporate or government activities, by company name, and by subject terms.

ECONOMICS ABSTRACTS INTERNATIONAL. The source of this DIALOG database is the Dutch Ministry for Economic Affairs, though some material is added by the producer, Learned Information, Ltd. It corresponds to portions of the printed publications *Economic Titles/Abstracts* and *Key to Economic Science and Managerial Science*. About 1,150 records are added to the file monthly. Coverage is provided back to 1974, with SDI available. Journals, books, government publications, reports, directories, and reference works are abstracted. Approximately 53 percent of these are in English, 20 percent in German, 17 percent in Dutch, and 9 percent in French. Titles are usually in the language of the original article although descriptive terms are all in English. Subject coverage includes economic aspects of labor, trade, finance, industries, public administration, markets, financial and corporate structure, management, advertising, policy, investment climates, and import regulations. In addition to the citation, the record includes short descriptive abstracts, document type, geographic codes, and language of the source article.

FINTEL COMPANY NEWSBASE. This BRS file, which began in 1981, is an index to 2 editions of the *Financial Times* of London: the final London edition and the International Frankfurt edition. Approximately 900 references are added weekly. Subject coverage includes 30,000 companies and their subsidiaries worldwide. Also included are references to all quoted sources of statistics or survey material and data regarding any charts or graphic presentations included in the articles. Abstracts are available and the records may be searched by geographic location, company name, people, product, industry, and subject terms.

LABORDOC. Available from SDC, this file corresponds to the printed publication *International Labour Documentation* and covers the years back to 1965, with SDI available. It is based on acquisitions of the library of the International Labour Organization and includes both books and journal articles, with emphasis on labor and labor-related materials. Approximately 400 citations are added monthly. Subjects included are industrial relations, management, human resources planning, economic and social development, demography, education, law, vocational training, and economics.

MANAGEMENT CONTENTS. All 3 vendors offer this file which corresponds to the printed publication with the same title. Coverage extends back to 1974, with SDI available. Sources include 300 international journals, proceedings, transactions, and some books. Approximately 1,000 citations are added per month. *Management Contents* was designed to provide current information on business and management topics to aid individuals and institutions in decision making and forecasting. Subjects included are accounting, decision science, economics, finance, government and public administration, industrial relations, management, social issues, marketing, operations, research, personnel, and production. The record contains concise, 3- to 4-sentence abstracts as well as document type and the number of cited references. Descriptor codes have been added to allow for access to more general concepts.

PETROLEUM/ENERGY BUSINESS NEWS INDEX. Available from SDC, this file is an index to 12 major publications in the field such as *Energy Asia, Platt's Oilgram News Service, National Petroleum News, Oil Daily, Lundberg Letter,* and *Oil and Energy Trends.* Approximately 650 citations are added per week. The file is retrospective to 1975. Records can be searched by company name, personal name, geographic location, and subject.

PTS F & S (FUNK & SCOTT) INDEXES. Corresponding to *Predicasts F & S Index of Corporate Change, Predicasts F & S Index International,* and *Predicasts F & S Index Europe,* this online file is available from both BRS and DIALOG. Domestic and international company product and industry information are covered with some citations dating back to 1972. Monthly updates add approximately 30,000 records each month. Sources include over 2,500 newspapers, trade journals, government publications, bank letters, reports, etc. Information contained in the publications includes corporation acquisitions and mergers, joint ventures, new products, technological developments, price changes, government antitrust actions, sales and licensing agreements, corporation management, labor relations, general economic factors, and business trends. Citations include brief descriptive annotations and may be searched by the Predicasts country, product, and event codes. A subfile contains the Source Directory, a listing of approximately 5,000 journals, government publications, newsletters, corporate annual reports, and other publications cited in the Predicasts files. Each source item lists full title, publisher and address, frequency of publication, cost, and codes for product, country, and language. The record for the bibliographic portion of the file includes citation; concise abstract; product, country, and event codes; and company name, with the structure of the record varying slightly for each vendor.

PTS PROMT (Predicasts Overviews of Marketing and Technology) provides information affecting markets for products. Coverage goes back to 1972 on all 3 vendors. Citations are selected from 800 worldwide journals, studies, and prospectuses. Approximately 3,000 records are added to the file monthly. SDC's PROMT file is updated weekly. Subjects included are new technologies, acquisitions and mergers, capacities, market data, new products, and processes and production for a broad range of products and services. These include food, agriculture, chemicals, communication, health services, governments, manufacturing, petroleum, transportation, wholesale and retail trade, and international groups. Thirteen percent of the records include tables of statistical information instead of abstracts, and these can be retrieved separately. Since 1980, Predicasts has added a note—"article contains little further information"—when the abstract incorporates most of the content of the article. The record does not include the title or personal author, but does have an informative abstract, the citation, document type, indexing terms, and product, country, and event codes.

STANDARD AND POOR'S. This DIALOG file holds records back to September 1979. The database, corresponding to the *Standard and Poor's Corporation Records Daily News and Cumulative News,* includes extensive coverage of more than 9,000 publicly held U.S. corporations. It is a major source of financial information for competitive analysis and investing. Approximately 1,500 records are added weekly. Sources of information (stockholder reports, reports to government bodies by the corporations, press releases, business wire services, and newspapers) cover acquisitions and mergers; changes in management, company names, product lines, and prices; financing arrangements; joint ventures; new products, contracts, construction plans, and addresses; bankruptcy and litigation; bond redemption; and the most recent Standard and Poor's ratings. The records include abstracts of varying length in either text or tabular form. Titles are not included. Records may be searched using subject terms, company name, or special features such as tables.

TRADE AND INDUSTRY INDEX. DIALOG's file includes material from January 1981, to the present. It is designed to provide trade- and industry-specific information for all Standard Industrial Classifications (SIC). Sources include (1) comprehensive indexing of 275 business, trade, and industry journals, (2) selective indexing of 1,200 more publications, (3) appropriate MARC records, (4) industry-related items from the MANAGEMENT CONTENTS database, and (5) all of the business-, trade-, and industry-related citations from the producer's other databases: MAGAZINE INDEX, NATIONAL NEWSPAPER INDEX, and LEGAL RESOURCE INDEX. Citations may represent journal or newspaper articles, books, or government publications. Approximately 10,000 records are added monthly. Daily updating for the current month is included in

DIALOG's NEWSEARCH file. General business information is included as well as information on taxation, banking, finance, real estate, insurance, wholesale and retail trade, manufacturing, transportation, oil and gas, agriculture, forestry, fishing, etc. Some records include abstracts, which vary in length and depth depending on the significance of the article. Captions for all tables, graphs, charts, and maps are included in the record, as are relevant SIC codes to the 4-digit level, geographic codes, and subject descriptors. The database may be searched by a long list of additional categories, including article type, Library of Congress call number or card number, personal name, statute citation, name, case, citation name, or jurisdiction.

Numeric Databases

BI/DATA TIME SERIES. This DIALOG file, available as of January 1982, consists of numerical data on more than 130 countries of the world for up to 315 economic indicators. Some of the data appear in the publication *Worldwide Economic Indicators*. The historical time series go back to 1960 if figures are available. The file is updated quarterly. Sources of information include the United Nations, the International Monetary Fund, the International Labour Organization, the World Bank, and national statistics. The data are particularly valuable for firms with international interests, banks, attorneys, consultants, research groups, and government bodies. Individual countries may be compared for specific data. About 20,000 time series provide figures on production and consumption, balance of payments, imports and exports, national accounts, demographics, labor force, wages, price indexes, and currency exchange rates. Financial records contain data on the currency of the country concerned, with prices current at the time of collection unless constant prices are requested. Searching can be done by country name or code and economic indicator or economic indicator code.

BLS CONSUMER PRICE INDEX. DIALOG provides this file on time series of consumer price indexes calculated by the U.S. Bureau of Labor Statistics (BLS). The data may appear in the BLS news releases and in publications such as the *Consumer Price Index, CPI Detailed Report,* and *Monthly Labor Review*. The file is completely reloaded monthly. Price data are collected by the BLS in 85 urban areas across the country from personal visits and mailed questionnaires. The time series show the average changes in prices for particular products or services. Prices were indexed to a base year of 1967 until 1982 and to a base year of 1977 after that date to conform with changes by the U.S. government. Figures for monthly, quarterly, and annual intervals are given when available. Major categories covered include food and beverages, housing, fuel and other utilities, apparel, transportation, medical care, and entertainment. Both more specific items and general groupings such as commodities, durables, nondurables, and services are also provided. The Consumer Price Index is calculated for 2 groups of population: (1) all urban consumers and (2) urban wage earners and clerical workers. Statistics are calculated for 4 geographical regions in the United States (northeast, north central, south, and west), 28 major urban areas, 16 regions designated by population size, and the U.S. city average. Searching can be performed using the geographic name or code, the product or services name or code, and one of the 2 subfiles: the index for "All Urban Consumers" or that for "Urban Wage Earners and Clerical Workers."

BLS PRODUCER PRICE INDEX. Time series of producer and industry price indexes which have been calculated by the U.S. Bureau of Labor Statistics are contained in this DIALOG file. The data may be printed in BLS news releases and in *Producer Price Index, Producer Prices and Price Indexes,* and *Monthly Labor Review.* The file is reloaded monthly with new data. More than 10,000 price quotations are collected by the BLS monthly, mainly by mailed questionnaire received directly from producing companies. Some prices come from trade publications and U.S. government agencies. The data are calculated to show average changes in prices received in primary U.S. markets for various commodities, agriculture, mining, gas and electric, public utilities, etc. All major industries are included. The figures follow the general economic pattern of a particular industry, with most data indexed to a base point, which is now 1977. Records contain monthly, quarterly, and annual data when available for the most recent 20 years annually and the most recent 10 years of monthly and quarterly data. Records can be retrieved by geographic name or code, product name, commodity code, SIC code, and BLS number. An adjustment code for seasonally adjusted or unadjusted data is available for some records. A subfile code will retrieve either the *Producer Price Index* or the composite *Industry Price Index.* Tables may be printed giving monthly data for the most recent year, monthly data for the most recent 3 years if available, monthly data for the most recent 5 years if available, quarterly data for the most recent 5 or 10 years if available, or annual data for the most recent 20 years if available.

DISCLOSURE II. DIALOG provides this extensive business and financial file on approximately 9,000 publicly owned companies, based on data secured from documents filed with the Securities and Exchange Commission (SEC)-10-K, 20-F, 10-Q, and 8-K forms plus proxy statements and registration information. The file is updated weekly with information on new registrants and changes or additions to existing company records. Reports on companies on the New York Stock Exchange and the American Stock Exchange go back to October 1980, over-the-counter company reports to January 1981. To be included in this file a company must have 500 shareholders of one type of stock and at least $1,000,000 in assets, and must have filed a 10-K or 20-F form in the past 18 months or a registration statement if it is a new company. DIALOG claims that the 10-Q data are added as received, making them available 2 to 3 weeks after receipt by the SEC. Disclosure has recently added quarterly information, beginning with the quarter ending June 30, 1981. Some companies (about 100) report their financial statements in non-U.S. currencies. The record available online is lengthy and includes basic information describing the company, location of the principal office, exchange, ticker symbol, and description of the business. Financial information includes balance sheets, income status, current assets, 5-year summary data, primary SIC field, people information such as name, age, title, and salary, and full text of the "management discussion" filed with the SEC. Searching can be by nearly 100 different categories, such as auditor, cash, total current assets, accumulated depreciation, number of employees, gross profit, income taxes, interest expense, inventories, total current liabilities, net sales, outstanding shares, raw materials, and telephone number. These are available in addition to the usual search terms such as company name, personal name, description of business, subsidiaries, etc. Various printing formats allow for selection of basic company information; filings listing; officers and directors; full company record excluding filings listing; company name, number, and cross-reference; company name and address; financial and auditor information, annual balance sheet and income statement, quarterly income statement, segment data, and 5-year summary; or ownership and subsidiaries.

PTS FORECASTS. Two files are available from DIALOG which contain abstracts of published forecasts: PTS U.S. FORECASTS, which corresponds to the print-form *Predicasts,* and PTS INTERNATIONAL FORECASTS, which corresponds to the print-form *Worldcasts.* The U.S. data go back to 1974; international data to 1971. Approximately 9,000 records are added to the U.S. file quarterly; about 7,000 monthly to the international file. Subjects covered include market information, imports, exports, prices, sales, profits, and other transactions of specific products. Statistical information is obtained from trade journals, business and financial publications, newspapers, government reports, and special studies. U.S. forecasts include data from the U.S. *Census of Manufacturers.* The record includes the source, author, the data on which the forecast is based, and the forecast, which may be short-range and/or long-range. Searching may be done by the Predicasts codes for country, measure, product, and event. Names of countries, products, and their uses in the language of the original article, as well as dates, growth rate, and measure name may also be used.

PTS TIME SERIES. Annual time series of historical data (Basebook records) and time series of historical and projected data (Composites records) are contained in these DIALOG files. The years included vary with each record. There are 2 files, one for the United States and one for international information. In the U.S. file, the earliest beginning date is 1957, the Basebook records are updated quarterly and completely replaced each year, and the Composites records are replaced quarterly. The international file includes an earliest beginning date of 1948, the Basebook records are replaced irregularly, and the Composites are replaced quarterly. The sources for U.S. Basebook records are U.S. government agencies and specialized subject sources; the international Basebook records come from international organizations such as the Food and Agriculture Organization, Organization for Economic Cooperation and Development, European Economic Community, and the International Monetary Fund. Composites are from the same sources with projections computed by the Predicasts Research Group. Subjects covered include production, consumption, price, and usage statistics for various industries, as well as general economic, demographic, and national income series. Time series can be used to determine a trend, measure fluctuations, or calculate a rate of growth. Records contain the source of information, descriptor subject terms, country name, years of coverage, and data. Currentness of the data varies according to country and topic—U.S. figures generally are available within a year or 2; data for other countries are not as current. Searching may be done by subject terms, country name, product name, event names, growth rate, measure name, and the Predicasts codes for country, event, measure, and product. There is a special ''Quick Code'' which will retrieve individual Composites records.

U.S. EXPORTS. DIALOG's file provides time series on exports of both domestic and nondomestic merchandise from U.S. customs territories to other countries. Sources are statistics compiled by the U.S. Bureau of the Census from Shipper's Export Declarations filed with Customs officials. The file contains annual data from 1978 when available. Its 750,000 records are updated monthly and reloaded annually. All commodities are included, and U.S. government shipments of all types, intra-company shipments, and purchases made in the U.S. by foreign governments or firms all are covered. Not only can data on individual commodities and individual countries be retrieved, but trends as well as totals can be determined for the United States and for all countries. Dollar values and shipping weights are given for commodities. The record includes product name, country name and code, and abbreviation for the measure, e.g., "lbs." or "no." Product codes according to the Bureau of the Census, Schedule B, *Statistical Classification of Domestic and Foreign Commodities Exported from the U.S.* are also included.

Directory Databases

EIS INDUSTRIAL PLANTS. This DIALOG file provides current information on 150,000 businesses operated by 67,000 firms with total annual sales of more than $500,000 and 20 or more employees. These firms are responsible for more than 90 percent of the industrial activity in the United States. The file is replaced 3 times a year. Sources of information are business and trade journals, clipping services, state and industrial directories, corporate financial reports, Census Bureau statistics, and direct input by companies. The record contains the name of the company or branch, address, telephone number, principal SIC code, annual sales, estimated share of the market, employment, and parent company information. Searching can be done by geographic location or region, product name or code, company names, sales, employee size, zip code, etc.

EIS NON-MANUFACTURING ESTABLISHMENTS. DIALOG has mounted this file, which is structured similarly to EIS INDUSTRIAL PLANTS, but which contains current information on more than 250,000 nonmanufacturing concerns that have 20 or more employees. All major nonmanufacturing categories are included and it is estimated that 85 percent of the industries' sales are represented. The records are replaced 3 times per year. New product codes have recently been added to this file, which allows retrieval by specific components of a large company. These segments include: headquarters of a company without the branches, subsidiary headquarters, headquarters location of a foreign owner of a United States company, and companies or subsidiaries that issue their own annual reports.

FOREIGN TRADERS INDEX. A listing of foreign business contacts is contained in this DIALOG file. These manufacturers, service organizations, agent representatives, retailers, wholesalers/distributors, and cooperatives in 130 countries outside the United States import merchandise from the United States or are interested in representing U.S. exporters. Source of the information is the U.S. Foreign Service, which has direct contacts with the firms as part of U.S. government trade promotion. Over 100,000 records representing the current 5 years are updated quarterly. The file is designed to aid in direct marketing in foreign countries or to find sales representatives. Each record includes company and personal names, addresses, telephone numbers, relative size, number of employees, nature of business, and date established. Use of the file is restricted to the United States.

FROST & SULLIVAN DM² (Defense Market Measures System). This DIALOG database provides information on announcements of U.S. government contract awards, requests for proposals, research and development sources wanted, sole-source negotiations, long-range planning estimates, and advanced planning procurement information for the engineered systems and services market. Sources are award and pre-award announcements of various government agencies. The file (1975 to present) is updated regularly, with about 15,000 announcements added per quarter. Aircraft, communications, data processing, transportation, military equipment, management services, basic research, and navigation are some of the categories included. The file is designed to help corporate planners, market analysts and researchers, and sales managers and representatives analyze and project the U.S. government market. It is possible to determine what systems are being studied, developed and operated; the companies producing the systems; and the agencies handling development and utilization. The record includes contract number, agency, contractor, amount of contract, the system, phase, and hardware, plus a brief abstract of the project, negotiation, or request.

TRADE OPPORTUNITIES. This DIALOG file, a listing of export opportunities for U.S. businesses, is restricted to U.S. users. Records contain descriptions of products and services which foreign governments or businesses want to purchase or represent. The file goes back to 1976 and is updated quarterly. It corresponds to the printed *TOP Bulletin*. The U.S. Foreign Service is the source of information through their direct contacts with local businesses. Embassies and consular posts around the world provide input. The historical data in the file can be used for market analysis, sales opportunities, and company information. Each record includes the type of opportunity, company or buyer, addresses, country of origin, date of information, specifications or quantities needed, product codes, and abstracts describing some of the particulars.

TRADE OPPORTUNITIES WEEKLY. DIALOG's file contains the newest export opportunities. After 3 months, the records are transferred to the TRADE OPPORTUNITIES file. Approximately 350 items are added each week. This allows the retrieval of the most recent information on export possibilities before it is available in printed copy. The file is restricted to U.S. users.

USGCA (U.S. Government Contract Awards). This SDC file lists grants by the U.S. government and its various agencies to both public and private recipients. The file corresponds to the printed *U.S. Government Contract Awards* from *Commerce Business Daily,* sections A, H, and U. These sections cover (A) experimental, developmental, test, and research work (both basic and applied research), (H) expert and consultant services, and (U) training services. Coverage goes back to 1978, and about 1,250 awards are added monthly. Records include a descriptive title, subject category, amount of award, name and location of recipient, date of award, granting agency, contract, and Request for Proposal (RFP) number.

Peripheral Databases

In addition to the heavily business-oriented databases noted above, many other databases offered by these vendors include business- or industry-related material along with scientific and technical information. These include among many others:

AGLINE (SDC) for agribusiness news from 1977 to present, produced by Doane-Western, Inc.

APILIT (SDC) covering petrochemicals and worldwide refining literature back to 1964, prepared by the American Petroleum Institute.

EPIA (SDC) for literature on electric power plants and related facilities beginning in October 1980, provided by the Edison Electric Institute.

FOREST (SDC) for literature on the wood products industry from September 1980 to the present, from the Forest Products Research Society.

FSTA (DIALOG and SDC) and FOODS ADLIBRA (DIALOG) covering the food industry. FSTA *(Food Science and Technology Abstracts)* covers literature back to 1969 and is prepared by the International Food Information Services.

PAPERCHEM (SDC) for literature back to 1969 on the pulp, paper, and board manufacturing industries, from the Institute of Paper Chemistry.

PHARMACEUTICAL NEWS INDEX (BRS and DIALOG) provides current news about pharmaceuticals, cosmetics, medical devices, and related health industries, from Data Courier, Inc., DIALOG from 1975, BRS from 1974.

PIRA (DIALOG) on the same subject as PAPERCHEM is produced by the Research Association for Paper and Board, Printing and Packaging Industries, England and begins in 1975.

TITUS (SDC) for textile industry information, going back to 1967, prepared by the Institut Textile de France. WORLD TEXTILE AB-STRACTS (DIALOG), 1970 to present, from the Shirley Institute, England, covers the same subject.

New Databases

A number of new databases announced for availability in 1982 include:

CATFAX: DIRECTORY OF MAIL ORDER CATALOGS. Mounted on DIALOG, this current listing of sources of 4,000 mail order catalogs, will provide access to suppliers of a broad range of products. The record will include the name and address, type of products included, frequency of publication, and type of payment required. The file corresponds to the printed *Directory of Mail Order Catalogs*. Fees are announced as $65.00 per connect hour and $.15 for the full record printed offline.

HARFAX INDUSTRY INFORMATION SOURCES. This database, produced by Harper and Row, will be mounted on BRS and DIALOG. It corresponds to the printed *Harfax Directory of Industry Data Sources*. The file, scheduled to begin with 25,000 citations and to be updated monthly with 2,000 new records, will provide comprehensive information on 60 industries in the United States and Canada. Each citation will describe the statistics or data contained in an article, conference report, book, dissertation, or report plus full information needed for ordering it. The item will be summarized, and indexed by SIC code, location, industry, and product. DIALOG intends to charge $75.00 per connect hour and $.30 per full record printed offline. BRS access will cost $67.50 per connect hour and $.30 per offline print.

INSURANCE ABSTRACTS. University Microfilms is producing this file which will be available on DIALOG. It corresponds to the printed indexes *Life Insurance Index and Property* and *Liability Index*. Beginning with 1979 records, the file will contain about 15,000 citations, each record including a short abstract. The cost is anticipated as $55.00 per connect hour and $.15 per full record printed offline. Emphasis will be on the literature of life, property, and liability insurance.

JOURNAL OF ECONOMIC LITERATURE. This database will be available on DIALOG in 1983. The file, corresponding to the journal part of the *Journal of Economic Literature* and the annual *Index of Economic Articles,* will cover from 1969 to the present, beginning with 100,000 records and adding 8,000 per year. Material included will be journal articles, book reviews, and articles in collected works from over 260 economic journals and 200 books. The charges will be $75.00 per connect hour and $.15 per full record printed offline.

Other Online Suppliers

Although the 3 major vendors have captured a great part of the market, there seems to be a trend toward producers of the printed form of a database offering online access directly for a subscription fee. It is difficult to keep up with the availability and costs of these more direct services, but they include:

- Data Resources, Inc., which offers (1) over 35 online business databases on specialized topics such as cost forecasting for the construction trade, (2) 3,000 time series on U.S. economic indices, (3) times series on nations in the European Economic Community, (4) data on exchange rates, (5) state and area forecasting, (6) commodities, and (7) *Value Line* and flow of funds. They have just added BUDGETRACK for data on the U.S. defense budget, covering line items as well as congressional activity.
- Dow Jones and Company, which put up their DOW JONES NEWS in 1982. The file includes articles added daily from the *Wall Street Journal, Barron's*, and the Dow Jones wire services and is also available through BRS upon suitable arrangements with Dow Jones. Also available from Dow Jones are WEEKLY ECONOMIC UPDATE for the latest summaries of financial and economic news and statistics and CORPORATE EARNINGS ESTIMATOR for forecasts of earnings and economic outlook of major corporations from research reports of leading U.S. brokerage firms.
- The Harvard Business Review, which started offering its own online database during 1981 covering all articles in the *Harvard Business Review* back to 1971 and an additional 400 articles published before 1971. The file has more than 1,200 records.
- InfoGlobe in Toronto, whose online database, MARKETSCAN, contains stock market quotations from major North American stock exchanges. There are daily updating and weekly summaries accumulated for 100 days.
- The New York Times, whose New York Times Information Bank includes abstracts of articles from more than 13 other newspapers and 40 magazines. This large database of more than 1.5 million entries covers publications such as the *Wall Street Journal, Business Week*, and the *Financial Times* of London.
- Predicasts, a number of whose files can be obtained directly by contract or subscription, offers a comprehensive selection of bibliographic, numerical, and directory files for current and retrospective company, product, and industry information. Computational services can be utilized

for inputing data, and for doing statistical analysis, tabulation, plotting, and graphing.

- THE SOURCE, produced by the Source Telecomputing Corporation, primarily as an inexpensive information service for home, business, and libraries, has announced plans to expand business-oriented service to provide some of the same databases as the 3 major vendors, plus commodity news, wire service reports, and stock market data.
- Standard and Poor's, whose COMPUSTAT provides information on annual and quarterly balance sheets and income statements from about 6,000 industrial bank and utility companies.

APPENDIX

TABLE 1. Business/economics databases available from the 3 major vendors: Dialog Information Services, Inc. (DIALOG), System Development Corporation (SDC), and Bibliographic Retrieval Services (BRS) as of January 1982.

DATABASE*	DIALOG	SDC	BRS†
	A. Bibliographic databases		
ABI/INFORM Data Courier, Inc. Louisville, KY 143,600 records	1971– Monthly updates $73/connect hour $.30/offline print $.20/typed or displayed record SDI available	1971– Monthly updates $75/connect hour $.30/offline print $.15/typed record SDI available	1971– Monthly updates $65/connect hour $.30/offline print $.15/typed record SDI available

ACCOUNTANTS
American Institute of
  Certified Public
  Accountants
84,000 records
		1974–
		Quarterly updates
		$95/connect hour
		$.15/offline print	

*Name of file, producer, approximate number of records. For each vendor: Years included, update schedule, cost per online connect hour, cost for full record printed offline, cost for full record typed or displayed if applicable, availability of SDI. Cost does not include communication charges of about $8.00 per hour via Telenet and Tymnet or $5.00 per hour via Uninet.

†BRS based on annual minimum subscription of $750.00 as of May 1982. Open access without subscription is possible, generally at about $5.00/file more than in the minimum subscription rate.

TABLE 1. Business/economics databases available from the 3 major vendors: Dialog Information Services, Inc. (DIALOG), System Development Corporation (SDC), and Bibliographic Retrieval Services (BRS) as of January 1982. (continued)

DATABASE	DIALOG	SDC	BRS
ADTRACK Corporate Intelligence, Inc. St. Paul, MN 163,000 records	October 1980– Monthly updates $95/connect hour $.25/offline print $.25/typed or displayed record		
BANKER Bell & Howell Co. Wooster, OH 27,000 records		1979– Monthly updates $90/connect hour $.15/offline print	
CHEMICAL INDUSTRY NOTES American Chemical Society 368,300 records	1974– Bi-weekly updates $69/connect hour $.20/offline print $.10/typed or displayed record SDI available		

TABLE 1. Business/economics databases available from the 3 major vendors: Dialog Information Services, Inc. (DIALOG), System Development Corporation (SDC), and Bibliographic Retrieval Services (BRS) as of January 1982. (continued)

DATABASE	DIALOG	SDC	BRS
ECONOMICS ABSTRACTS INTERNATIONAL Learned Information, Ltd. London, England 113,600 records	1974– Monthly updates $65/connect hour $.20/offline print SDI available		
FINTEL COMPANY NEWSBASE Fintel, Ltd. London, England 30,000 records			January, 1981– Weekly updates $78/connect hour $.46/offline print
LABORDOC International Labour Organization 77,000 records		1965– Monthly updates $105/connect hour $.20/offline print SDI available	

TABLE 1. Business/economics databases available from the 3 major vendors: Dialog Information Services, Inc. (DIALOG), System Development Corporation (SDC), and Bibliographic Retrieval Services (BRS) as of January 1982. (continued)

DATABASE	DIALOG	SDC	BRS
MANAGEMENT CONTENTS Management Contents, Inc. Northbrook, IL 90,100 records	1974– Monthly updates $75/connect hour $.30/offline print SDI available	1974– Monthly updates $80/connect hour $.25/offline print SDI available	1974– Monthly updates $75/connect hour $.25/offline print SDI available
PETROLEUM/ENERGY BUSINESS NEWS American Petroleum Institute 210,000 records		1975– Weekly updates $105/connect hour $.15/offline print $.05/type or display print to subscribers $.25/offline print $.15/type or display to nonsubscribers	

TABLE 1. Business/economics databases available from the 3 major vendors: Dialog Information Services, Inc. (DIALOG), System Development Corporation (SDC), and Bibliographic Retrieval Services (BRS) as of January 1982. (continued)

DATABASE	DIALOG	SDC	BRS

PTS F & S INDEX
Predicasts, Inc.
Cleveland, OH
1,750,000 records
	1972–
	Weekly updates
	$90/connect hour
	$.20/offline print
	$.50/type, display,
	   print for
	   nonsubscribers
	SDI available
			1972–
			Monthly updates
			$90/connect hour
			$.20/offline print
			$.10/typed record
			SDI available

PTS PROMT
Predicasts, Inc.
Cleveland, OH
381,500 records
	1972–
	Weekly updates
	$90/connect hour
	$.20/offline print
	$.50/type, display,
	   print for
	   nonsubscribers
	SDI available
			1972–
			Monthly updates
			$90/connect hour
			$.30/offline print
			$.20/typed record
			SDI available

STANDARD AND POOR'S NEWS Standard & Poor's Corp New York, NY 156,000 records	Sept. 1979– Weekly updates $85/connect hour $.15/offline print SDI available		

TABLE 1. Business/economics databases available from the 3 major vendors: Dialog Information Services, Inc. (DIALOG), System Development Corporation (SDC), and Bibliographic Retrieval Services (BRS) as of January 1982. (continued)

DATABASE	DIALOG	SDC	BRS
TRADE & INDUSTRY INDEX Information Access Corp. Menlo Park, CA 140,000 records	1981– Monthly updates $85/connect hour $.20/offline print SDI available		
B. Numeric databases			
BI/DATA TIME SERIES Business International Corp. New York, NY 20,300 records	Dates vary Quarterly updates $85/connect hour $1.50/type, display, or offline print		
BLS CONSUMER PRICE INDEX U.S. Bureau of Labor Statistics 8,800 records	Dates vary Monthly updates $45/connect hour $.50/type, display, or offline print		

TABLE 1. Business/economics databases available from the 3 major vendors: Dialog Information Services, Inc. (DIALOG), System Development Corporation (SDC), and Bibliographic Retrieval Services (BRS) as of January 1982. (continued)

DATABASE	DIALOG	SDC	BRS
BLS PRODUCER PRICE INDEX U.S. Bureau of Labor Statistics 6,000 records	Dates vary Monthly updates $45/connect hour $.50/type, display, or offline print		
DISCLOSURE II Disclosure, Inc. Bethesda, MD 8,500 records	Current Weekly updates $60/connect hour $10.00/offline print $6.00/type or display record		
PTS INTERNATIONAL FORECASTS Predicasts, Inc. Cleveland, OH 278,600 records	1971– Monthly updates $90/connect hour $.20/offline print $.50/type, display, or offline print for non-subscribers		

TABLE 1. Business/economics databases available from the 3 major vendors: Dialog Information Services, Inc. (DIALOG), System Development Corporation (SDC), and Bibliographic Retrieval Services (BRS) as of January 1982. (continued)

DATABASE	DIALOG	SDC	BRS
PTS INTERNATIONAL TIME SERIES Predicasts, Inc. Cleveland, OH 136,285 records	Dates vary Replaced periodically $90/connect hour $.20/offline print $.50/type, display, or offline print for non-subscribers		
PTS U.S. FORECASTS Predicasts, Inc. Cleveland, OH 193,200 records	1971– Quarterly updates $90/connect hour $.20/offline print $.50/type, display, or offline print for non-subscribers		

TABLE 1. Business/economics databases available from the 3 major vendors: Dialog Information Services, Inc. (DIALOG), System Development Corporation (SDC), and Bibliographic Retrieval Services (BRS) as of January 1982. (continued)

DATABASE	DIALOG	SDC	BRS

PTS U.S. TIME SERIES
Predicasts, Inc.
Cleveland, OH
37,784 records
	Dates vary
	Replaced regularly
	$90/connect hour
	$.20/offline print
	$.50/type, display,
	  or offline
	  print for non-
	  subscribers		

U.S. EXPORTS
U.S. Department of
  Commerce
750,000 records
	1978–
	Monthly updates
	$45/connect hour
	$.25/offline print
	$.25/type or
	  display record		

C. Directory databases			

EIS INDUSTRIAL PLANTS
Economic Information
  Systems, Inc.
New York, NY
150,000 records
	Current
	Replaced 3
	  times/year
	$90/connect hour
	$.50/type, display,
	  or print record		

TABLE 1. Business/economics databases available from the 3 major vendors: Dialog Information Services, Inc. (DIALOG), System Development Corporation (SDC), and Bibliographic Retrieval Services (BRS) as of January 1982. (continued)

DATABASE	DIALOG	SDC	BRS
EIS NONMANUFACTURING ESTABLISHMENTS Economic Information Systems, Inc. New York, NY 251,879 records	Current Replaced 3 times/year $90/connect hour $.50/type, display, or print record		
FOREIGN TRADERS INDEX U.S. Department of Commerce 109,612 records	Current 5 years Quarterly updates $45/connect hour $.25/offline print		
FROST & SULLIVAN DM2 New York, NY 339,925 records	1975– Quarterly updates $90/connect hour $.25/offline print		

TABLE 1. Business/economics databases available from the 3 major vendors: Dialog Information Services, Inc. (DIALOG), System Development Corporation (SDC), and Bibliographic Retrieval Services (BRS) as of January 1982. (continued)

DATABASE	DIALOG	SDC	BRS
TRADE OPPORTUNITIES U.S. Department of Commerce 82,189 records	1976– Quarterly updates $45/connect hour $.25/offline print		
TRADE OPPORTUNITIES WEEKLY U.S. Department of Commerce 7,800 records	Current 3 months Weekly updates $45/connect hour $.50/type, display, or print record		
USGCA Washington Represen- tative Services 60,000 records		1978– Monthly updates $105/connect hour $.20/offline print	

Business Periodicals: A Core Collection for the Smaller Library

by Louise S. Sherby

Periodicals in business, as in any area, serve several different purposes: (1) they disseminate the results of research in the field in its primary form; (2) they serve as a forum for discussing new ideas, new theories, and new techniques; (3) some, particularly those written in a more popular or readable form, provide news and articles aimed at the general or practice-oriented rather than the research-oriented reader; (4) they provide information on topics that are too specific in nature to warrant a full-length study; and (5) they act as a means of communication within a specific trade or industry between groups of businesspersons with the same interests.

A number of standard sources list periodicals in the field of business. *Ulrich's International Periodical Directory* (21st edition, 1982) lists approximately 720 titles under the heading Business and Economics, not including the titles listed under the various subheadings under Business and Economics or those titles listed under related topics such as Management. The *Standard Periodical Directory, 1981-82* (7th edition) lists approximately 1,000 titles under its Code 0360 for Business and Industry. *Magazines for Libraries* (3rd edition, 1978) lists approximately 300 titles under the heading Business, including all of its subheadings.

The range of titles (300–1,000) identified in the above sources is far too large for a smaller library to consider buying. This study sought to identify a small core collection of journals in business that the smaller library could use for its collection development decisions. In order to arrive at the core list, the following procedure was used.

The list of titles from the *Ulrich's Directory* was checked against the latest available serials list for a large academic library in an institution offering an accredited MBA degree. This provided a list of about 250 titles. The same method was applied to the data from the *Standard Periodical*

Directory and *Magazines for Libraries*. This resulted in a collection of approximately 400 titles that were owned by the large academic library and were listed in at least one of the standard sources used. These titles were checked against current serials lists available from a very large academic research library, a state college library in an institution offering a wide range of business courses, and the Business, Industry, and Science Department of a large public library.

The titles to be included in the final list were selected on the basis of 2 conditions. First, the titles had to be owned by at least 3 of the libraries whose serials lists were checked. Second, the title had to be indexed in either the *Business Periodicals Index* or the *Public Affairs Information Service Bulletin (PAIS)*, which are considered by the author to be the 2 most important of the general indexes relevant to the field of business. A few exceptions were made, however, the first in the case of the *Wall Street Journal*. As a newspaper, it would not fall within the scope of either of the 2 indexes, but because of its importance in the field it was included anyway. Three additional exceptions were made because the titles appear in the core list included as Part I of this volume. This was done because the the titles are considered to be of importance to the smaller business library even though they do not fulfill both conditions for inclusion in this list. These exceptions are *Advertising Age, Monthly Bulletin of Statistics,* and the *Monthly Labor Review*.

There have been a few attempts recently to examine the characteristics of the business literature. Popovich, in a study done in 1975, analyzed 31 dissertations done in the fields of business and management to discover the pattern of citations given.[1] Of the 62 titles he found cited most frequently in those 31 dissertations, 17 are included in the core list presented here. Cox, Hamelman, and Wilcox also looked at the characteristics of the business literature using a multidimensional scaling technique.[2] Of the 38 journals they examined, nearly half (16) are included here. In 1976, Moyer and Crockett examined 56 journals in management and business with regard to policies and trends in publishing and the acceptance of manuscripts.[3] Sixteen of the journals included in this core list also appear on their list, although a number of the titles they studied could be said to be outside the strict realm of the fields of management and business (e.g., *American Journal of Psychology* and *American Sociological Review*). In 1977, Tega published a monograph study of the most important journals in management and economics.[4] He listed 161 periodicals in that volume. Of the 49 titles included in this core list, 42 appear in his list of important journals. Richard King also compiled a list of business serials found among U.S. government publications.[5] Only 4 of the titles included here also appear in his list. One of the most recent lists of business periodicals is the one compiled by Richard Behles.[6] His list includes 24 titles, of which 50 percent also appear in this list.

It must be remembered that any core list of titles, whether it be of books or periodicals, is an arbitrary one. Core lists should be reviewed frequently as new journals appear and older ones fade in importance or disappear. All fields, including business, should be seen as if they were "emerging" fields. New concepts and ideas are always being developed, tested, and eventually accepted. As these new ideas develop, new journals appear to fill the information needs created. The 49 titles suggested here are available for the total annual sum of $1,680,000 (at current subscription rates)—not an unreasonable amount for the smaller business library. With these cautions in mind, the suggested core list of business periodicals follows.

Accounting Review. American Accounting Association. 1926–. Quarterly. ISSN: 0001-4826. $25.00.

Published by the American Accounting Association, the journal emphasizes articles on accounting education and on current trends in accounting. Regular features include book reviews and research notes on current research projects in the field of accounting.

Administration and Society. Sage Publications. 1969–. Quarterly. ISSN: 0095-3997. $42.00 institutions. Formerly: *Journal of Comparative Administration*.

This journal "seeks to further the understanding of public and human service organizations, their administrative processes, and their effect on society." Emphasis is on empirical research and theoretical articles that contribute to that understanding.

Administrative Management: The Systems Magazine for Administrative Executives. Geyer-McAllister Publications. 1940–. Monthly. ISSN: 0001-8376. $18.00.

In this independent journal, which focuses on office equipment, personnel, and overall office management, emphasis is on the practical aspects of office operations with many regular features that focus on news, events, equipment, and personnel problems.

Administrative Science Quarterly. Cornell University, Graduate School of Business and Public Administration. 1956–. Quarterly. ISSN: 0001-8382. $40.00 institutions.

"Dedicated to advancing the understanding of administration through empirical investigation and theoretical analysis," the emphasis in this quarterly is on research articles. Each issue contains several lengthy, critical book reviews and a list of current publications received.

Advanced Management Journal. Society for Advancement of Management. 1935–. Quarterly. ISSN: 0036-0805. $13.00 members; $16.50 nonmembers.

This official journal of the Society for Advancement of Management focuses on clear, reliable, and practical information in the field of management. Regular features include both national and international notes.

Advertising Age: The International Newspaper of Marketing. Crain Communications. 1930–. Weekly. ISSN: 0001-8899. $40.00.

Actually a weekly newspaper, *Advertising Age* is one of the most important journals for the fields of advertising and marketing. Section 1 contains news items covering advertising campaigns, personnel changes, account changes, and new products; Section 2 contains a special report on a single topic of current interest to the advertising professional.

American Economic Review. American Economic Association. 1911–. Quarterly. ISSN: 0002-8282. $100.00 institutions.

One of the most prestigious economics journals, this covers all areas of economics, with articles written primarily by outstanding researchers in the field. Each issue contains 12–14 lengthy articles and 8–10 shorter papers. Also included is an annual list of doctoral dissertations.

Barron's National Business & Financial Weekly. Dow Jones. 1921–. Weekly. ISSN: 0005-6073. $55.00.

This weekly review of business and finance information, including trends in the stock market, is published in a newspaper format and written primarily for private investors, professional money personnel, and business executives.

Bell Journal of Economics. American Telephone and Telegraph Co. 1970–. 2/year. ISSN: 0361-915x. $5.00. Formerly: *Bell Journal of Economics and Management Science*.

Published by the Bell System, the journal hopes to "expand scholarly interest—and creative thinking—in the application of economics, finance, and management science to the problem areas of the regulated sector."

Black Enterprise. Earl G. Groves Publishing Co. 1970–. Monthly. ISSN: 0006-4165. $10.00.

Published "for black men and women who want to get ahead," the journal is of particular use to those interested in a business career. The June issue, "Black Enterprise 100," lists the top 100 Black-owned businesses in the United States.

Business America: The Magazine of International Trade. U.S. Department of Commerce, International Trade Administration. 1978–. Biweekly. SuDocs No.: C61.18:B. $55.00. Formerly: *Commerce America, Business Today, Commerce Today*.

A review of activities relating to private enterprise by the U.S. Department of Commerce, this biweekly includes information on exports, overseas activities, and international business opportunities.

Business and Society Review: A Quarterly Forum on the Role of Business in a Free Society. Warner, Gorham and Lamont. 1972–. Quarterly. ISSN: 0045-3609. $48.00.

Directed toward the business professional and the public interest group, articles in this forum are wide-ranging in subject matter. Included are a periodical listing of women currently serving on corporate boards and a "quarterly review of notable company achievements and failures in areas of public concern."

Business Conditions Digest (BCD). U.S. Department of Commerce, Bureau of Economic Analysis, Statistical Indicators Division. 1961–. Monthly. SuDocs No.: C 59.9: $60.00. Formerly: *Business Cycle Developments.*

BCD emphasizes the "cyclical indicators approach to the analysis of business conditions and prospects" and includes information on national income, measures of prices, wages, and productivity, and other data on the labor force, along with other economic measures.

Business History Review. Harvard University, Graduate School of Business Administration. 1926–. Quarterly. ISSN: 0007-6805. $15.00.

The focus in this quarterly is on business and economic history in the United States and abroad and on the "scholarly investigation and analysis of the interactions of business and its environment. Several critical and lengthy book reviews are included in each issue.

Business Horizons. Indiana University, School of Business. 1958–. Bimonthly. ISSN: 0007-6813. $15.00.

Written for businesspersons, teachers, and advanced students of business administration, issues of this bimonthly normally have a "feature" topic with 2–4 articles plus several articles on other areas of interest and include book notes and reviews.

Business Week. McGraw-Hill. 1929–. Weekly. ISSN: 0007-7135. $34.95.

The general business magazine, which covers all areas of interest to the business community worldwide, has weekly departments on such topics as finance, international business, marketing, and technology. The articles are clear, concise, and intelligible for the layperson.

California Management Review (CMR). University of California, Berkeley, Graduate School of Business Administration. 1958–. Quarterly. ISSN: 0008-1256. $18.00.

"An authoritative source of information and ideas contributing to the advancement of management science, it is directed to active managers, scholars, teachers, and others concerned with management."

Columbia Journal of World Business. Columbia University, Graduate School of Business. 1965–. Quarterly. ISSN: 0022-5428. $32.00. Formerly: *Journal of World Business.*

Aimed at the business executive, scholar, and government official interested in an international or comparative approach to business, the articles in this journal deal primarily with practical experience or applied theory and include lengthy and critical book reviews.

Dun's Business Month. Dun and Bradstreet. 1893–. Monthly. ISSN: 0012-7175. $24.00. Formerly: *Dun's Review.*

Written for the business executive, feature articles cover such areas as the economy, management, companies, industries, marketing, technology, money and markets, and the international business market. Shorter news reports cover the latest events in the same areas to keep the executive up to date.

Economist. Economist Newspaper Ltd. 1843–. Weekly. ISSN: 0013-0613. $85.00.

This provides a good summary of the British point of view concerning current economic and political affairs, as well as that of other countries and areas of interest to the British businessperson. Regular features cover world politics and current affairs, as well as business, finance, and science, including the "American Survey," which provides an overview of the current economic and political situation in the United States.

Federal Reserve Bulletin. U.S. Board of Governors of the Federal Reserve System. 1915–. Monthly. SuDocs No. FR 1.3: ISSN: 0014-9209. $20.00.

This official publication of the Federal Reserve Board is a reliable source for statistical information concerning the areas of national and international banking, economics, and business.

Finance and Development. International Monetary Fund. 1964–. Quarterly. ISSN: 0145-1707. Free. Formerly: *Fund and Bank Review.*

A joint publication of the IMF and the World Bank (International Bank for Reconstruction and Development), this is published in English, Arabic, French, German, Portuguese, and Spanish editions. It covers international economic developments and provides the latest information on the activities of the 2 sponsoring organizations.

Financial Analysts Journal. Financial Analysts Federation. 1945–. Bimonthly. ISSN: 0015-198x. $36.00.

The journal covers a wide range of topics related to the stock market and investment handling and provides unbiased reporting on the corporate and economic outlook and on money management techniques.

Forbes. Forbes. 1917–. Biweekly. ISSN: 0015-6914. $33.00.

One of the most important general business magazines, *Forbes* is known for its good, concise articles covering a wide range of topics from the point of view of the executive. Special features include personal profiles and case histories.

Fortune. Time. 1930–. Biweekly. ISSN: 0015-8259. $33.00.
Another important general business magazine, *Fortune* covers the business news from a broad point of view. A recent issue included articles on the automobile industry, computers, nuclear weapons, air cargo, and hospitals. It is also known for its *Fortune 500* directories.

Harvard Business Review. Harvard University, Graduate School of Business Administration. 1922–. Bimonthly. ISSN: 0017-8012. $27.00.
A scholarly journal with an emphasis on research articles covering all aspects of business and other related topics, its articles attempt to supply real solutions to everyday business problems.

Industrial and Labor Relations Review. Cornell University, New York State School of Industrial and Labor Relations. 1947–. Quarterly. ISSN: 0019-7939. $14.00 institutions.
A major journal in the field of industrial and labor relations covering all areas of interest, its major features include "Recent Publications," which lists new items of interest, "Research in Progress," and "Book Reviews."

Industrial Marketing: Selling and Advertising to Business, Industry and the Professions. Crain Communications. 1916–. Monthly. ISSN: 0019-8498. $20.00.
This general magazine dealing with all aspects of marketing and advertising covers general business trends and developments and government activities that affect business and publishes an annual issue on "Advertising Budgets."

Journal of Accountancy. American Institute of Certified Public Accountants. 1905–. Monthly. ISSN: 0021-8448. $20.00.
The official journal of the American Institute of Certified Public Accountants and a major journal in the field of accounting focuses primarily on the information needs of CPAs and can be somewhat technical at times.

Journal of Business. University of Chicago, Graduate School of Business. 1928–. Quarterly. ISSN: 0021-9398. $27.00 institutions.
The journal covers the "entire range of business topics, including finance, accounting, marketing, security markets, administration, industrial organization, banking, management, and economics," and tries to maintain a balance between theoretical and practical information.

Journal of Finance. American Finance Association. 1946–. 5/year. ISSN: 0022-1082. $35.00.
As the official publication of the American Finance Association (AFA), the journal includes scholarly articles on all aspects of finance as it affects business, and also publishes abstracts of completed dissertations in the field as well as the proceedings of the annual meeting of the AFA.

Journal of Marketing. American Marketing Association. 1936–. Quarterly. ISSN: 0022-2429. $40.00 institutions.

Published by the American Marketing Association, this journal's objective is "to serve as a bridge between the scholarly and the practical." Areas of interest include consumer behavior, all aspects of marketing, legal developments, and methodology, measurement, and models.

Journal of Retailing. New York University, Institute of Retail Management. 1925–. Quarterly. ISSN: 0022-4359. $18.00.

Devoted to those interested in the retail trade, this scholarly journal tries to promote new ideas and concepts related to the marketplace. Special issues on specific topics are occasionally published. Regular features include "Retail Abstracts" and "Book Reviews."

Management Accounting. National Association of Accountants. 1919–. Monthly. ISSN: 0025-1690. $42.00 nonmembers. Formerly: *NAA Bulletin—Management Accounting*.

Addressed to a broader audience than *Journal of Accountancy* and somewhat less technical, this is concerned primarily with the practical aspects of management accounting. Articles are normally written by members of the NAA.

Management Science. The Institute of Management Sciences (TIMS). 1954–. Monthly. ISSN: 0025-1909. $65.00 institutions.

A scholarly journal that "seeks to identify, extend, or unify any scientific knowledge pertaining to management," its emphasis is on theory and applications of management science and operations research. Articles are addressed to those with an undergraduate mathematics background.

Monthly Bulletin of Statistics. U.N. Department of Economic and Social Affairs, Statistical Office. 1947–. Monthly. ISSN: 0027-0229. $8.00.

Published in English, French, and Spanish, this journal provides a monthly statistical update for the *U.N. Statistical Yearbook*. It provides statistical data for approximately 70 subjects for over 200 countries. Emphasis is on population, economic, and trade statistics. Data are collected from official publications of each country.

Monthly Labor Review. U.S. Department of Labor, Bureau of Labor Statistics. 1915–. Monthly. SuDocs No.: L 2.6: ISSN: 0098-1818. $23.00. Indexed: *American Statistics Index*.

An official publication of the Bureau of Labor Statistics, this covers all aspects of labor in the United States. Areas of special interest include wages, productivity, legislation, collective bargaining, and consumer prices.

Nation's Business. Chamber of Commerce of the United States. 1912–. Monthly. ISSN: 0028-047x. $49.75.

The official organ of the Chamber of Commerce of the United States, the journal covers all aspects of commerce and industry and provides up-to-date information on the activities of the Chamber of Commerce as well as monthly reports on economics, legislation, politics, etc. as they affect business activities.

OECD Observer. Organization for Economic Cooperation and Development. 1962–. Bimonthly. ISSN: 0029-7054. $15.85.
Published in English and French, the journal provides concise reporting on the activities of the OECD. Subjects covered are diverse, and the articles are written primarily by the OECD staff. An annual feature is the "OECD Member Countries," which provides a statistical summary of the economic conditions of member nations.

Operations Research. Operations Research Society of America. 1952–. Bimonthly. ISSN: 0030-364x. $65.00.
A scholarly journal, this aims to publish "quality operations research and management science work of interest to the OR practitioner and researcher in the three substantive categories: operations research methods, data based operational science, and the practice of OR."

Personnel. AMACOM. 1919–. Bimonthly. ISSN: 0031-5702. $28.50 nonmembers; $24.25 members.
This publication of the American Management Association, designed for the personnel specialist, covers all aspects of personnel administration with an emphasis on practical applications. Its "Bookshelf" provides brief reviews of new books dealing with personnel management.

Personnel Journal. A.C. Crofts. 1922–. Monthly. ISSN: 0031-5745. $32.00.
Aimed for the practitioner in the field, the journal is subtitled "The Magazine of Industrial Relations and Personnel Management." Articles are both scholarly and popular and cover all aspects of personnel management.

Public Personnel Management. International Personnel Management Association-U.S. 1940–. Quarterly. ISSN: 0091-0260. $25.00. Formerly: *Personnel Administration, Public Personnel Review*.
Directed toward the personnel manager in the public sector, the articles tend to be practical in nature and cover all aspects of personnel administration as related to the government employee.

Review of Economics and Statistics. Harvard University, Department of Economics. 1919–. Quarterly. ISSN: 0034-6535. $62.50. Formerly: *Review of Economic Statistics*.
Considered one of the most important journals in the field of theoretical and applied economics, the emphasis is on econometrics and methodology; articles also cover new and unusual topics.

Sales and Marketing Management: The Magazine of Marketing. Sales Management. 1918–. 16/year. ISSN: 0163-7517. $38.00. Formerly: *Sales Management.*

Aimed toward all those involved in marketing operations, this is the major journal in its field and covers all aspects of the process of marketing: evaluation, planning, packaging, etc. It is noted for its annual series of surveys on selling, buying, and purchasing power.

Sloan Management Review. Massachusetts Institute of Technology, Alfred P. Sloan School of Management. 1960–. Quarterly. ISSN: 0019-848x. $26.00. Formerly: *Industrial Management Review.*

This aims to "provide the practicing manager with the latest tools and information needed for effective problem solving and decision making," and includes "Book Reviews" and "Recent Management Publications."

Supervisory Management. AMACOM. 1955–. Monthly. ISSN: 0039-5919. $18.00 nonmembers; $15.25 members.

Another publication of the American Management Association designed "for the continuing education of the professional manager," this easy-to-read, practical journal covers key problem areas in personnel supervision. A recurring feature is "Let's Get Down to Cases," a series of case studies of tough situations one is likely to face.

Survey of Current Business. U.S. Department of Commerce, Bureau of Economic Analysis. 1921–. Monthly, with weekly supplements. SuDocs No.: C 59.11: ISSN: 0039-6222. $50.00.

One of the most useful sources for current business statistics, this periodical divides each issue in 2 sections; the first deals with general business topics and the second, "Current Business Statistics," provides current data for more than 2,500 statistical series.

Wall Street Journal. Dow-Jones. 1889–. 5/week. ISSN: 0043-0080. $77.00.

Although primarily a newspaper covering topics of interest to the business/investment world, the *Wall Street Journal* also provides excellent coverage of other news items of importance. Known for its investigative reporting and objective viewpoint, it remains a newspaper of importance for nearly all libraries.

REFERENCES

1. Charles J. Popovich, *Business/Management Research Characteristics and Collection Evaluation: A Citation Analysis of Dissertations* (ERIC document ED 136 835).

2. Eli P. Cox, III, Paul W. Hamelman, and James B. Wilcox, "Relational Characteristics of the Business Literature: An Interpretive Procedure," *Journal of Business*, 49 (April 1976): 252–65.

3. R. Charles Moyer and John H. Crockett, "Academic Journals: Policies, Trends and Issues," *Academy of Management Journal*, 19 (September 1976): 489–95.

4. Vasile G. Tega, *Management and Economics Journals: A Guide to Information Sources* (Detroit, MI: Gale, 1977).

5. Richard L. King, ed., *Business Serials of the U.S. Government* (Chicago: American Library Association, 1978).

6. Richard J. Behles, ed., "Business Periodicals," *Serials Review*, 6 (April 1980): 9–16.

A Business Marketplace: Step Ahead with U.S. Government Information

by Roberta A. Scull

As a collective body of federal departments, agencies, offices, printing offices, and so on, the U.S. government is almost certainly the most prolific disseminator of printed publications in the world, in both the public and the private sector. While numerous individual federal agencies publish, have printed, and distribute their own publications, 2 major government bodies print, warehouse, and sell government publications. These are the U.S. Government Printing Office and the National Technical Information Service.

VOLUME OF PUBLICATION

The Government Printing Office (GPO) is the official printing organ of the U.S. government, printing and distributing over 29 million copies of approximately 70,000 depository titles during 1981 alone. Most of these publications are made available through a free depository program to over 1,350 (1981) depository libraries throughout the United States or through the GPO-administered sales program. These publications range from such useful items as "Fifteen Ways the Department of Commerce Can Make Your Business More Profitable Through Exports" (Stock number 003-009-00260-5) to the most detailed statistical, technical, and regulatory information imaginable, such as "Study of Dynamic Flu-Gas Temperature and Off-Period Mass Flow Rate of a Residential Gas-Fired Furnace" (Stock number 003-003-02092-3).

The National Technical Information Service (NTIS), an agency of the U.S. Department of Commerce, is probably the world's largest collector and distributor of government-sponsored research and development reports. NTIS alone has available over one million titles and adds to this sum at a rate of approximately 70,000 reports per year. Each title in this collection is available for purchase as either microfiche or paper copy.

Additionally, it is estimated that at least another 80,000 government publications are produced annually outside both the GPO depository program and the NTIS program, totaling more than 200,000 U.S. government publications each year. Most of these are accessible, if one knows which bibliographic tools to search.

BIBLIOGRAPHIC TOOLS (COMMERCIAL)

Government regulations require that many types of social, demographic, business, regulatory, trade, technical, and statistical data and information be gathered. Therefore, it is not surprising that the government generates studies and statistics on gross national product; government, business, and consumer finances and expenditures; banks and other financial institutions; construction and housing; various price and wage indices; foreign and domestic trade and aid; management, labor, and personnel problems; manufacturing, business, and industry; energy and natural resources; and so on. Even though some of the government's publishing efforts seem to be frivolous, there is so much of value in recurring government statistics, monographic reports, serial and journal articles, congressional hearings and committee prints that one must survey the government literature when preparing economic and statistical analyses of forecasts, developing product designs, marketing reports, making management decisions, surveying business opportunities, conducting technical evaluations, writing grant proposals, and the like. A good rule of thumb is that if the public or business is considering a problem, the government has studied it or is in the process of investigating it.

Bibliographies

Because of the extensiveness of this information, bibliographic tools are essential to the researcher, and since the government produces bibliographies as prolifically as any other type of material (1,374 bibliographies appeared in the 1981 *Monthly Catalog of United States Government Publications*), one could reasonably hope to find a monographic or recurring bibliography on virtually any topic. These bibliographies generally include citations to commercial as well as government publications. The area of government-produced bibliography is so vast and important that several commercial reference tools are published just to provide access to government-produced bibliographies. Among these are:

Body, Alexander. *Annotated Bibliography of Bibliographies on Selected Government Publications and Supplementary Guides to the Superintendent of the Documents System.* Kalamazoo, MI: Western Michigan University, 1967; Suppl. 1, 1968; Suppl. 2, 1969; Suppl. 3, 1973; Suppl. 4, 1975; Suppl. 5, 1977.

This is one of the first efforts at compiling any type of annotated subject guide to the rich area of government-produced bibliography. Body's is a highly selective, well-annotated aid from 1967 through 1977. Since the fifth supplement in 1977, the biennial supplement has been continued by Gabor Kovas in Greeley, Colorado.

Kanely, Edna. *Cumulative Subject Guide to United States Government Bibliographies 1924-1973.* 7 vols. Arlington, VA: Carrollton Press, 1976.

Using the GPO shelflist and the *Monthly Catalog*, Kanely compiled a comprehensive unannotated list of all government-produced bibliographies cataloged by the GPO from 1924 to 1973.

Larson, Donna. *Guide to U.S. Government Directories, 1970-1980.* Phoenix, AZ: Oryx Press, 1981.

This annotated bibliography to directories published by the GPO since 1970 contains a large number of directories related to business concerns.

Scull, Roberta A. *A Bibliography of United States Government Bibliographies 1968-1973.* Ann Arbor, MI: Pierian Press, 1975.

———. *A Bibliography of United States Government Bibliographies 1974-1976.* Ann Arbor, MI: Pierian Press, 1979.

———. "A Bibliography of United States Government Bibliographies— 1979." *Reference Services Review*, Vol. 8 (January/March 1980): 49–77.

Picking up where Body left off in 1967, Scull lists with brief annotations every government bibliography (except for NTIS bibliographies) which comes to her attention, mostly through the *Monthly Catalog*. Bibliographies are grouped by broad subject categories and indexed by title and subject.

Zink, Steven D. *United States Government Publications Catalog*. (SLA Bibliography No. 8). New York: Special Libraries Association, 1982.
Zink, in one concise little reference work, describes over 200 current titles of U.S. government agency publications catalogs. The primary emphasis here is on recurring catalogs that announce a particular agency's publications.

In addition to the bibliographies of U.S. government-produced bibliographies, several outstanding bibliographic tools increase access to U.S. government publications. These are: *The American Statistics Index* (ASI), *The Congressional Information Service Index* (CIS), and *The Index to United States Government Periodicals*.

Other Bibliographic Tools

American Statistics Index: Comprehensive Guide and Index to the Statistical Publications of the United States Government. Washington, DC: Congressional Information Service, 1975–. Monthly, with quarterly and annual cumulations.
ASI first became available in 1975, though some publications date retrospectively to the 1960s. Virtually every statistic published by the federal government in a publication or monographic report is referenced. Accompanying the bibliographic citation to the source are lengthy abstracts that detail the information and further assist researchers in determining the usefulness of a report or table without necessarily examining the document. If a publication needs to be viewed, it is comforting to know that all publications mentioned are available in printed or microfiche format. In addition to standard subject and title indexes, ASI has separate indexes by geographic area and economic topic, and by demographic considerations such as age, disease, education, race, and sex. Hence, this may very well be deemed the single most important bibliographic source of instant access to federally produced statistical information.

Congressional Information Service Index to Publications of the United States Congress. Washington, DC: Congressional Information Service, 1970–. Monthly, with quarterly and annual cumulations.
As a companion to ASI, CIS indexes all congressional hearings, committee prints, Congressional Budget Office publications, and numerous public laws, as well as congressional reports and documents. Indexing is by name of business or individual, subject, title, and legislative number.

Frequently, the congressional publications contain valuable studies and/or statements by or on businesses such as Exxon, Gulf States Utilities, American Petroleum Institute, and Arthur D. Andersen, Inc. The congressional publications portray contemporary concerns of banking, small business, food shortages, exports to the Soviet Union, the Eastern European economy, the automobile industry, IRAs, etc. CIS is a bibliographic key to our times.

Index to United States Government Periodicals. Chicago: Infordata International, 1970–. Quarterly, with annual cumulations.

Almost 200 of the most popular government periodicals are indexed here. One might expect to find a great deal of nonstatistical business information included. Pertinent topics might be false advertising, consumer information, corporate finance, enterprise zones, recruiting, and occupational safety and health.

BIBLIOGRAPHIC TOOLS (GOVERNMENT)

While these commercial reference tools are valuable in approaching government-produced reports and bibliographies, the government issues thousands of single-topic bibliographies and numerous recurring bibliographic tools that are essential to locating current government and nongovernment publications, articles, and additional bibliographies of interest to the business and technical communities.

The following is a brief description of selected bibliographic tools produced by the U.S. government which are important for the technical and nontechnical spheres of business. All of the bibliographies mentioned are available from the Superintendent of Documents, United States Government Printing Office, Washington, DC 20402, unless otherwise indicated. The "S/N" number is the GPO stock order number. The "Catalog No." is the Superintendent of Documents classification number, which is used by many Government Printing Office depository libraries.

Board of Governors of the Federal Reserve System. Office of Special Assistants. *Federal Reserve Board Publications.* Irregular. Available from agency. Catalog No. FR 1.45:year.

Complete citations and prices are provided for all currently available Federal Reserve Board Publications.

Department of Commerce. Bureau of the Census. *Bureau of the Census Catalog.* 1947–. Quarterly issues cumulative to annual volume. Annual volume only is available from GPO. S/N 003-001-8001-2. Catalog No. C 3.163/3:year/issue.

In addition to being a traditional catalog of the Census Bureau's publications, this catalog describes in detail available data files and special tabulations that may be subscribed to through the Census Bureau or individual request. This work provides—according to subject—the telephone numbers of key Census Bureau personnel who can assist data users. Access is by subject and geographic indexes and is essential for locating trade, business, and marketing information not found in printed form.

Department of Commerce. International Trade Administration. Office of Export Development. *Index to Foreign Market Report.* 1973–. 10 per year. (International Marketing Information Series.) No longer available. Catalog No. C 61.16:date.

This publication, which announces reports on foreign markets, is to be replaced by *International Market Research (IMR) Index* by the International Trade Administration. IMR will be available from the agency.

Department of Commerce. National Technical Information Service. *Government Reports Announcements and Index.* 1946–. Biweekly. Catalog No. C51.9/3:vol/no.

Government Reports Announcements and Index (GRA&I) announces, summarizes, and makes available some 70,000 new research and development reports per year which have been made by local, state, and federal government agencies, private researchers, universities, and special technology groups. These reports are divided into 26 major subjects and therein subdivided. One might also subscribe to a weekly single abstracting service on one of 26 major subjects, among which are: Administration; Administration and Management; Behavior and Society; Building Industry Technology; Civil Engineering; Communications; Computers, Control, and Information Theory; Electrotechnology; Energy; Environmental Pollution and Control; Government Inventions for Licensing; Health Planning and Health Services Research; Industrial and Mechanical Engineering; Information for Innovators; Medicine and Biology; Natural Resources and Earth Science; Ocean Technology and Engineering; Problem Solving Information for State and Local Governments; and Transportation. Since GRA&I includes the citations for all of the above and is subdivided by specific category, it is unnecessary to have a subscription to a single abstracting service as well as GRA&I.

Department of Energy. *Energy Abstracts for Policy Analysis: A Monthly Abstract Journal for the Analysis and Evaluation of Energy Research, Conservation, and Policy.* 1975–. Monthly, with annual cumulative index. S/N 061-000-80003-4. Catalog No. E 1.11:vol./no.

Presented are nontechnical articles and reports on all phases of energy analysis and development considered to have significant reference value. Technical aspects of energy development can be found in *Energy Research Abstracts* (ERA) below.

Department of Energy. *Energy Research Abstracts.* 1975–. Semimonthly. S/N 061-000-80002-6. Catalog No. E 1.17:vol.

ERA abstracts and indexes "all scientific and technical reports, journals, articles, conference papers and proceedings, books, patents, theses, and monographs originated by the U.S. Department of Energy, its laboratories, energy centers, and contractors. ERA also covers other federal and state government organizations, foreign governments, and domestic and foreign universities and research organizations."

Government Printing Office. *GPO Sales Publications File.* Microform. S/N 021-000-80004-0. Catalog No. GP 3.22/3:mo.

This is a catalog of all publications currently offered for sale by the Superintendent of Documents and is issued in microfiche (48X) only. The file is arranged in 3 sequences: (1) GPO stock numbers, (2) Superintendent of Documents (SuDocs) classification numbers, and (3) alphabetical arrangement of subjects, titles, agency series and report numbers, key words and phrases, and personal authors. A bimonthly—February, April, and so on—update to the GPO *Sales Publications Reference File* is included in the subscription and contains only new items received in a month's period following issuance of the regenerated master file. Not only is this an excellent reference aid for searching subjects and titles of GPO publications, it is a "must" as an acquisitions tool because it gives price and order information for all publications currently available from the GPO.

Government Printing Office. *Monthly Catalog of United States Government Publications.* 1895–. Monthly, with semiannual and annual indexes. S/N 021-000-80002-3. Catalog No. GP 3.8:date.

Cataloged monthly in machine readable cataloging (MARC) format are U.S. government publications that have been entered into the OCLC database by the Government Printing Office. Included are publications sold by the Superintendent of Documents, those for official use, and those which are sent to depository libraries. Indexes are by author, subject, title, series number, and key word in title.

Government Printing Office. *Selected United States Government Publica- tions.* 1928–. Monthly. Available on request to libraries. Catalog No. GP 3.17:vol./no.

Listed and briefly annotated are currently available publications which the GPO feels might be of interest to the public. Subject matter varies widely, and the types of materials range from highly technical texts to coloring books. Current order information is provided for each item.

Government Printing Office. *Subject Bibliography Series.* Free for indi- vidual title requests. Catalog No. GP 3.22/2:no.

This series, which replaces the *Price List Series,* encompasses thousands of available GPO publications, which are listed with order information and SuDocs classification in one or more of over 300 individual "Pathfinder"–type bibliographies. The following are a few titles that may be of interest to business librarians:

3. *Highway Construction, Safety, and Traffic*
4. *Business and Business Management*
13. *Aircraft, Airports, Airways*
21. *Patents and Trademarks*
27. *Customs, Immunization and Passport Publications*
40. *Shipping and Transportation*
42. *Accounting and Auditing*
44. *Manpower, Employment, Occupations, and Retirement*
51. *Computers and Data Processing*
56. *How to Sell to the Department of Defense*
87. *Stenography, Typing and Writing*
90. *Federal Government Forms*
97. *National and World Economy*
100. *Federal Trade Commission Decisions and Publications*
108. *Workers' Compensation*
109. *Weights and Measures*
120. *Insurance and Securities*
123. *Foreign Trade and Tariff*
125. *Marketing Research*
126. *Copyrights*
128. *Banks and Banking*
138. *Building Science Series*
146. *Census of Manufacturers*
152. *Census of Business*
156. *Census of Governments*
157. *Census of Construction*

Department of Health and Human Services. National Institute for Occupational Safety and Health. *NIOSH Publications Catalog.* 1977–. Irregular. Available from agency. Catalog No. HE 20.7114: P96/2/yr.

Each edition of this catalog is a cumulative listing of all NIOSH numbered publications, health hazard evaluations, technical assistance reports, and education and training materials. Each publication has a complete bibliographic citation with availability and ordering information provided. An extremely thorough index by industry, process, hazard, chemical, etc. enhances the use of this catalog.

Department of Housing and Urban Development. *Housing and Planning References, New Series.* July/August 1965–. Bimonthly. S/N 023-000-80002-1. Catalog No. HH 1.23/3:date.

Covered are current publications and articles received by the HUD library. Entries, most of which are briefly annotated, are arranged by subject groups covering all aspects of architecture, building, design, planning, urbanology, home financing, and so forth. Author and geographical indexes facilitate its use.

Department of Labor. Office of Information. *New Publications*. Monthly. Available from agency. Catalog No. L 1.34/3:date.

To keep abreast of labor problems, wage surveys, and the like, this monthly publication is most useful.

Department of Labor. Office of Information. *Publications of the United States Department of Labor: Subject Listing*. 1948–. Irregular. Available from agency. Catalog No. L 1.34: P96/yr.

This irregular catalog generally covers a 5-year period and lists the department's publications by subject during that period. Also mentioned are periodical and subscription services. Price and availability for all publications are given.

Federal Home Loan Bank Board. Office of Communications. *List of Publications Available*. Irregular. Available free from FHLB.

Listed are the Federal Home Loan Bank Board's publications, most of which are free on request.

Federal Trade Commission. Office of the Secretary. *List of Publications* 1957–. Irregular. Available from agency. Catalog No. FT 1.22:date.

Listed by subject are the reports, studies, instructional aids, and pamphlets of the FTC. Pricing and order information are provided.

General Accounting Office. Document Handling and Information Service. *GAO Documents*. 1977–. Monthly. S/N 020-000-80003-8. Catalog No. GA 1.16/4:vol./no.

The GAO has several publications catalogs, but for comprehensiveness, indexing, and a good abstract, this catalog is the best. If currency is not critical, one might prefer to use the semiannual *General Accounting Office Publications* (GA 1.16/2:nos. and V. no5.)

Office of Personnel Management. *Personnel Bibliography Series*. 1960–. Irregular. Order individually by S/N. Catalog No. PM 1.22/2:nos.

These individual bibliographies are compiled periodically, usually on an annual basis, by the U.S. Office of Personnel Management from

Personnel Literature and deal with special aspects of management and personnel relations. The literature coverage is broad and covers government, nongovernment, and occasionally foreign publications. The following are a few select titles:

121. *The Federal Civil Service—History, Organization and Activities*. 1981. S/N 066-000-01241-8.
122. *Labor-Management Relations in the Public Service*. 1981. S/N 006-000-01242-6.
123. *Executive Personnel*. 1981. S/N 006-000-01243-4.
125. *Self-Development Aids for Supervisors and Middle Managers*. 1981. S/N 006-000-01236-1.
126. *Equal Opportunity in Employment*. 1981. S/N 006-000-01237-0.
127. *Personnel Management Function*. 1981. S/N 006-000-01238-8.
128. *Personnel Policies and Practices*. 1981. S/N 006-000-01239-6.
129. *Work Force Effectiveness*. 1981. S/N 006-000-01239-6.

Office of Personnel Management. *Personnel Literature*. 1941–. Monthly with annual index. Available on subscription from GPO. Catalog No. PM 1.16:date.

Personnel Literature is one of the oldest and certainly one of the best bibliographic current awareness tools in the areas of personnel management and problems of and with the employed and unemployed in both the public and private sectors. Since the formation of the Civil Service Commission in 1941, *Personnel Literature* has remained virtually unchanged in function and form. The only substantial change is in the name of the office producing it: the Civil Service Commission has changed to the Office of Personnel Management (OPM). Included are selected books, pamphlets, and other publications received in the library of the Office of Personnel Management during the previous month. Periodical articles, unpublished dissertations, and microforms are also listed. This superb index gives in-depth coverage on hundreds of job-related topics such as career planning, hours of work, political activity, retirement, women, and youth.

Small Business Administration. *Small Business Administration Publications*. 1960–. Quarterly. Available free from agency. Catalog No. SBA 1.18:year/no.

This quarterly listing of publications available free from the SBA covers marketing and management reports, aids, and bibliographies.

Small Business Administration. *Small Business Bibliographies Series.* Available from agency. Catalog No. SBA 1.3:No. ed.

These pamphlets briefly discuss the business topics under consideration and give bibliographic and purchasing information for government, nongovernment, and trade publications. In most instances, addresses are provided for additional information contacts. The following are a few of the more than 100 subject bibliographies related to business:

   3. *Selling by Mail Order*
   9. *Marketing Research Procedures*
   12. *Statistics and Maps for National Market Analysis*
   13. *National Directories for Use in Marketing*
   18. *Basic Library Reference Sources*
   80. *Data Processing for Small Business*
   87. *Financial Management*
   90. *New Product Development*

In addition to the bibliographic publications mentioned, today's business searcher may utilize numerous computerized bibliographic databases to locate information rapidly and in a timely fashion. In fact, of the publications mentioned above, the following may be searched online: *American Statistics Index* (ASI) (available on DIALOG, SDC); *Congressional Information Service Index* (CIS) (available on DIALOG, SDC); *Energy Research Abstracts* (DOE Energy) (available on DIALOG, SDC, BRS); *Monthly Catalog of United States Government Publications,* (GPO *Monthly Catalog*) (available on DIALOG, SDC, BRS); *GPO Publications Reference File* (available on DIALOG); and *Government Reports Announcements and Index* (NTIS) (available on DIALOG, SDC, BRS).

Going a step further, some government information is *only* readily accessible through computerized bibliographic and data files. Among the databases of particular interest that are publicly available to business are files from the Bureau of Labor Statistics (BLS) and the Patent Office. The BLS provides the following files through commercial database vendors: *BLS Consumer Price Index, BLS Employment, Hours and Earnings, BLS Labor Force,* and *BLS Producer Price Index.* All are available through DIALOG.

The CASSIS (Classification and Search Support Information Service) file of the U.S. Patent Office is a cumulative file of all United States patents. In addition to being used by the Patent Office, this data file is available to the public at officially designated U.S. Patent Depositories. At this time, it is not available through a commercial database vendor.

Government information for business is abundant. Knowledge and use of the indexes, bibliographies, and databases accessing this information open the door to the marketplace of this wealth to which all are freely entitled.

Making the Business Library Visible

by Janet L. Harrington and Bernard S. Schlessinger

Library literature in the past 20 years[1] has noted the change in emphasis in libraries from the storage house concept to the service concept. But what should have been, in the minds of the authors, a concurrent interest in publicizing and increasing both visibility and use of the library has been far less intense than would have been expected. This is especially true when one considers business libraries, which operate on a literature base that emphasizes sales and marketing. Further, it is especially important to address publicizing the business library, since recent studies indicate that the overriding factor influencing an individual's use of the library is not its quality but the amount of information possessed by the individual about the library.[2]

THE LITERATURE

The general literature dealing with publicizing libraries provides a considerable body of good information on the subject both for libraries generally and for business libraries specifically. The most important points from the literature, along with some contributions from the authors, have been gathered under the following categories of "What Should Be Publicized?" "Who Should Be Approached For Help?" and "How Should Publicity Be Accomplished?"

What Should Be Publicized?

—Effective planning, through inventory of the assets and liabilities of the collection.[3]

—Photocopying services.[4]

—Referral services, to fill in gaps in the patron's knowledge.[5]

—Cost savings through cooperation, such as the establishment of a business library cooperative that collects less-used materials at one location to improve backruns of journals.[6]

—Accountability in acquiring, storing, and discarding materials to improve holdings and achieve the most economical use of funds and space.[6]

—Availability of computer databases and the information they contain, as well as the fact that the technology exists to access them.[7]

—Availability of information to small businesses on (1) government agencies that would buy their goods and services, (2) government purchase offices to approach, and (3) government specifications that apply to their products and services.[8]

—Use of business information resources in carrying out training programs in business and industry.[9]

—The long hours that library resources are available.

—Facilities and equipment available for use: meeting rooms, projectors, and other AV aids.[10]

—Information from daily press and wire services.[11]

—Budget problems—honestly, but never as an excuse for poor service or inferior collections.[12]

—The willingness to think in terms of cost relative to number of requests, time spent to fill requests, ease of access, user satisfaction, and accuracy.[13]

Who Should Be Approached for Help?

—Consultants from the Special Libraries Association, to assist in structuring the business collection.[14]

—Trade and professional organizations in the area, for opinions and advice about collection building.[14]

—The Chamber of Commerce.[14]

—Business firms, to cut down on overhead by providing their own pickup of materials. Libraries have reported the loss rate on such transactions to be as low as 2 percent.[14]

—Groups of local businesses, to support the cost of expensive titles and subscription services.

—Businesses that might be willing to contribute superseded copies of expensive publications on a regular basis.

—Other business reference specialists working in a team effort.[15]

—Budget authorities—with an honest recital of budget problems.[15]

—The Business Reference Services Committee of ALA (and their literature).[16]

—National sources, to fund acquisition of overseas materials.[16]

—Local businesses willing to give support. One library found a bank which offered any customer opening a new $100 account the opportunity to donate $5 of the bank assets to a local library.[17]

How Should Publicity Be Accomplished?

—Within the library, by helpful, creative shelving and a simple cataloging scheme.[17]

—Geographic location, advertising in itself, with the heart of the business community presenting the ideal.[18]

—Emphasis on "market research projects," which result in action and more effectively reach potential clients, rather than on "user studies," which only describe situations.[19]

—Business and industry fairs in the library.[20]

—Displays highlighting local firms and their contributions to the community.[20]

—Billboard advertising.[21]

—Publication of community information pamphlets. An example of this is *Open Dallas,* published in Texas at $2 per copy.[22]

—One-on-one meetings between the librarian and businesspersons at the places of business.[23]

—Informal breakfasts with businesspersons, to identify staff and resources.[24]

—Lunchtime film programs on topics of special interest to the small businessperson.[24]

—Talks on library services to business given to seniors in local business colleges and to seniors in high school work-study programs.[24]

—Mailing or having available at the desk peel-off telephone labels printed "For business information, call _____."[24]

—Library information booths at local business conferences and trade shows. A major advantage here would be the contact one would have with those staffing other booths. Particularly attractive would be the advantage in selling the "free" library's resources, in the presence of other fee-based services surrounding the booth. Video would be especially useful in this enterprise.[25]

—Follow-up notes, including an annotated list of business and legal information sources, to businesspersons who are contacted in any way.[26]

—Ads in the yellow pages.

—A campaign of advertising "business reference by telephone." Business people are accustomed to the use of phones in advertising.[27]

—Creation of a regular mailing list for information. Friends groups' and trustees could be asked to support the funding for mailings.[28]

—Distribution of information flyers with city paychecks.[29]

—Library business cards, embossed scratch pads, pencils, stationery, and notices.[29]

—Banners flying outside the library building displaying the availability of business information services within.[29]

—Mailing of questionnaires to all households which will provide details of the community and which, more importantly, will alert residents to the existence of a valuable source of information.[30]

—In-house business and financial services workshops.

—Presenting information in attractive packaging—being careful to guard against bulk, especially for special libraries.[31]

—Traditional bulletin board efforts within the community—the display, the poster. A coffee mug designed to promote the library's wares is another possibility.

—A newsletter used as a guide to the business collection mailed by bulk rate or distributed at lunch counters, bookstores, and gathering places in the business community. In a public library, the Friends of the Library could support the effort.[32]

—Public service announcements on radio and TV. Use cable and local talk shows as well.[32]

—Press releases available from salespeople on new business reference items. These can be mailed to selected audiences.[32]

—Continuing contact with local newspapers—articles, ads, supplements, and perhaps regular reviews of business sources.[33]

—Custom-designed form letters detailing business services available, sent to persons who are reported in the new appointments business section of local newspapers.[34]

The literature provides, as noted above, a wide variety of suggestions for possible implementation. One must, in addition, avoid waste arising from such errors as uniform provision of services for differing needs, outdated or false assumptions about user behavior, inappropriate application of international or national standards, frustration of human talents through bureaucratic administration, and prevention of learning and change due to rigidity.[35]

THE REALITY

To attempt to determine what is the reality in practice, the authors surveyed 6 different business libraries, including a small, a medium-sized, and a large public library, an industrial (computer manufacturer and sales) library, an information broker, and a business school library. The results of the interviews are presented below in summary.

Perceptions of Strengths and Trends

The 2 smaller public libraries agreed that their greatest asset for the business community was the completeness of their collections; the industrial library noted the special importance of the collection of conference proceedings; the business school library emphasized the strong support of the curriculum; immediate delivery was stressed at the large public library; and a broad range of experience within the organization was the major asset identified by the information broker.

As for trends, (1) the business school library and the 2 larger public libraries all remarked on the low demand for information dealing with foreign economies in a time of inflation; (2) the industrial library and the information broker indicated that they were moving away from use of traditional printed matter toward greater use of computer databases; and (3) the smaller public library noted that insurance resources were used decreasingly and that market logic surveys had recently been eliminated from their holdings.

Clientele and Capacity

The large public library held 40,000 noncirculating items, provided an emphasis on microfiche service (featuring American and New York Stock Exchange data and annual reports over a 10-year period), and noted 120 in-person and 93 telephone requests per day. Surprisingly, student usage was reported as greater than that of the diffuse business community in which the library is located. It was further indicated that future outreach would probably not be possible with the severe budget cutbacks recently experienced.

The medium-sized public library characterized itself in terms of its 293 noncirculating items, 40 business-specific periodicals (some circulated), loaning of business pamphlets, and handling of 14 in-person and 8 telephone requests per day. The librarian described the clientele as older men in search of information about stocks and people of all ages seeking employment. Her hope for the future was to attract the interest of wealthy community members who might help finance a portion of the library's business collection.

The smaller public library identified 628 items (any of which could be circulated overnight) and the handling of 5 in-person and one telephone request per day. The heaviest use of its collection was by a combination of the town's business groups and job seekers. The hope was to capture the interest of the general consumer.

The business school library pointed out its 54,000 books and 40,000 journals, stressed the circulation of its reference collection to faculty, the availability of databases, and in-house recording of journal use, and reported 57 in-person, one telephone, and 4 computer-search requests per day. It was proud of its service to undergraduates, graduate school students, faculty, and alumni, and saw the possibility of developing its gradually increasing service to the corporate community into a reciprocal support system.

The industrial computer manufacturer's library used 2,265 circulating items, an overnight-circulating reference collection, and database availability to service 5 in-person and 15 telephone requests daily. In addition, they indicated "many" requests via electronic mail. The computer engineer was noted as a more frequent user than the computer programer.

The information broker served primarily librarians, using a 1,500-item collection and databases. Thirteen telephone and 13 written requests were received daily. Future plans included service to personnel groups and general records people.

Promoting the Product

The business libraries interviewed have implemented a myriad of diverse techniques for promoting their services and making themselves visible. These included business seminars, library brochures aimed at the business community, appearances at businesspersons' luncheons, memberships in business groups, publication of annotated lists of new acquisitions, distribution of information on library activities, coursework on business reference, bulletin boards, open houses, production of library user manuals, tours, and direct mailings on services offered.

Most of the librarians interviewed believed it was both necessary and desirable to increase the visibility of the library and the use of its services. However, they concurrently expressed the fear that such use would almost force the charging of fees for service, a practice they all decried.

SUMMARY AND CONCLUSIONS

The literature reveals much that could help the business librarian in promotion of his/her product. The reality indicates that business libraries are trying, but even taken collectively, the efforts to make the library visible fall far short of what could be done. The future would seem to be one of cautious hope that service can be expanded, coupled with equally cautious optimism that present collections and services can be maintained adequately.

Some general comments, based on the interviews and on observation of business libraries over the years, seem warranted.

1. Business librarians balance a desire to expose their services and expand their clientele with a fear that the resulting use will overwhelm their limited capacities to serve.
2. Database availability and manipulation by and for users will probably be part of every business library's future. So will other forms of advanced technology, although most librarians are only mildly supportive of technology's use in libraries.
3. The marketplace, in terms of collection unit prices, database use, and staff involvement in service, would seem to predict (a) greater cooperative efforts among libraries and (b) development of fees for some services, but cooperative endeavors were notable only by their limited number, and fees were decried by almost all of the librarians surveyed.
4. The ambitions of business librarians are limited, and promotion efforts are mostly passive in nature.
5. In-house accountability (usage and statistical reporting of such) remains very low.

The 1980s will be a time of challenge and of learning to live with static (or reduced) budgets for all libraries. Business libraries have a unique opportunity to provide leadership in coping with these challenges. How well they respond will be eagerly monitored by their peers.

REFERENCES

1. Jesse Shera, *The Foundations of Education for Librarianship* (New York: Becker & Hayes, 1972), pp. 163–94.

2. Alice Norton, "Why Does A Public Library Need Public Relations?" *Catholic Library World* 49 (February 1977): 290.

3. "Highlighting Libraries at Business Expo," *American Libraries* 6 (March 1975): 147.

4. "How to Service the Information Needs of Businessmen," *Unabashed Librarian* 16 (Summer 1975): 19.

5. Malcolm J. Campbell, "Structure and Distribution of Business Information: Some Problem Areas," *Aslib Proceedings* 27 (November/December 1975): 433.

6. Eric Stevens, "Not Only . . . But Also . . . ," *New Library World* 80 (9 January 1979): 142.

7. Louisa D. Spencer, "Growing Demand for Information-to-Order," *Savvy* 2 (January 1981): 23.

8. O. J. Delaney, "Selling to the Government," *Oklahoma Librarian* 28 (January 1978): 15.

9. S. V. S. Sharma, "Training Small Scale Industry Extension Workers in Information Use," *Library Science with a Slant to Documentation* 15 (December 1978): 174.

10. "Publicizing Library Service to Business," *RQ* 13 (Spring 1974): 239.

11. J. D. L. Patterson, "Designing a Business Information Service for Top Management," *Aslib Proceedings* 30 (April 1978): 144.

12. Norton, pp. 289–91.

13. N. E. Heiser, "Cost Effective Analysis for Reference Departments," *Library of Congress Information Bulletin* 39 (5 September 1980): 348.

14. "How to Service . . . ," p. 20.

15. "Serving Business and Government: Studies in Illinois," *Library Journal* 99 (1 September 1974): 2026; Norton, p. 290.

16. "Publicizing Library Service . . . ," p. 239; Campbell, p. 431.

17. "Selling the Library: Fund Raising and PR," *Library Journal* 99 (15 December 1974): 3166; Side Graves, "In the Small and Medium Sized Library: Business and Financial Workshop," *Mississippi Library News* 41 (October 1977): 138.

18. Alexander Wilson, "Marketing of Library Services," *Canadian Library Journal* 34 (October 1977): 375.

19. Alan Armstrong, "Information Centres and Their Uses to Business," *New Library World* 74 (September 1973): 208–09.

20. Sara Kerr, "Your Business and Theirs: Business and Industry Fair," *Ohio Library Association Bulletin* 48 (April 1978): 26.

21. "Selling the Library . . . ," p. 3166.

22. J. N. Berry, "Building an Information Constituency," *Library Journal* 100 (15 April 1975): 705.

23. "Librarians Advised Against Too Little PR Too Late," *Library Association Record* 78 (September 1976): 394.

24. "Publicizing Library Service . . . ," p. 240.

25. "Highlighting Libraries at . . . ," p. 148.

26. "Librarians Advised Against . . . ," p. 395.

27. "Serving Business and . . . ," p. 2026.

28. "Publicizing Library Service . . . ," p. 239.

29. Susan DiMattia, "Business Books of 1979," *Library Journal* 105 (1 March 1980): 582.

30. "Serving Business and . . . ," p. 2026.

31. Patterson, p. 144.

32. "Publicizing Library Service . . . ," p. 239.

33. Spencer, p. 21.

34. "Highlighting Libraries at . . . ," p. 147.

35. Wilson, p. 375.

Index to Part III

This index refers to Part III only. For indexes to Parts I and II, see pages 63–69 and pages 101–06.